Au

D1615033

EAST SUSSEX~~~
WITHDRAWN

02759379 - ITEM

EAST

V DON

SUS # 385.09422

02759379

EAST SUSSEX

WLR

25 SEP 2024

BRN

DATE

07/03   AT VEK VCKS   11/14

34

A REGIONAL HISTORY OF
THE RAILWAYS OF GREAT BRITAIN

General Editors
DAVID ST JOHN THOMAS AND J. ALLAN PATMORE

VOLUME II
SOUTHERN ENGLAND

An idealized view of an early excursion train on the South Eastern Railway (c. 1845) on the cover of a sheet of music. It was trains such as this which, for the first time in history, made possible the habit of travel among the ordinary people of England. They also indirectly created in their modern forms Brighton, Margate, and many other resort towns.

A REGIONAL HISTORY OF
THE RAILWAYS OF GREAT BRITAIN

Volume II

SOUTHERN ENGLAND

by
H. P. White

WITH FRONTISPIECE AND 46 PLATES
9 ILLUSTRATIONS IN TEXT
INCLUDING REGIONAL MAPS
AND LARGE FOLDING MAP

DAVID & CHARLES

NEWTON ABBOT   LONDON   NORTH POMFRET (VT)

British Library Cataloguing in Publication Data
White, H. P.
    Southern England.—4th ed.—(A Regional history of
the railways of Great Britain; V.2)
    1. Railroads—England—History
    I. Title   II. Series

ISBN 0-7153-8365-5

© H. P. White 1961, 1970, 1982

First published 1961
Second edition 1964
Third edition 1969
Fourth edition 1982

All rights reserved. No part of this
publication may be reproduced, stored
in a retrieval system, or transmitted,
in any form or by any means, electronic,
mechanical, photocopying, recording or
otherwise, without the prior permission
of David & Charles (Publishers) Limited

Printed in Great Britain
by Redwood Burn Ltd   Trowbridge   Wilts
for David & Charles (Publishers) Limited
Brunel House   Newton Abbot   Devon

Published in the United States of America
by David & Charles Inc
North Pomfret   Vermont 05053   USA

Contents

     Southampton · cross-country links · Isle of Wight

VII WEST HAMPSHIRE   153
     The drive to the west · Bournemouth

VIII DEVELOPMENT OF MAIN LINE SERVICES,
     1845–1923   164
     The South Eastern · the London, Chatham & Dover
     · the Managing Committee · the Brighton · the
     London & South Western · postscript

IX   THE 'SOUTHERN' AND ELECTRIFICATION
     POLICY   179
     The creation of the 'Southern' · suburban electrifi-
     cation · the effects of electrification · main line
     electrification · 'Southern Electric' · Southern Region
     —the early years · the Beeching period

X   1965–80: THE UNFINISHED STORY   207
     Changes in government policy · changes in pas-
     senger traffic · changes in freight traffic · changes
     in international traffic · other changes and rational-
     ization · military lines · industrial lines · preserved
     lines · conclusion

     BIBLIOGRAPHY AND ACKNOWLEDGMENTS   222

     INDEX   226

Illustrations

IN TEXT

Sources of the Photographs

Thanks are due to the following for providing material: The
Curator of Historical Relics, British Transport Commission
(frontispiece, plates 9, 17, 18, 19, 20, 21, 24, 25, 28); the Public
Relations department, Southern Region (plate 16); Locomotive
& General Railway Photographs (plates 1, 3, 4, 5, 6, 7, 8, 11,
12, 26, 29, 30, 31, 32, 33, 34); J. S. Gilks (plate 36); J. G.
Glover (plates 37, 38, 40, 41, 43, 44, 46); B. N. Nunns (plates
42, 45). Other photographs are by the author.

CHAPTER I

Railways and the Personality of Southern England

In the days when freight was the life-blood of British railways a Frenchman stood on the platform at Thirsk, on the main line north of York. Gradually he became aware of an apparently endless succession of heavy freight trains passing through. Eventually the exclamation was wrung from him of '*Quel pays industriel!*'

It is unlikely that he would have made any such remark were he waiting on a station of similar size and importance in Southern England. On few, if any, lines in those parts would there have been a similar procession. But the significance of the story goes deeper than that. At few stations would there have been more freight trains than passenger trains passing, while it would be most unlikely that our Frenchman would have had long to wait before the arrival of his train, for, on anything like a main-line service intervals are frequent, even at intermediate stations.

Just as the railways on and around the coalfields of Britain, and those connecting them with London, were principally concerned with moving freight, the railways of Southern England have always been mainly engaged in the transport of passengers. In 1957 over ten million *more* passenger journeys originated on the Southern Region than on any other. In that year the Region also carried as many passengers as all the Class I railways of the U.S.A. put together. This preponderance of passenger traffic distinguished the Region from all others. It seemed that a higher proportion of the population served by the Southern was on the move, and on the move by train, than in other parts.

To take some random examples. The ancient town of Berwick-upon-Tweed had an estimated population of 12,160 in 1961. It is an important market town and is railhead for a very extensive, though somewhat thinly populated area. The summer timetable for that year showed 18 trains calling, 7 terminating and 6 starting their journeys from the station on an ordinary weekday. In contrast East Grinstead can be selected. With a population of 15,421 in 1961, it was a typical South Country market town, though admittedly almost a suburb of London these days. The summer timetable of 1961 revealed that on an ordinary weekday 39 trains called, 22 terminated and 20 started. Horsham was a similar town with 21,155 inhabitants in 1961. In the same timetable 82 passenger trains were scheduled to call, 65 to terminate and 59 to start their journeys. Lest these last two towns be considered as special cases by their comparative proximity to London, it may be added that Lewes with 13,637 inhabitants had 214 trains advertised in the summer of 1961, while the far more famous junction of Grantham (population 25,030) had 110.

Compared with the trunk routes to the North, the casual observer perhaps saw everything on a deceptively small scale. The trains were for the most part short and with the possible exception of Clapham Junction there were no junction stations to compare in size and atmosphere with Crewe, York or Carlisle. Yet more passenger trains passed through East Croydon with its three island platforms than any of these. There is some truth in the remark reputed to have been made by a Great Western officer when introduced to an opposite number from Waterloo: 'How interesting to meet a tramwayman!' But all that was before the time when more frequent, lighter and fixed-formation passenger trains and declining freight traffic tended to bring other Regions in line with the Southern.

But the consequences of railway development upon the personality of Southern England have been no less than on any other parts of Britain. That they have been different is due to the nature of the region itself. On the one hand it has only limited coal and other mineral deposits and on the other hand most of its soils are highly fertile. While dominating it all is the metropolis of London.

In the last 130 years a network of railways has been laid over the region – a network growing piecemeal and influenced in the direction of its individual lines, not only by the pre-existing social and economic conditions, but also by the physical structure of the area. In its turn this rail net has profoundly altered the society and economy and has helped change the landscape out of all recognition. The railways themselves have merged into the landscape, urban and rural, to become an integral part of it. The London Road viaduct is now as much a part of the Brighton scene as the Georgian 'Front' of Kemp Town, while the Ouse viaduct is a complement to rather than a violation of the Sussex Weald.

Perhaps because of this, but also because the Railway Age is only just receding into history, it is only recently that serious study is being made of this interplay of cause and effect, which it is a part of our purpose to examine. Even the second transport revolution, brought about by bus, lorry and car, until recently did not receive the attention it deserved.

Yet the effects of developments in transport have been far-reaching in any age, for men and goods, and with the men ideas, have been exchanged between the various regions of the world. Such traffic currents existed in Southern England long before the coming of the railway, as attested by the Neolithic trackways converging on Salisbury Plain no less than by the Roman roads, the turnpikes and the canals. The railway net was created to reinforce these pre-existing currents, but as a result of its creation new currents were set up, sometimes obliterating the old.

The 'Sabbath-breaking railway' which served the city of Barchester (surely the Bishopstoke–Salisbury branch of the London & South Western) which so incurred the wrath of Mrs Proudie and Mr Slope would eventually have altered the way of life of Archdeacon Grantly and his friends far more than ever the Palace faction were able to do. Today, a century after these fictional events, the family from the Midland industrial town enjoying its annual holiday on the beach at Bournemouth, the cursing infantryman returning to Aldershot after manœuvres on the Hampshire heaths, and the fruit-farmer of Mid-Kent supervising the harvesting of his apples, no less than the business man in the electric train from the City to his suburban villa, are all doing what they are, where they are, largely because of the currents set up by nineteenth-century railway building. This remains true even if the holiday-makers came down by car, the soldier is returning on a bus and the farmer loading his fruit on a lorry. For

Bournemouth, Aldershot and the Mid-Kent fruit belt as well as the close-built inner suburbs of London came into existence only during the Railway Age and very largely as a direct consequence of it.

For the remainder of this introduction, therefore, it may be profitable to pick out some of these currents of traffic, for it is these currents, created and nurtured by the railway, which have loomed so large in developing the personality of Southern England as we now know it.

Overshadowing all else is the dominating and all-pervading influence of London, ever since its foundation in Roman times the largest and most important town in Southern England. But a boundary has to be drawn somewhere, and Greater London together with the lines and services as far out as Dartford, Orpington, Purley, Epsom, Surbiton and Twickenham is excluded from this book. The railways' influence upon the metropolis as a whole has been dealt with in Volume III, *Greater London*. But it must be remembered that London is everything to Southern England: as any traveller by train or car quickly discovers to his cost, for there are few important cross-country routes. So though London is technically outside our area, its influence is continually present and to make the history intelligible it is sometimes necessary to trace events in outline to the respective termini of the main lines.

At the dawn of the Railway Age, though castigated by Cobbett as 'The Great Wen', London south of the Thames was no more than an extended bridgehead. Even in 1857 Dickens in describing a railway journey to Dover could speak of the train 'passing into the country about New Cross'. Since then building has spread ever southward: extensive as was the London of 1914, areal growth since has been spectacular, very largely stimulated by the constant extension of electric services. The continuously built-up area now extends right up on to the North Downs beyond Orpington and Croydon. Rural villages of 1914, among them Bexley, West Wickham, Sutton, Malden and Ashford (Middlesex), have become large towns with thousands of small or medium-sized houses. Beyond the North Downs and far up the Thames erstwhile market towns, Sevenoaks, Dorking, Guildford and Wokingham among them, have swollen to several times their population of a century ago. Scattered semi-rural suburban areas such as Crowborough and Haslemere have come into being and even coastal towns, Brighton, Bognor and others, harbour their quota of London commuters. There are few stations in the whole of Southern England at which the booking-clerk would not treat a request for a season ticket to London as a matter of course. To go 'up to Town' universally means to go up to London. While there are numerous local centres of business, industry, entertainment and culture, major regional centres may scarcely be said to exist, although some towns may claim to be such. Outside London Southern England has no newspapers of more than local standing; in 1969 there was only one team in the First Division of the Football League and but four Universities – and those among the newest in the country.

Besides its administrative, commercial and entertainment functions, London is also the chief port of the region and of course the greatest in the country. But there are many others of importance, some with a long history of maritime activities. These were naturally the goal of several of the main lines radiating from London.

The greatest of these is Southampton. While it was not born of the railway, it was certainly nurtured by it. Since medieval times it has been a focus of cross-channel traffic, but it fell on evil days with the discovery of the New World and the growth of the Atlantic trade in the British economy. It was revived by the intimately linked growth of the docks and the London & South Western Railway until it again achieved a full tide of prosperity as the principal Atlantic terminal. It became the premier ocean passenger port of the country, ranking second in the tonnage of shipping handled, and trading with nearly all important world ports. In 1952 13,480 vessels used it, carrying 650,000 passengers and 12 million tons of cargo. By 1966 cargo handled reached 25 million tons. Southampton is now a city of 206,300 people and is the focus of some of the region's few cross-country rail routes.

Though many of the ports of Southern England had long engaged in ferry or 'packet' services with their Continental opposite numbers, it was the railway which developed the cross-Channel traffic to its present enormous proportions. The railway companies introduced the idea of the Continental holiday to the middle classes of the later nineteenth century just as they had already fostered the seaside habit among them – and were now doing so among the working classes. In the twentieth century to go abroad came within reach of all and sundry. Nor is the traffic one way, for increasing numbers of Continentals appear to be defying the traditional rigours of tourism in Britain. In 1958 3,503,000 people crossed the Channel in ships of British Railways or of their Continental associates, and in 1966 over 5 million.

The greatest of these packet ports has always been Dover. Its development has proceeded apace since it was first reached by rail in 1844, until in 1966 3·9 million passengers used it. But other ports have been brought into being by the railway, Folkestone and Newhaven among them. Southampton also came into its own again as a cross-Channel port. But though the Continent was thus made accessible to an ever-wider section of the community, the majority of Britons have of course, always taken holidays at home. One of the consequences of the Railway Age was that to take a holiday in Britain meant doing so at the seaside. As a result the railway created, occasionally from no pre-existing nucleus, large towns whose sole function was the lodging and entertaining of visitors.

Right round the region's coasts, save only along the muddiest and most polluted shores of the Thames estuary, these towns, villages and mere groups of caravans and bus-bodies extend in an almost continuous line. The greatest of them all is Brighton. Though pre-railway in origin, its later development and its rise to greatness is so inextricably bound up with that of the London, Brighton & South Coast Railway, that the history of the one cannot be considered in isolation from that of the other. Modern Brighton is at the same time the creation and the creator of what has always been popularly known as the 'Brighton Railway'. In 1841 the town had a population of 46,661, in 1931 it had grown to 147,427, while the present population of the conurbation which includes Hove, Portslade and Shoreham exceeds 280,000.

On the other hand Bournemouth – Brighton's chief rival – is virtually the creation of the railway. In 1841 less than thirty houses stood in the area now occupied by the Borough. Even in 1881 the town was still only served by a branch line, but it had grown to 15,000. In 1961 the County Borough of Bournemouth

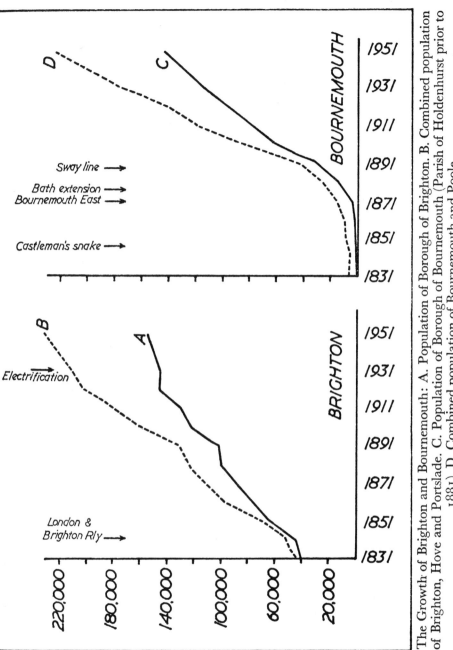

The Growth of Brighton and Bournemouth: A. Population of Borough of Brighton. B. Combined population of Brighton, Hove and Portslade. C. Population of Borough of Bournemouth (Parish of Holdenhurst prior to 1881). D. Combined population of Bournemouth and Poole.

had 153,965 inhabitants while the conurbation had over 250,000.

The Victorian era also saw the increasing complexity of modern war and the consequent growth of the armed forces. Though the final emergence of total war was to be delayed until the present century, steam had transformed the Navy, the period was not without its invasion scares, and troops were needed to bear the growing burdens of Empire. The proximity of Southern England to the Continent meant it shared very fully in this new current. The dockyard towns of Portsmouth, Chatham and Sheerness grew apace, while in the mid-century the remote village of Aldershot became the country's chief military centre. The southern railways have thus always had a considerable naval and military traffic, a traffic which reached enormous proportions whenever the country became involved in a war.

The extensive areas of fertile soils in Southern England and the great London market nearby have long made the region agriculturally important. The coming of the railway not only increased the ease with which the market could be reached, but the closely associated industrialization of Britain brought about a revolution in farming by expanding the town demand for vegetables, fruit and milk. Two writers of 1910, D. Hall and J. Russell, are of the opinion that

> Many continental travellers on the . . . South Eastern Railway, which between Tonbridge and Ashford runs along the Wealden plain, must wonder where the boasted fertility of Kentish land exists.

But today there would be no such question, this part of the Weald being as intensively cultivated as the older fruit-growing areas of North Kent. After Tonbridge the line traverses at least 15 miles of what appears to be one vast orchard and hop garden. Similarly the 'Chatham' line is bordered throughout the 40 miles from Swanley to Faversham by intensively cultivated fruit and vegetable farms with scarcely a grass field the whole way.

It may be considered significant that so far no current set in motion by industrialization has been mentioned. But, if it were ever true to talk of an industrial North and Midlands and an agricultural South, it is certainly no longer true now that most industries are not tied to the coalfields. In addition to all its other functions, London is the country's largest single centre of manufacturing industry, employing in 1956 nearly 15 per cent of its total payroll. The industrial development of London was, of course, based on a stream of sea-borne coal, later supplemented by rail-borne coal. Generating stations, producing power for Southern England, now line the lower Thames, burning coal brought direct by coastal steamer and fuel oil from the Thameside refineries. Thus the region has been through a second industrial revolution and has outstripped its coalfield rivals.

In 1955 there were 13,300 industrial establishments employing 1,569,000 workers in the then London and South East Region of the Ministry of Labour (the administrative counties of London, Kent, Middlesex, Surrey and East and West Sussex, together with the inner parts of Herts and Essex). Almost every industry other than textiles was represented, but there was a particular concentration of engineering of all kinds, especially electrical and automobile, also metals, food processing, clothing and printing.

Almost every town in the region has at least one manufacturing industry. Some of the products were used throughout the world: motor-cycles from Ashford (Kent), fire-engines from Guildford, airliners from Weybridge, and cricket-balls from Tonbridge. At Grain (Kent) and Fawley (Hants) are two of the largest oil-refineries in the country with a combined capacity in 1966 of 16·7 million tons a year, each with associated chemical industries. Other modern industries such as electronics and plastics are also widely represented. The variety of products from towns large and small is bewildering: bus bodies from Brighton, lorries from Basingstoke, fireworks from Richborough, pharmaceuticals from Folkestone, glass from Queenborough, banknote paper from Overton, flour from Southampton, beer from Alton, electric motors from Oxted.

All this was grist to the mill of the Southern Region, which, though it hid much of its freight traffic under cover of darkness, moved 2·7 million tons of merchandise in 1957, much of it industrial traffic originating on its own system or raw materials conveyed to lineside factories. Along the North Kent line some 40 daily freight trains were scheduled each way, and may at times be more frequent than passenger trains.

In short, the influence of railways on the region is all-pervading. It would be too long a task to pursue the matter systematically, but two final instances, not wholly unrelated, can be mentioned, for they have done much to alter the appearance of the countryside.

Prior to the coming of the railway the haulage of building materials was tedious and expensive. Most buildings were therefore in local materials. They merged most satisfactorily into their countryside – the wooden 'clapboard' houses of North Kent, the half-timbered houses of the Weald Clay, the 'tile-hung' dwellings of the High Weald, and the thatched villages of the Hampshire Downs.

But the railway spread a dull uniformity everywhere. It was now cheaper to build in mass-produced rail-transported bricks, first the yellow London stocks and later the reddish Flettons, roofed either in Welsh slate or red tiles. Almost all towns and villages have such an area, large or small, around the Victorian railway station, which incidentally can itself be admirable architecturally.

In the present century outer suburban rail services and the ubiquitous private car, this time in the role of feeder rather than rival, have led to the spread of building throughout the rural areas of the region. It has been termed the 'rurbanization' of Southern England. Thus we return to our starting point: for better or for worse the whole region is overshadowed by and in the grip of the 'Great Wen'.

Before turning to a study of the development of the rail net and of the relationship between the railway in particular and the economy and society in general some mention of the physiography of the region is necessary, for it is an integral part of the personality of Southern England. It has also exerted a profound influence on the development of the railway system.

Many millions of years ago Southern England was covered by a vast sheet of chalk up to a thousand feet thick. At the time of the building of the Alps this sheet was thrown up by the 'outer ripples of the Alpine storm' into a great upfold along the axis of Salisbury Plain and the Weald. This was flanked on either side by downfolds or basins, the London Basin to the north and the Hampshire Basin to the south. These basins were later filled by deposits of clays, sands and gravels. The eastern part of the upfold was eroded away to expose concentric rings of rocks older than the chalk, mainly clays, sandstones and limestones. Throughout the region the clays generally form low-lying vales and plains, while the harder rocks stand up as steep-sided ridges and plateaux. Thus between Thames and Channel are four differing types of country: the rolling chalk plateau centred on Salisbury Plain, the Weald with its concentric ridges, the chief of which are the North and South Downs, the Thames basin with its flat clay lands and its gravel-capped heights, and finally the rather similar Hampshire Basin.

The 'grain' of the country is therefore east–west. But the main lines of movement are north–south, or more accurately, between Thames and Channel. These are thus interrupted by barriers of ridge and plateau, always less than 900 feet, but disturbingly numerous. Not that they were ever insurmountable to the early engineers who had experience of building the Kilsby and Box Tunnels and the Menai Bridge or of crossing the Pennines. But these south country barriers required much cutting and tunnelling and some heavy grades. They were surmounted only at a cost, a cost that the companies were not always able to bear.

Fortunately however the high chalk ridges and plateaux are deeply seamed by valleys, while the ridges are broken in places by 'gaps'. The gradients through the ridges up to the gaps were thus eased, while the latter allowed access to the clay vales and coastal plains where lines could be laid out easily and cheaply.

Thus did the events of many millions of years influence the laying out of the railway system in the nineteenth century and its development in the twentieth.

CHAPTER II

The Dawn of the Railway Age

When the nineteenth century began, Southern England was entirely without railways. Save for the horse-operated Surrey Iron Railway, it was to remain so during the next quarter-century. Many proposals were made but, at a time when railways were already commonplace in several parts of the country and were rapidly becoming so in others, no construction was achieved.

The Northumberland and Durham coalfield was exploited by a very fully developed private railway system; in South Wales many miles of line had been built; and in the Midlands lines were rapidly developing as feeders to the excellent canal system. Even the West Country had its tramways. True, some of Southern England's roads had been improved, but generally there had been little change in the transport system since the Middle Ages. Wherever possible heavy goods, such as iron, coal and grain, and passengers too were moved by coasting vessel. Small ports were dotted along the coast between London and Poole and served a very large proportion of the population. In 1731 fifteen vessels a month were entering Chichester, bringing coal from the Tyne, salt from the Isle of Wight, cheese from Poole and cloth and wines from London, returning with grain, flour, malt, timber and beer. In addition some of the rivers were navigable for a short way above the estuaries.

The roads were among the worst in England. They were badly surfaced and had to cross wide outcrops of clay where they became all but impassable during wet weather. Defoe, writing in 1724, says of Wealden roads:

> In dry Summers, indeed a great deal [of timber] is carried away to Maidstone and sometimes I have seen one tree on a Carriage, which they call there a Tug, drawn by 22 oxen, and even then it is carried so little a way, being thrown down and

left for other Tugs to take up and carry away that sometimes it
is two or three years before it gets to Chatham, for if once the
rains begin, it stirs no more that year, and sometimes a whole
Summer is not dry enough to make the roads passable.

It is small wonder that there was little development in the economy, and that the larger towns were confined to the coasts and
estuaries. However, by 1820 almost all the main roads had been
turnpiked. The roads to Dover, Portsmouth and Brighton, via
Cuckfield, were excellent, while even in the backward Weald
there was a considerable mileage of turnpikes. In some cases the
turnpikes were not merely improvements of existing roads, but on
new alignments and well engineered. Such a one is the A229 from
Maidstone to Hastings. This has heavy cuttings and embank-
ments through the ridges of the High Weald and even crosses
two roads by 'underpasses'. By 1835 there were 810 miles of turnpikes in Hampshire and most of what are now the class 'A' roads
had been improved.

Inland water transport had been aided by river 'navigations'.
The first Act for a navigation in Southern England was obtained
in 1651 for improving the $15\frac{1}{2}$ miles of the Wey from its junction
with the Thames at Weybridge to Guildford. By 1800, reaches of
the Wey, Medway, Arun, Adur and Western Rother were improved, a total length, according to the canal historian Charles
Hadfield, of $93\frac{3}{8}$ miles. These brought the advantages of water
transport to inland market towns such as Tonbridge, Midhurst
and Godalming. But few canals were cut to feed these navigable
rivers with traffic – only seven, with a total length of $142\frac{1}{2}$ miles,
and none were financially successful. Three, the Arun & Wey, the
Basingstoke, and the Portsmouth & Arundel, perished miserably.
Three more, the Croydon, the Thames & Medway, and the
Andover, were converted to railways. Only the Royal Military
Canal at Hythe survives in good order. Southern England thus
missed the Canal Age. By the time the urge to improve the transport system became irresistible, the railway was available – a far
more efficient mover in this region of broken terrain.

Even when steamers were introduced, after 1815, to carry the
important coasting traffic – over a million passengers annually
used the 'long ferry' between London and Gravesend – the transport system of the early nineteenth century was quite inadequate

to deal with any expansion of the economy. Elsewhere expansion was rapid as a result of the Industrial Revolution; but in Southern England many of the traditional industries were in full decay. The last furnaces smelting Wealden iron had been extinguished; the textile mills of Kent and Hampshire were dying in the face of the mechanized production of the North; and the wooden boat-building industry of the estuaries was yielding before the coming of iron. There were, of course, still industries based on local agriculture and supplying local markets, such as milling, malting and brewing, butter- and cheese-making. There were also brick and tile works, and so on. But the region could not share in the Industrial Revolution without railways.

In addition to these economic needs for transport improvements, there was a strategic need. Britain was at war with Napoleon, who controlled the whole of the opposing Channel shore. The coastal route, the strategic and economic lifeline of Southern England, was under constant pressure from the French army. The whole country feared invasion.

Speedy communication with the naval bases of Portsmouth and Dover and means of diverting commerce from the Dover Straits were urgent objectives. Thus there were numerous schemes afoot for linking Portsmouth with London, both by canal and railway. The immediate danger was averted by the victory at Trafalgar in 1805, but the economic compulsion remained.

THE SURREY IRON RAILWAY

The pioneer Surrey Iron Railway grew out of a proposal of 1799 to open a part railway, part canal, route between London and Portsmouth. The railway portion was to be open to the public, who would use their own horses and wagons, on payment of tolls. In short it was to be a public railway and not one of the private canal-feeder or mineral lines, hitherto the only ones known.

The first part of the new route, from the Thames at Wandsworth to Croydon, was to have been a canal, but William Jessop and later John Rennie, both retained as consultants, decided the water requirements of a canal would be harmful to the industries of the Wandle valley, even then an important manufacturing area. James Malcolm, in his *Survey of Surrey*, reported 38 factories along the banks of the Wandle, employing between them 1,700 people and representing a capital investment of a half to one million pounds. This concentration of industry was in itself justification for improved transport, even if the eventual aim of reaching Portsmouth was rather more doubtful economically. At a shareholders' meeting at Wandsworth on 3 June 1800 a railway was finally decided upon and next year the Surrey Iron Railway Company, the world's first public railway, was incorporated under an Act of 21 May 1801. At a meeting of 4 June that year, William Jessop, part-owner of the Butterley Iron Works, was appointed engineer.

The Wandle Valley presented few obstacles, and the railway was formally opened, with due ceremony, on 26 July 1803. It is probable that public traffic had already been passing to and from 'Mr. Henckell's iron mills' at Garret, near Wandsworth. A branch to Carshalton was opened on or about 1 June 1804.

The Surrey Iron Railway was of double track, laid with plate rails on stone sleepers, many of which can be seen in rockeries and walls along the course today. The cost of construction worked out at about £7,000 per mile. Four-wheeled wagons, the wheels flangeless and iron-tyred, were used, drawn by horses. They were provided by merchants and carriers who paid tolls calculated on tonnage, commodity and distance. The opening of the Surrey Iron Railway marks a most important stage in transport history, being not only the first public railway in the world, but the first line of any kind in Southern England. The fact remains, however, that it partook more of the features of the early mineral tramways of northern England than of the modern railway.

On 17 May 1803 the Royal Assent was given to an Act incorporating the Croydon, Merstham & Godstone Iron Railway Company to extend the Surrey Iron Railway up the dry valley south of Croydon to the Merstham Gap in the North Downs and then on to Reigate, en route for Portsmouth. In the event, the urge to reach Portsmouth and even Reigate faded with Nelson's victory and with the high cost of construction. The line never got beyond the Greystone Lime Works at Merstham, a vast gash in the face of the North Downs alongside the Merstham and Quarry Tunnels of the present Brighton line. The route – mostly of single track –

can still be traced on the side of the valley opposite that of the Brighton line, having become a series of footpaths and rights of way. South of Coulsdon, however, while some remains exist, it has been largely obliterated by rail and road construction.

At least for a few years the Surrey Iron Railway served its purpose, though it was never financially successful. It was abandoned in 1846 – the Croydon, Merstham & Godstone had already been closed, in 1838 – the Act of Dissolution reciting that 'traffic along the line ... has of late years been diminishing'.

THE CANTERBURY & WHITSTABLE RAILWAY

The first public, steam-powered, passenger and freight line in Southern England was opened in 1830, the opening year for the Liverpool & Manchester Railway and nearly a quarter of a century after the Surrey Iron Railway's appearance. It was a short line, 6 miles long, and of purely local import, but its place in the history of railway development in Southern England remains assured. It had a long life, for though it was always a backwater it remained part of the rail network until 1953.

In 1820 the cathedral city of Canterbury, East Kent's most important market centre, was in many ways typical of the inland towns of Southern England. Though it had some local industries such as milling and brewing, its textile industry had died and its main function was to collect the agricultural products of the surrounding countryside – cattle, grain, fruit and hops – and to export the surplus, in return importing and distributing coal and manufactures from other parts of Britain. For this, the city depended on its river, the Stour, and its port, Fordwich.

But throughout historical times the Stour estuary had been silting up, depriving Canterbury of its principal link with the outside world. Since the reign of Henry VIII, if not earlier, there had been many proposals for improving the river, but little was achieved even after an 1811 survey for a canal from Ashford, down the Stour Valley to Canterbury and out to the Thames estuary at St Nicholas Bay. But Telford was later invited to plan a navigation below Canterbury and as a result of his survey an Act was obtained in 1825.

That this scheme fell through is symptomatic that the Railway

Age was dawning. That this dawn illuminated an oligarchical provincial city council of the early nineteenth century was largely due to the personality of William James, one of the minor prophets of the Age, whom some call the 'father' of railways in preference to George Stephenson. James had visited the city in 1823 and strongly urged a railway directly out to the Thames, where a harbour could be built at the fishing village of Whitstable.

His arguments were so persuasive that they eventually carried the day. After he had surveyed the line a Bill was successfully promoted in opposition to the Telford scheme, and the Canterbury & Whitstable Railway Company was incorporated by an Act of 10 June 1825. The original capital as proposed by James was £25,000, but doubts on its adequacy led to the calling in of George Stephenson as consultant. He endorsed James's alignment, but raised the estimates by £6,000. This resulted in his replacing James as engineer, but after one visit he sent an assistant, Joseph Locke, to lay out the line.

Work went ahead steadily and on 3 May 1830 the formal opening ceremony took place amid general rejoicing. The solitary locomotive was driven by no less a person than Edward Fletcher, later locomotive superintendent of the North Eastern. Public traffic began next day.

The line was single and just over 6 miles long. Its Canterbury terminus was in North Lane, across the river from Westgate Towers. All traces of the original station have been destroyed in laying out the present goods yard. Athwart the short run to the coast was the 300-foot plateau of the Blean Forest, entailing heavy gradients on either approach to a gable summit, including 836 yards at 1 in 31. Under Tyler Hill was a 1,012-yard tunnel. Some writers have neither referred to a good map nor walked the line, for they quote the apocryphal story that Stephenson built the tunnel not because it was necessary, but at the insistence of the citizens of Canterbury, who felt no good railway was complete without one. The Canterbury & Whitstable seems to have been one of the first to issue season tickets; 'family' and 'personal' tickets were available from 25 March 1834.

During its independent existence the railway owned only one locomotive, the *Invicta*, an 0-4-0 with outside cylinders at the

leading end, built by Robert Stephenson. The first to be so
equipped, it is thus the direct ancestor of the modern steam locomotive. After long exposure in the Moat Gardens, Canterbury,
it was brought under cover in 1981. It was not successful, even
on the level stretch outside Whitstable, and the line was soon
worked entirely by stationary engines (the engine-man's cottage
at Tyler Hill is still inhabited), a state of affairs which lasted
until the line was taken over by the South Eastern in 1844. It
was closed to passengers from 1 January 1931, and for freight
from 1 December 1952. It was temporarily reopened to supply
Whitstable during the floods of the following January.

At Whitstable a small harbour was excavated in the muddy
foreshore, capable of receiving small coasters and colliers. This
harbour was served by extensive sidings and a simple stone-
built station which still survives, though in a very derelict condition. Across the road stands the 1894 South Eastern station, built
to obviate passenger trains having to use the level-crossing. The
track has disappeared off the whole line. In 1957 the harbour was
sold by the British Transport Commission to Whitstable Urban
Council for £12,500. It is now used by increasing numbers of
yachts.

THE LONDON & GREENWICH AND
LONDON & CROYDON RAILWAYS

Even now the Railway Age had not fully dawned. The first two
lines which might be described as the immediate ancestors of the
present system were opened during the decade following the
Canterbury & Whitstable venture. They were both built on the
then outskirts of London, and foreshadowed the Southern Region
by being interested chiefly in passenger traffic – and suburban
traffic at that, catered for by an intensive service at regular intervals. However, their promotion was of more than local interest,
for they were also designed to provide an approach to London for
trunk lines from the south and east. This they eventually did and
they are now vital links in the approaches to London Bridge
station. Though they are strictly outside our area, some details
must be noticed here.

The London & Greenwich Railway was incorporated by an

Act of 17 May 1833 to build a line 3¾ miles long from London Bridge to Greenwich, then not only important for its riverside activities, but as a fashionable residential area. There is no doubt, however, that the promoters intended to project the line on to Dover. This was logical enough. The southern shores of the Thames estuary form the natural route to Dover, followed by the Dover Road since Roman times. Many important riverain towns, Dartford, Gravesend, Rochester and Faversham among them, would be served and would provide a source of heavy traffic. But, as we shall see, this route to Dover only became possible after many years as a result of piecemeal construction. In consequence no through train traverses it from end to end. It must therefore be regarded as one of the failures, failures surprisingly few in view of haphazard development, that instead of a quadruple-track exit from London down the great riverain routeway, there is but a sinuous, heavily occupied and severely graded double-track on which high speeds are impossible even for electric trains.

The line was planned by G. T. Landmann, a retired Colonel of Engineers, who described his scheme before the Committee of the proposed Company in October 1831. He suggested that the track should be built on a viaduct, to facilitate crossing the numerous roads and lanes at the approach to London. This idea was accepted.

The railway was formally opened by the Lord Mayor on 14 December 1836, though a part of it had been opened since 8 February that year, and it was not until 24 December 1838 that the final half mile to Greenwich was ready. Once the novelty had worn off, traffic was disappointing. The capital cost worked out at over £266,000 per mile, and at first dividends were low and intermittent. Soon the line was to be used by other companies, however, and income from tolls soared. Eventually the South Eastern, which never wittingly over-valued any property it took over, leased the line for 999 years at 4½ per cent of the total capital, which the shareholders drew until the Company was dissolved in 1923, though of course it had lost its commercial and operating identity seventy-nine years before.

The market town of Croydon lay in the upper, dry valley of the Wandle and thus the natural approach was up that river from its junction with the Thames at Wandsworth. This was the

way the Surrey Iron Railway reached the town in 1803. Four
years later a rival route became available with the opening of the
Croydon Canal from what is now New Cross. The new canal was
not a success, for it had to surmount the heights of Forest Hill.

By now the railway was becoming a more efficient and economic form of transport and it was decided to replace the canal.
Croydon was, as today, the most important town immediately
south of London and a goal in itself. But in between lay those
gravel-capped clay hills which proved the undoing of the canal,
but which estate agents were wont to describe as 'salubrious'.
Already the wealthier merchants and professional men were escap-
ing from their homes above their businesses in the City and were
building villas on this line of heights whose very names – Den-
mark Hill, Sydenham Hill and Forest Hill – were to typify
Victorian suburbia. Here was an opportunity for traffic. There
was yet a third objective. Like the Greenwich line, the London
& Croydon was to be an approach line for trunk routes from the
south.

The Act of 12 June 1835 required the purchase of the whole
canal undertaking for £40,250 – plus another shilling for loss of
profits. From West Croydon to Corbett's Lane was 8¾ miles and
thence the trains would have running powers for 1¾ miles over
Greenwich metals to a separate station at London Bridge.

The engineer was William Cubitt, who soon found difficulty
in excavating the deep clay cutting from New Cross (now New
Cross Gate) to near the summit of the bank at Forest Hill. Severe
slips occurred on this section even after opening. The line's formal
opening was on 1 June 1839, 150 guests, including the Lord
Mayor, being conveyed to Croydon in two special trains to view
'the extensive station . . . excellently arranged and containing
every comfort that can be desired'. Public traffic began on 5 June,
a service of 12 trains a day, virtually on a time-interval basis,
being provided. The Railway Age had at last fully dawned.

THREE TRUNK LINES

The way was now clear for the next stage in the historical development of the railway system, the building of trunk lines on which
branches were later grafted to make up a dense network. In the

late 1830s, three trunk lines were almost simultaneously promoted, each connecting London with an important point on the Channel coast, Dover, Brighton and Southampton respectively. These three lines were to become the backbones of the three major companies which went to form the Southern Railway and whose ghosts are still discernible in some features of the Southern Region.

Dover, taken first only because it is intended to start at the east and work westward, was an obvious goal. The gateway to England since the Romans founded it, alone of the medieval Cinque ports, at one time paramount in defence and commerce, its importance has remained undiminished. Permanent peace in 1815 led to a great increase in traffic. In 1824 8,000 people crossed the Channel from Dover alone. Moreover, the traffic, passenger and freight, was of the kind which could afford to pay for speed. The traditional route, by the Roman Watling Street, lay over the Kentish Downs to Canterbury and on to Faversham, whence the south bank of the estuary was followed, the Medway being crossed at Rochester. The logical step would have been to have built a railway along this long-established and busy route. In 1824 the first scheme was launched with Telford as engineer. Similar schemes were put forward in 1832 and 1835. But all foundered on the barriers of the Medway and the Kentish Downs or upon Admiralty intransigence (Vol. III, p. 45), which held up any extension of the London & Greenwich until 1878.

Meanwhile the legend that was Brighton was growing apace, and the town with it. The insignificant fishing village of Brighthelmstone, built on the edge of a shingle beach where a small stream entered the sea from a steep-sided valley in the South Downs, had grown into a town of 24,429 in 1821. A decade later it numbered 40,634 and was the largest town in Southern England outside London. This was largely the work of a Lewes doctor, Richard Russell, who advocated sea bathing as a cure for all manner of the ills that eighteenth-century flesh was heir to, and who founded there a bathing establishment. Aided by its proximity to London it was now the resort of fashionable society, led by the Prince Regent himself. Nash had been commissioned to extend Holland's fabulous Sino-Indian Pavilion and around it High Society lodged in the elegant Georgian terraces which have become the glory of Brighton.

Communications with London were on a lavish scale for the period. It was reported to a Parliamentary Committee in 1836 that 36 coaches were on the London and Brighton run with a licensed capacity of 3,400 passengers a week. The actual number of passengers carried in 1835 was 117,000, the average fare being 21s. inside and 12s. outside, the average time 6 hours. Then, as now, speed was the order of the day on the Brighton Road. In 1784 the Prince of Wales had driven himself down in 4½ hours and in November 1830 the *Red Rover* coach, bringing the text of the King's speech, arrived in Brighton in 4 hours 20 minutes. Coaches were doing the round trip in a day and Cobbett painted in his usual sour manner a picture of commuting 'stock-jobbers' living in Brighton and doing business in London.

Here then was a prize for the early railway promoters. Soon a number of rival schemes were mooted. The interesting point historically is that a line to Brighton would, with the doubtful exception of the Oystermouth horse tramway, be the first ever built primarily to serve and develop a holiday resort, itself a relatively new social concept.

The third of the chief objectives of the promoters was, of course, Southampton, one of the most important ports in the country. Yet there were fears that the traffic potential would be insufficient to justify the construction of a trunk route, and there was some evidence to support this.

In the first place, Southampton had declined in importance since it had attained prosperity in medieval times exporting wool and importing wine across the Channel. It had not shared in the growing Atlantic trade of the eighteenth century to the extent of Bristol, Liverpool and Glasgow. For although trade had grown to some extent, the passage up Southampton Water was difficult for large sailing ships. The days of steam, however, had by now arrived and the port had the unique advantage of double high tides, increasing the period of high water and reducing the tidal range, thus rendering enclosed docks unnecessary.

In the second place the countryside between Southampton and London was then sparsely peopled. In 1821 there were only 135,000 people living within 10 miles of the route finally selected. London had not yet begun to spread south-westward up the slopes of the Thames Basin, and Surbiton, Weybridge and Woking were either non-existent or small villages, and though there was much good farming land, Hampshire then, as today, had much unproductive heathland, and it also still had 100,000 acres of forest, preserved for naval timber.

But the citizens of Southampton were rapidly regaining confidence in the future of their town, which by 1831 had doubled its 1801 population of 8,000. In 1803 the Harbour Commissioners were constituted and had obtained powers to build docks. But it was obvious there must be an overland link with London before any large expansion could take place. Delays to shipping passing through the Straits of Dover through fog and contrary winds added weight to the argument. Meanwhile in 1830 about 100,000 passengers had used the port (probably mostly cross-Channel passengers) and 30,262 tons of goods had passed by road in the area. According to Colonel Henderson, first chairman of the London & Southampton railway, in 1831 coal cost 23s. to 30s. a chauldron (25½ cwt.) at Southampton, but 50s. to 60s. in the heart of Hampshire. An economic rail charge would add but 6s. to the Southampton price.

Further evidence of traffic potential is provided from a meeting of gentlemen connected with a number of western counties held in 1832 to discuss the effect of the railway. One cattle salesman estimated that 6,000 sheep and 50,000 cattle were driven up to London annually from the area concerned and that droving losses were heavy. In addition nearly 3,500 tons of grain were sent up.

Taking it all round there was much hope for the new trunk lines to Dover, Brighton and Southampton.

CHAPTER III

Kent and the 'Feud'

The bastion of England in war, Kent is the gateway of England in peace. But it is more than this: its fertile soils have for long made it one of London's chief larders, while more recently its coastal towns have become holiday resorts and its north-western portion has been invaded by the sprawling suburbs of London.

The general pattern of communications and of the railway system in particular can be explained in terms of the three ribs of upland which stretch eastward, separating three bands of lowland into which the main routes are channelled. The most northerly of the three ribs is the broad plateau of the North Downs, which slopes gently down to the Thames marshes which lie to the north. The crest of the Downs falls in a steep scarp into the narrow Vale of Holmesdale, beyond which rises a second, narrower and lower upland, the Greensand or Ragstone Ridge. This in turn is separated from the ridge and valley country of the High Weald by the broad Vale of Kent.

Along the northern flanks of the Downs and through the Vale of Kent respectively run two main lines, each linking London with Dover, while through Holmesdale runs what has become a secondary through route to Dover. From each main line spring a number of branches, in many cases respectively serving the same towns, for the main lines were built by rival companies. Finally, in the remoter areas several small independent companies built and operated their own small systems.

But, while each main and branch line follows routes influenced by the physical features just described, the growth of the system can only be explained in terms of the ruinous warfare waged between the Companies owning the two main lines. Instead of dealing with a series of self-contained areas as is general in this series, the approach in Kent must be at least partly chronological,

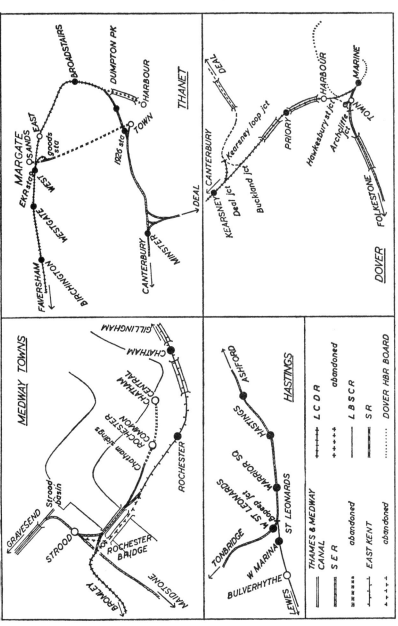

The Dover and Deal joint railway (represented by a broken line) is a unique example of co-operation between the warring companies.

MEDWAY TOWNS

GRAVESEND
Strood basin
STROOD
Chatham sidings
ROCHESTER COMMON
ROCHESTER BRIDGE
ROCHESTER
MAIDSTONE
BROMLEY
CHATHAM CENTRAL
CHATHAM
GILLINGHAM

MARGATE

FAVERSHAM
BIRCHINGTON
WESTGATE
EKR stage
WEST
OSANDS
EAST
goods sta
1926 sta
BROADSTAIRS
DUMPTON PK
HARBOUR
TOWN
MINSTER
CANTERBURY
DEAL

THANET

HASTINGS

TONBRIDGE
ASHFORD
HASTINGS
WARRIOR SQ
ST LEONARDS
W ST LEONARDS
Bopeep jct
W MARINA
BULVERHYTHE
LEWES

DOVER

KEARSNEY
CANTERBURY
Deal jct
Buckland jct
Kearsney loop jct
DEAL
PRIORY
HARBOUR
Hawkesbury st jct
Archcliffe jct
TOWN
MARINE
FOLKESTONE

THAMES & MEDWAY CANAL
S E R
S E R abandoned
EAST KENT
L C D R
L C D R abandoned
L B S C R
S R
DOVER HBR BOARD

the story being divided into three main periods. Some aspects, however, such as Folkestone and Dover and their Continental traffic, have their own sections; and as in other books in this series branch lines are listed separately at the chapter's end.

The first of the three main periods is dominated by the building of the first trunk line to Dover and the subsequent expansion of the South Eastern Railway which built it. This period ends in 1861 with the establishment of the London, Chatham & Dover's competing service from Victoria to Dover. The second period is that of the calamitous feud between the Companies, and ends with the fusion of 1899. The third period is one of consolidation by the South Eastern and Chatham Managing Committee, but it is also marked by the rapid increase in traffic brought about by the outward spread of London.

FIRST PERIOD: TRUNK LINE TO DOVER

Mention has already been made of the reasons for promoting a line from London to Dover and of the fate of the schemes seeking to follow the road route (page 21).

Success was finally won by the South Eastern. Originally this line was to cross the North Downs by the dry valleys leading up to the gap in the summit at Oxted. Thence the low-lying Vale of Kent, the outcrop of the Weald Clay, was to be used as far as Ashford. From here the line was to run under the Downs to Folkestone and so along the sea-shore to Dover. The route was circuitous in the extreme and passed through few towns but it traversed relatively easy country. The promoters also had their eye on Brighton, which could be reached by a branch line from Edenbridge.

There was some indecision about the approach to London. The Act of Incorporation, 21 June 1836, specifies an end-on junction with the London & Croydon. A further Act altered the junction to Jolly Sailor (now Norwood Junction) and finally the passage of the London & Brighton Act of 1837 altered the situation once more, for Parliament were insistent that only one approach to London from the south and south-east was needed. The South Eastern was not averse to this, as it reduced costs, even though lengthening the London–Dover run. Accordingly a junction was authorized at a lonely spot which is now Redhill but was then referred to as Earlswood Common.

Ownership of the approach to the common terminus of London Bridge was as follows:

London Bridge to Corbett's Lane	1¾ miles,	London and Greenwich
Corbett's Lane to Jolly Sailor	7¾ ,,	London and Croydon
Jolly Sailor to Stoat's Nest	5 ,,	London and Brighton
Stoat's Nest to Earlswood Common	6½ ,,	South Eastern

So from its earliest days the South Eastern was nurtured in the atmosphere of unpunctuality for which it was later to become notorious. There could be no other result when up to four mutually hostile Companies were using the same metals with no other train-control methods than time-table and time-interval, for there were not even telegraphs to convey information of the whereabouts of trains. From this too sprang the tradition of bad relations between the South Eastern and the Brighton, bad relations which affected the long-suffering travelling public as much as the bickering parties themselves. Though only a single instance, the ridiculous feud over the unimportant Caterham Railway (page 89) typifies the sad story.

The new Company seemed curiously slow to start work on the line. It was not until its first meeting that the appointment of William Cubitt as engineer was announced and not until the one of 25 November 1837 was it announced that the work had actually started. This may have been due to a project surveyed by Sir John Rennie, details of which were made public in 1838 – the Central of Kent. It was to be an extension of the London & Greenwich and was to run via Lewisham, the Darenth Valley to Otford and thence along Holmesdale through Maidstone to Ashford. At one time it was hoped to interest the South Eastern sufficiently to alter its Oxted route, but the project perished.

From the accounts of succeeding meetings we can build up a picture of the organization of railway construction in those hopeful early days when earthworks were formed by the picks and shovels of thousands of 'navigators', though it is hard fully to recapture the excitement – not to mention the inconvenience to the ordinary population – in the countryside intersected by the route. In November 1838 it was stated that work had commenced at Tunbridge (the old spelling) and that Shakespeare Tunnel was 'progressing'. In November next year it was reported that from the 'Brighton Junction' to Tudeley (a locality east of Tonbridge), a distance of 22 miles, 'the works were everywhere active in 12 divisions or contracts and will be ready for permanent way next summer'. As to the section Tudeley to 'Staplehurst Road' (the site of Staplehurst Station), the 'line was being formed'. Thence to Ashford the 'works' would be light and there would be no cause for worry if they had not yet been started. 'Heavy work' was in progress between Folkestone and Dover.

In May 1841 it was reported that one of the twin bores of Shakespeare Tunnel had been completed and that the sea wall between the various tunnels was in a 'formed state'. The 'preliminaries' of the other two tunnels on this section were completed. Nothing had been done between Ashford and Staplehurst, half the work had been done thence to Tonbridge and the remainder should be open to traffic the following year. Permanent way was being delivered at Tonbridge, by the Medway Navigation. From Tonbridge to 'the Brighton line not a single spot [was] unoccupied with workmen and contractors'.

The engineer's report of 20 November 1841 stated that 3 miles of permanent way had been laid between Tonbridge and Edenbridge, 'on which the locomotive engines of Messrs. Betts [the contractors for ballasting and permanent way] are at work night and day'. Bletchingley Tunnel was ready.

The next report, that of 31 May 1842, gave the long-awaited news of the opening of the line for passenger traffic as far as Tonbridge on 26 May. Stations were provided at Reigate, Godstone, Edenbridge and Tonbridge and were erected at 'moderate cost'. The only one of these still in its original form is at Edenbridge and here we can appreciate the 'moderate cost' when we examine the staggered platforms, with level-crossing instead of a footbridge, and the simple single-storey wooden clapboard building. Staggered platforms were common on the South Eastern outside the London area and until 1961 Marden, Staplehurst and Pluckley, all on the main line, were without footbridges.

The line was opened to Headcorn on 31 August and to Ashford on 1 December 1842. The report of 2 December gives the first revenue account, from 26 May to 30 October 1842:

RECEIPTS

	£	s.	d.
Passenger traffic	16,012	17	7
Carriages	277	14	6
Horses and dogs	214	4	0
Parcels	725	1	10
Carrying a/c (i.e. goods)	128	7	5
	17,358	5	4

EXPENDITURE

	£	s.	d.
Maintenance of Way	682	15	1
Locomotive power	3,120	8	0½
Coaching Dept.	1,793	8	9
Police (mainly signalling)	556	7	3
Duty (Govt. tax on passengers)	765	1	8
Tolls (to Croydon and Greenwich Coys.)	2,902	13	0
Rates	58	3	11
Lighting stations with gas	38	9	0
General charges	1,125	8	11½
Balance (surplus)	6,315	9	8
	17,358	5	4

On 28 June 1843 the line was extended to a temporary station at Folkestone: the 19-arch, 100-foot-high Foord Viaduct was not ready until 18 December, when the permanent station (Folkestone Junction) was opened. *Bradshaw* of September 1843 shows 8 trains each way, 3 conveying third-class passengers. The fastest trains covered the 91¾ miles in 3 hours 5 minutes, an average speed of 29·6 m.p.h.

This may not seem particularly impressive. It must however be remembered that it was nearly three times the speed of a mail-coach. It must also be remembered there was another side to coach travel from that given by film producers in which coaches for ever bowl along good roads in brilliant sunshine. On the whole coach travel was slow, uncomfortable and expensive. In 1840 it cost as much to travel the 30 miles from Tunbridge Wells to St Leonards as it did to stay for a fortnight in good lodgings at the latter. The new railway might have been primitive, but was an advance over the coach greater than that of aircraft over surface transport, for hitherto no one on land had travelled faster than a horse. Mechanical transport was a completely new conception.

The railway hurried on with its extension to Dover, one of the last obstacles being overcome on 26 January 1843, when the Round Down cliff was destroyed by a vast blasting operation involving 18,500 lb. of powder. The contemporary Press spread itself on the spectacle, but the whole line below the cliffs is an impressive feat, considering the limited tools and engineering experience of the day. It had one unusual feature; its cost was less than was estimated.

Trains began to run into Dover on 7 February 1844. Down trains left London Bridge at 8.0, 9.30 and 11.30 a.m., 1.30, 4.0 and 5.30 p.m. The 8.0, 11.30 and 4.0 ranked as expresses, taking 3 hours, and did not convey third-class passengers. These latter could only travel to and from New Cross until Bricklayers Arms was opened the following year. The South Eastern was not going to pay high Greenwich tolls on low third-class fares (Vol. III, p. 13).

Cubitt laid out the line well, to the great advantage of present-day operation. Save for very slight deviations at Staplehurst and Headcorn, the latter dating only from 1924, it is dead straight over the 26 miles from Tonbridge to Ashford. This came to be a well-known racing ground and, incidentally, a navigation aid for aircraft. Aided by the very gently rolling terrain of the Vale of Kent all this was accomplished without extensive earthworks or gradients more severe than short undulations at 1 in 220 to 250. At Redhill the line diverges sharply from that to Brighton and after an initial rise, descends gradually all the way to Tonbridge. Bletchingley Tunnel (1,327 yards), between Nutfield (opened 1883) and Godstone, is the only engineering feature. It figured in an early text-book on tunnelling by F. W. Simms, the resident engineer. Lyghe Halt dates from 1911.

Beyond Tonbridge the line undulates gently all the way to Ashford but thereafter rises continuously for eight miles, mainly at 1 in 250 and 280, to a summit immediately beyond Westenhanger. Then comes a twelve-mile descent to sea-level at Dover. Near Sandling are two short tunnels, but of course the chief engineering works lie beyond Folkestone at the foot of the 'white cliffs'. The 532-yard Martello Tunnel gives access to the hummocky area of the Warren, a former landslip. After this the track is carried on an artificial shelf, reinforced by a sea wall up to and between the 1,942-yard Abbotscliff and 1,387-yard Shakespeare

Tunnels. The entry into Dover from the latter was originally over a timber trestle.

The principal stations were well designed with the main platforms reached by loops off the through roads. Originally Tonbridge, Paddock Wood and Ashford were so equipped. Redhill was rebuilt in this style probably in 1844 and Headcorn as late as 1924. The fullest use of these loops is made at peak periods, particularly to allow the non-stop boat trains to overtake stopping trains. Most of the larger stations have been rebuilt but Paddock Wood retained until about 1968 the dignified Italianate red-brick of many early South Eastern stations.

Tonbridge (30,325 in 1971) is an ancient market town which grew up round the Norman castle guarding the Medway crossing. Its importance preceded the coming of the railway, but its subsequent growth was due to the latter. Tonbridge became an important junction and the railway was the largest employer in the town. As late as 1963 there were 150 men under the stationmaster. In addition there was a large goods depot (the East Yard) and a locomotive shed, which closed with electrification. In 1934 the station was rebuilt, the approach curve from Sevenoaks eased, and a new marshalling yard (the West or 'Jubilee') laid out. The area has since been provided with multiple-aspect signalling (m.a.s.) and yet another signal box. There was commuting to London from the 1930s on, but it grew to large proportions in the 1950s, and still further after electrification in 1962. By 1963 there were 2,300 season-ticket holders, a 44 per cent increase over 1957.

Paddock Wood, a junction since the Maidstone branch opened in 1844, was, until then, officially Maidstone Road. But a handbill of 11 October 1842 advertising coach connections to Maidstone shows that Paddock Wood (a wood of that name had been cleared to build the station) was already in popular use. When the railway arrived, there was no nearby dwelling, but by 1971 the village had grown to 4,805, having doubled since 1951. It has a number of industries and is the centre of thousands of acres of orchards and hop gardens, almost all of which have been planted since the coming of the railway. Though little produce is now railed, during the 1930s a control office was set up during the fruit-picking season.

For many years the station has been a busy one. In 1951 53,000 tickets were issued and 73,000 collected and traffic has grown considerably since. In 1952 23,620 loaded wagons were dealt with in the goods depot and 144,320 wagons passed through the small Keylands Yard to and from other stations in the fruit belt and in the industrial area of the Lower Medway. The picturesque seasonal influx of hop-pickers from London is however no more. As late as 1952 4,442 pickers and 23,000 friends travelled in 56 special trains. But even then the 'hopping' traffic was a pale shadow of its former self due to rising living standards and greater moderation in the Bacchanalian ceremonies which accompanied the hop-harvest. Mechanization has rendered the pickers largely unnecessary and the few still employed bring their impedimenta in motor vans.

In the half-yearly report of May 1842 it was announced that an agreement had been drawn up for pooling the South Eastern's stock of 34 locomotives with the Croydon, under the South Eastern's locomotive superintendent, Benjamin Cubitt. The Cubitts seem to have been well established on the South Eastern. In March 1844 the Brighton Company joined the pool, which lasted until 31 January 1846. By that time the Companies were establishing works at Brighton and Ashford, so what was probably the main reason for the pool, the single works at New Cross (now New Cross Gate), had passed away.

Ashford locomotive works had been planned in February 1846, Ashford then being a small market town (3,082 inhabitants in 1841) in a comparatively impoverished area. There was thus an adequate supply of unskilled labour, though key men had to be obtained from the North of England. One hundred and eighty-five acres were purchased for works and housing and by the autumn of 1847 all work had been transferred from New Cross Gate. The carriage and wagon works were established in 1850.

Ashford New Town (originally Alfred Town) remains as a complete example of a planned Victorian industrial housing estate. Built round a green, it included public baths, an inn and a general store, a row of what are reputed to be the only 'back-to-back' houses in Southern England, presumably originally for labourers, larger terrace houses for the skilled men, very large villas for the works manager and other officers, a school and a mechanics' institute. Around the outskirts are more recent houses built by the Managing Committee for the men from Longhedge transferred when the Chatham's works were closed in 1913. It is still said in the New Town that for many years the children of the original South Eastern employees were not allowed to play with those of 'the Battersea folk'.

The locomotive works closed in 1962, but the wagon works are still active and electric stock is serviced at the Chart Leacon shops, opened in 1961. The railway introduced the concept of manufacturing industry to this southern market town, an important aspect of its present functions. An agreed site for London overspill, the town grew from 24,783 in 1951 to 36,380 in 1971. Between 1961 and 1967 ticket sales rose by 54 per cent to 400,000 and those of season tickets by 24 per cent. In 1966 21 freight trains were despatched daily from Ashford Sidings. The passenger station was rebuilt and enlarged in the early 1900s and again completely rebuilt in 1961–3, when the bays at the country end of each main platform were converted to through platforms.

THE EXPANSION OF THE SOUTH EASTERN: HASTINGS

Even before the main line was open all the way, the directors had plans afoot for numerous extensions. Many of these came to fruition during the boom in railway promotion known as the Railway Mania. This culminated in the 1845–46 Session, when 815 Bills were deposited, of which 280 received the Royal Assent, thus authorizing the building of 4,450 route miles in Britain as a whole.

Though not the first branch, that to Hastings was certainly one of the more important. In 1845 the Brighton, Lewes & Hastings Company obtained powers to extend its line from Lewes to Ashford via Hastings, keeping close to the coast for most of the way. The South Eastern deposited counter-proposals in the shape of a branch from Headcorn to Hastings via Tenterden. Preference was given to the coastal scheme on strategic grounds, but Parliament was persuaded that the South Eastern could better operate the section from Ashford to Bopeep Junction, slightly west of Hastings. (The Junction was named after an inn on what is now the outskirts of St Leonards, frequented by shepherds from the nearby marshes.) Powers for it were therefore transferred. The LBSCR, which had meanwhile absorbed the Brighton, Lewes & Hastings, thus lost its independent access to the ancient Cinque port of Hastings. The extent of this loss may be overlooked today, although as many as 758,000 tickets were collected in 1957, but at that time Hastings (population 11,617 in 1841) was the only place with over 5,000 people all the way along the coast between Lewes and Hythe. It had gained some note as a resort as well as being a fishing town. James Burton was laying out St Leonards as a speculation. Bexhill-on-Sea did not exist, Bexhill being a small village clustered round the ancient parish church on a ridge over a mile inland, and the shores of Pevensey and Pett Levels were deserted.

On Friday, 13 February 1851, a crisis was precipitated by the simultaneous opening to Bopeep of the 28-mile South Eastern line from Ashford and the quarter-mile link of the Brighton from its Hastings and St Leonards station. The Brighton had already tried to delay the opening of the Ashford line by various pretexts, for though in an isolated spot, it was then the nearest station to Hastings. But the Brighton route via Cooksbridge was 76½ miles as against the 94 miles from London of the South Eastern. The latter was already complaining of declining traffic at Staplehurst, on the London–Dover line, which though 32 miles from Hastings had been the railhead for the town before Bulverhythe, the first BL & H terminus, ¾ mile west of Bopeep.

On opening day a Brighton train was held so long at Bopeep it had to set back into Hastings & St Leonards station (renamed St Leonards from that date) and unload there. An immediate approach was made to Finnegan, the South Eastern superintendent, who 'happened' to be in Hastings. He made the excuse that he had no proof the Brighton was the legal successor of the Brighton, Lewes & Hastings and of its running powers. He also said, which was likely enough, the Brighton had not provided him with a copy of its working time-table. This was eventually forthcoming and on the Saturday and Sunday a few trains worked through. Two engines and 17 coaches were then stabled at Hastings for Monday's traffic. Early that day the South Eastern tore up the track at Bopeep, stood a ballast train across the sidings at Hastings and marooned the Brighton agent in his office there, cutting off the gas on this February morning. The Brighton hired a bus, a move countered by the South Eastern erecting a barrier across the station approach, thus preventing its departure. The Brighton speedily got an injunction against the South Eastern and was able to run its trains again, but not until 5 December 1870 were they allowed to stop at St Leonards (Warrior Square). On that day St Leonards station became West Marina (closed 10 July 1967).

For a large part of its length the Ashford–Hastings line crosses the dead level of Romney Marsh, though there are severe gradients at either end. The Marsh is a world apart socially, where malaria died out only two generations ago. Its rich pastures support many thousands of sheep, which once were a source of considerable traffic, though today they are taken by lorry to the market at Ashford. Since the war hundreds of acres have come under the plough for a whole range of new crops, including asparagus. The station at Rye blends well with a town widely known for its architectural glories, its well-balanced features standing at the head of a tree-lined avenue. This came to be used as a bus terminal, a too-rare example of a convenient interchange. In 1958 an interval service of diesel-electric trains was inaugurated. From 1963 to 1980 the line has survived repeated closure threats. Proposals to single were made in 1979.

A shorter South Eastern route to Hastings also had its beginnings as far back as 1845, when powers were obtained to start it. The 5¾-mile branch from Tonbridge to Tunbridge Wells was steeply inclined, and as a safety measure trailed into a siding 50 chains east of Tonbridge station, an arrangement superseded in 1857 by the existing spur leading straight up from Tonbridge station. Opening day for the double-track branch as far as a temporary station at Jackwood Springs was 20 September 1845. The half-mile extension through the 823-yard Wells Tunnel under Mount Pleasant to the present Central station, then on the outskirts of the town, was opened on 25 November 1846. Southborough (renamed High Brooms from 21 September 1925), the only intermediate station, was not opened until 1893 to serve a growing suburb of Tunbridge Wells.

By 1845 Tunbridge Wells had come a long way from the 'rustick' encampment round the chalybeate spring developed by Lord Abergavenny in the early seventeenth century. In the face of competition from the seaside its function as a resort was declining. This, however, was soon offset by its becoming a place of retirement for people from elsewhere. There was pre-war commuting to London, but it increased steadily after 1950, with 1,800 season-ticket holders in 1963 (1,350 in 1957).

The continuation from Tunbridge Wells, the $27\frac{1}{4}$ miles on to Bopeep, near Hastings, followed in stages a few years later – the $15\frac{1}{4}$ miles to Robertsbridge being opened on 1 September 1851, the 6 miles thence to Battle on the following New Year's Day, and the final 6 miles on 1 February 1852. The South Eastern's route to Hastings was thus reduced to $73\frac{1}{4}$ miles, and, ending a rate-cutting war with the Brighton, a fifty-fifty division of receipts was agreed after much discussion.

The shorter route involves crossing the High Weald with its deep valleys and narrow ridges. Gradients are arduous, in spite of heavy earthworks. There is an almost continuous climb from Tonbridge up through Tunbridge Wells to Wadhurst, after which the line descends to the Rother Valley on an $8\frac{1}{4}$-mile bank inclined at 1 in 97 or more. There is then another, though lower, gable summit at Crowhurst. There are four tunnels which, except for Grove Tunnel immediately south of Tunbridge Wells Central, are built to a very restricted gauge. Battle station, by William Tress, is a masterpiece, perhaps the finest example of a gothic roadside station. In 1957 an interval service of diesel-electric multiple-unit trains was introduced. This has been much modified over the years (page 210). In 1966 400,000 tons of gypsum were railed from the Mountfield mine. In 1970 a merry-go-round service began to the Northfleet cement plant (page 212).

On 1 June 1902 a branch was opened by the Managing Committee from a new and spaciously laid-out junction at Crowhurst, a few miles short of Hastings, to Bexhill. This had been authorized by the Crowhurst, Sidley & Bexhill Railway Act of 1897, the local Company later being vested in the South Eastern. Bexhill had just become the first British resort to allow mixed bathing, and was now brought within 62 miles of Charing Cross compared with the 72 (or 78 if the reversal had to be made at Eastbourne) from Victoria by the ex-LBSCR. Through coaches ran on the branch until 1940, but thereafter a self-contained shuttle service, dieselized in 1958, ran until 15 June 1964.

THE EXPANSION OF THE SOUTH EASTERN: OTHER LINES

Another of the South Eastern's important branches was one of 34 miles from Ashford to Margate. Authorized on 23 May 1844, it kept to the Stour valley through Canterbury (14¾ miles) to Minster (25¾ miles) and thence across the low chalk downs of the Isle of Thanet. Construction therefore was easy and the line was opened to Canterbury (West) on 6 February 1846, to Ramsgate (Town) on 13 April, and to Margate (Sands) on 1 December. East Kent was now in communication with London by rail as well as steamer, but by a most roundabout route.

Canterbury was provided with loops to the platforms and a Doric portico was included in the frontage of perhaps the most impressive of the original South Eastern stations. In those days the city was the largest town in East Kent, and it was only exceeded in the whole county by the riverside towns near London. Its growth however has been very much slower than other Kent towns, several of which have overtaken it. This was mainly due to its reluctance in developing industrial or resort functions. Even so its two stations dealt with 430,000 arriving passengers in 1951. The West station, on which general goods traffic was concentrated, became railhead for the despatch of fruit, flowers and vegetables from the market gardens along the Sandwich Road. A connection was made with the pioneer Canterbury & Whitstable line (see page 16), converted to locomotive haulage by April 1846. The Deal branch, another example of the South Eastern's addiction to circuitous routes, was opened from Minster in 1847. These lines are described in more detail later.

North Kent was the scene of long and bitter battles dating back to the 1845 Session, which saw extensive but mutually destructive proposals not only by the South Eastern but by the London & Croydon and by the London, Chatham & North Kent. Among those of the South Eastern was a cut-off, to shorten the London–Dover line, from Greenwich to Paddock Wood. Already the long Redhill route was proving tiresome. All the Bills were rejected, which at least served to consolidate the South Eastern's position.

The struggle for North Kent was renewed in the Mania Session of 1846 in which the South Eastern had several Bills affecting the county as a whole. In the face of threatened competition the

Company was now bent on shortening its routes and issued a pamphlet throwing the blame for their length on Maidstone's opposition to the Central of Kent.

On the whole the Company had reason to be satisfied with its year's legal work for it obtained authority for the 22½-mile North Kent line, from North Kent East Junction, near London Bridge, via Lewisham and Dartford to Gravesend. Beyond that town it was to join the 7 miles of line operated by the Thames and Medway Canal. The canal, opened in 1824, was built to save barges the long and exposed detour round the Isle of Grain. Between Higham and Strood two tunnels, now 1,531 and 2,329 yards, separated by a 50-yard opening which served as a passing-place, were bored through the chalk. On 31 July 1845 the Canal Company obtained powers to maintain a single-line railway along the towpath and on a stage erected over the water in the tunnels. This legalized a situation already in being, for a service of 6 trains a day had been operated since 10 February of that year. In 1846 canal and railway were bought by the South Eastern for £310,000. The canal in the tunnels was filled in and a double track laid throughout. North Kent trains began a through service between London and Rochester on 30 July 1849. Actually the station was at the canal basin at Strood and a ferry was provided to the cathedral city.

In the 1847 Session, the South Eastern sought authority for the remainder of its projects, which included Strood to Chilham on the Ashford–Margate line, Lewisham to Tonbridge, and a predecessor of the present Dartford Loop. Unfortunately for both the Company and the county a national financial crisis now occurred. The remedy was one with which we are all too familiar: Parliament immediately discouraged the investment programme. Among others these three projects were suspended. Had the first one come to fruition, the South Eastern's position would have been assured and Kent would have been spared the 'Feud'.

Thus ended the first phase of the South Eastern's development. In 1852 it owned 267½ route miles, as against the Brighton's 160 and the South Western's 249. It enjoyed the monopoly of the territory east of the Redhill–Tonbridge–Bopeep line. It was led by the energetic J. M'Gregor as chairman, while the young and enthusiastic J. I'A. Cudworth, the locomotive superintendent, was

SEVENTY YEARS OF CHANGE AT TONBRIDGE

(1) *The top-hatted station-master of 1890 watches the Continental 'Club' train making for Dover, while a local train loads up in the Redhill bay. The express has* wagons lits *coaches and is hauled by a Stirling '240' class 4–4–0.*

(2) *His successor of 1958, in more sober uniform, watches the 9.20 a.m. diesel-electric train from Charing Cross to Hastings preparing to stop at the down platform. Note the more spacious platforms of the new station, rebuilt to deal with heavier trains, the contrasts in signalling, and the westward growth of the town. The two photographs were taken from exactly the same viewpoint.*

CONTRASTS AT TUNBRIDGE WELLS

(3) *Trains were being marshalled by manpower at Tunbridge Wells when this unknown artist was at work shortly after the opening of the line in 1845.*

(4) *A present-day view of Tunbridge Wells Central. The original buildings survive on the up side, those on the down were built by the Southern Railway. Note the growth of the town.*

(5) *Luxury travel in 1900. The up 'Club' train from Hastings to Charing Cross near Grove Park, formed of a set of seven 'Gilberts' (vehicles owned by the Gilbert Car Co.) hauled by a Stirling 4–4–0 of the '440' class built by James Stirling and rebuilt by Harry S. Wainwright. The grassy slopes behind the train are now covered with houses and recreation grounds.*

successfully operating one of the best fleets in the country. The schedules of the Dover trains were drastically cut and the Folkestone traffic was developing apace. It is true there was some trouble. In 1850 William Barlow, the engineer, began laying the Barlow patent rails. After laying 67 miles he was hauled before a Committee of Investigation and forced to retire. In 1855 M'Gregor also had to resign over the purchase of the Reading Line. But the South Eastern's reputation stood high and if left alone it showed promise of becoming a really good railway. It had been gratuitously praised by the *Westminster Review* for its equitable treatment of passengers, which would have seemed incredible to the travelling public of the 'seventies and 'eighties.

GENESIS OF 'THE CHATHAM', 1853–64

But the South Eastern was to be denied both prosperity and public acclaim. On 4 August 1853 a cloud no bigger than a man's hand appeared in the clear skies of the South Eastern's monopoly. On that day the Royal Assent was given to the Bill incorporating the East Kent Railway Company and authorizing it to build a 48½-mile line from the North Kent at Strood to Canterbury with a 1-mile branch down to the Swale at Faversham Quay, and another to the South Eastern at Chilham.

Though originally a 'Landowners' line', promotion was soon in the hands of Morris, a contractor, and Crampton of locomotive fame, who considered it a good speculation to continue the natural route to Dover. They were joined by another contractor, Burge, who had invested heavily in speculative building at the new resort of Herne Bay. He had also built part of the Great Western's Box Tunnel. They were vociferously supported in the East Kent towns, but subscriptions were slow to follow. Burge and Morris withdrew, but Crampton persuaded the well-known contractors, Peto and Betts, to join – and also Lord Sondes, an East Kent landowner, who was chairman from 1852 to 1866.

The East Kent Railway's Act gave it the right to use the South Eastern's station at Strood, while the South Eastern gave an undertaking not to oppose any East Kent extension from Canterbury to Dover. As things turned out this was a grave error, but at the time there was no doubt that Parliament, the public and the South Eastern alike considered the East Kent to be nothing more than an extension of the North Kent. It is true the new Company failed to get running powers over the latter, but it did get a facilities clause, whereby the South Eastern agreed to handle its traffic as expeditiously as its own.

The Chatham-Faversham section was opened on 25 January 1858 and extended to Strood across the new Medway Bridge on 29 March, while the Faversham Quay goods branch opened on 12 April 1860. Meanwhile the extension on to Canterbury languished for lack of funds. The line was single and the 5 through trains each way, supplemented by a Strood-Sittingbourne round trip, were worked by 6 'small Hawthorns', borrowed from the Great Northern Railway. The South Eastern waited in the background for the onset of bankruptcy, hoping to absorb the new line at a substantial discount.

But it waited too long. In 1855 the East Kent obtained powers to reach Dover and, flushed with success, determined on an attack on London. Accordingly next year it again sought running powers over the North Kent to Dartford and a line thence to the West End of London & Crystal Palace Railway, which was eventually to give access to Victoria. The South Eastern opposed this on the grounds that the North Kent had all the traffic it could carry. This argument was two-edged, for it allowed the East Kent to obtain powers in 1858 for an independent route from Strood to St Mary Cray, there to link with the Mid-Kent (Bromley and St Mary Cray), incorporated in 1856 as part of a tentative incursion into Mid-Kent. This line in turn made connection with the West End of London & Crystal Palace and, piecemeal indeed, a line from Victoria to Dover was authorized. (Fuller details are in Vol. III, pp. 31-4.) On 1 August 1859 the East Kent changed its name to the London, Chatham & Dover.

The line from Faversham was opened to Canterbury (East) on 9 July 1860, but the Chilham branch was not made. From Bromley (now Shortlands) the line had been opened to Southborough Road (now Bickley) on 5 July 1858 and the first train from Rochester reached Bickley on 3 December 1860. Regular through services were now possible between Victoria and Canterbury (East) and were inaugurated on the same date.

Some of the stops of the fastest train (130 minutes) seem rather odd today: the stations served were Crystal Palace, Bickley, St Mary Cray, Farningham Road, Chatham, Sittingbourne and Faversham. Bromley and Gillingham were ignored, but then New Brompton, as the latter was then called, was but a very minor suburb of Chatham. But the Bickley stop, unless one of the officers lived there, seems inexplicable. The LCDR was fully launched as an independent concern and only one train a day now connected with the North Kent at Strood.

Dover was reached on 22 July 1861 and the rival route to the South Eastern was complete. The 'Chatham Line', as it is still invariably called, has always been difficult to operate, for its piecemeal origin and construction on the cheap has resulted in fierce gradients and appalling curves. From Shortlands over 2 miles of 1 in 95-100 lead up to Bickley Junction. Thence the line traverses the plateau of the North Downs against the grain of the deep and steep-sided valleys, crossed at St Mary Cray and Farningham Road by high viaducts. There is thus a savagely saw-toothed profile, with gradients mostly at 1 in 100. Sole Street station is the highest point and from there the 5 miles at 1 in 100 of Sole Street Bank go down almost to sea-level at Rochester Bridge. With undersized locomotives the operating expenses of this, the most difficult of all the exits from London, were a drain on an impoverished company. Also, this high-level line through lonely country brought in little local revenue.

From Rochester to Faversham the line is reasonably level, but curvature prevents high speeds. Thence to Canterbury there is a gable summit involving 4 miles up at 1 in 100-110 and as many down at 1 in 132. Then comes a steady climb out of the Stour Valley up to Shepherd's Well high in the Kentish Downs. Finally there is a 7¾-mile descent through the 2,369-yard Lydden Tunnel and down the Dour Valley.

The original stations are simple to the point of meanness, a plain Victorian lower middle-class villa with a single-storey booking hall attached. They can be best appreciated awaiting a train late on a stormy night at Sole Street or Bekesbourne. The larger stations had a short overall roof, which Canterbury East retained until 1958. This funnelled any wind there was into a howling gale such as is experienced in a wind-tunnel of an aerodynamics laboratory.

SECOND PERIOD: 1864–99: THE PROTAGONISTS

There are two distinct elements in the history of the second period, that between 1864 and 1899. The more obvious is the mutually destructive feud, but underlying its spectacular manifestations was a continuous progress towards the inevitable fusion of the exhausted parties. That this was so long delayed was due to a number of factors, but not the least was the clash of personalities between the two men who dominated their respective companies for most of the period. Sir Edward Watkin and James Staats Forbes were almost lifelong rivals, with violently contrasting characters, but each with a ruthless determination to get the better of the other. Their quarrels over Central London are traced in Vol. III.

Watkin, son of a Manchester businessman, was born in 1819 and, as a boy, attended the opening of the Liverpool & Manchester. At twenty-six he came under the influence of Captain Mark Huish, serving for a year as secretary of the Trent Valley and from 1851 as a minor officer of the LNWR. Thus was added to his family background of nineteenth-century mercantilism, experience in the Huish school of railway management, a ruthless imperialism which neglected equally the short-term interests of the shareholders and any interests at all of the travelling public. In 1854 he became general manager of the Manchester, Sheffield & Lincolnshire, and in 1864 chairman, an office he held for thirty years. In the same year he was invited to join the Board of the South Eastern. Two years later he became chairman, also holding that office until 1894. As well as being chairman of the Metropolitan from 1872 to 1894, he was a director of the Great Eastern and Great Western Railways and of the Channel Tunnel Company; retiring from public life after an illness in 1894, he died in 1901.

Forbes was born at Aberdeen of a professional family in 1823, and trained under Saunders of the Great Western, rising to chief goods manager. He then became general manager of the British-owned Dutch Rhenish Company, and in 1861 was appointed general manager of the London, Chatham & Dover, becoming chairman in 1873, when at last he could meet Watkin on an equal footing. His tact at meetings contrasted with Watkin's bullying but it was coupled with guile and it was he who, behind the scenes, probably turned War Office opinion against the Channel Tunnel, a Watkin scheme. The *Dictionary of National Biography* describes him as 'suave and charming'. He was a well-known connoisseur of art and a broadly cultured man. Watkin was more a stern Cobdenite Liberal of the Manchester school, but not a complete philistine: in his younger days he had organized musical soirées in Manchester.

For thirty years these men steered their companies through an amazing series of financial crises, using all their resources in vain attempts to crush each other. The cost was a stagnation in services. Fares were high, the result of enormous capital expenditure on new lines, while some of the coaches on the North Kent reached their half century. The third-class accommodation was shocking, for Watkin held that to improve it would encourage the lower middle class to desert second and the Chatham had no money for new rolling stock. Unlike fares, speeds showed no tendency to increase. In the late 'eighties Acworth and Foxwell, the railway writers, were commenting fairly but devastatingly. Ahrons writing in 1917 says:

> The S.E.R. of 25 to 35 years ago was a railway combining a number of good features with many exceedingly bad ones and at one time the Company, with its younger Chatham brother, was held to be ——. Here the reader had better choose his own adjectives, of which a choice and lurid selection was at one time obtained from most regular travellers.

SECOND PERIOD: 1864–99: THE CAMPAIGN IN THE FIELD

The most permanent legacy of the 'feud' was the spate of new construction thus engendered. Logically much of this new mileage was quite unjustifiable. The over-capitalization rendered the Chatham bankrupt, and kept the SER poor, but by one of the ironies of history, subsequent economic developments eventually led to most of the apparently redundant lines becoming vital links in the present system.

Spurred on by the coming of the Chatham, the South Eastern at last shortened its trunk route to Dover by cutting out the Redhill detour. On 30 June 1862 the 24 miles from St Johns on the North

Kent line to Tonbridge were authorized, reducing the distance from London Bridge to Tonbridge and all places beyond by 12½ miles and avoiding congestion north of Redhill. In February 1865 it was announced: 'There is in direct work 5 locomotives, 16 pumping and winding engines, 12 brickmaking and sawing machines, 500 earth wagons, 150 horses and 1,500 workmen, bricklayers, carpenters, miners and navvies.' 1 July 1865 saw the opening to Chislehurst. Goods trains ran throughout from 3 February 1868. For passengers, openings were: 2 March to Sevenoaks and 1 May to Tonbridge. Though some trains from London still ran that way, the 'Old Road' from Redhill to Tonbridge now lost its main-line status.

The Sevenoaks Cut-off is by no means easy and earthworks are heavy, for the parallel crests of the North Downs and Greensand Ridge must be crossed and there are no convenient gaps in them. From New Cross there is an unbroken climb of 11¾ miles, mainly at 1 in 120–140, to just beyond Knockholt station (Halstead until 1900). The final 3 miles are in a deep chalk cutting. Beyond the summit is a downhill run through the 2,610-yard Polhill Tunnel, wet, noisy and illuminated by arcing from the shoes of electric trains. A short rise leads through the four-road Sevenoaks (Tubs Hill) station to the mouth of the 3,454-yard Sevenoaks Tunnel. This is at the top of the 6-mile Hildenborough Bank, mainly at 1 in 122, which was a formidable obstacle to up steam trains which could not 'rush' it owing to the 40 m.p.h. slack out of Tonbridge.

When the line was opened, the market town of Sevenoaks, with an 1861 population of 4,800, was the only place on the line larger than a village, while Chislehurst, Orpington, Chelsfield and Dunton Green were the only intermediate stations on the 17 miles between New Cross and Sevenoaks. In 1956 there were ten intermediate stations; 244,000 tickets were issued and 482,000 collected at Sevenoaks (including the much less important Bat and Ball station on the line from Swanley), while 20,041 seasons were sold, and there was heavy freight traffic, particularly in agricultural lime. By 1963 season ticket sales had swollen to 29,000 and at the other stations traffic also grew as more commuters drove their cars to them from homes scattered beyond Chelsfield.

The Chatham's main lines were completed by the 27 miles from

Faversham to Ramsgate harbour, destined to become far more important than the Company's original main line to Dover. Short though it was, promotion was piecemeal. The Herne Bay & Faversham Company was incorporated in 1857, in the teeth of South Eastern opposition on the grounds that the resort was adequately served by its Sturry station, six miles across the Blean plateau! Then, in 1859, an extension to Margate and a change of name to the Margate Railway was authorized, while construction of the original section went slowly forward. Faversham to Whitstable was opened on 1 August 1860, but the South Eastern delayed the opening to Herne Bay until 13 July 1861 on the pretext that the. bridge under the little Canterbury & Whitstable was unsafe. In 1861 authority was obtained to push on to Ramsgate and to change the name of the Company to the Kent Coast. The extension to Ramsgate was opened to public traffic on 5 October 1863. The line was worked from the start by the Chatham and vested in it in 1871.

By its Dover and Kent Coast lines, the Chatham carried the attack squarely and with much justification deep into South Eastern territory. But over the twenty years after 1865 the Company promoted a number of competing lines which were at the time of doubtful utility. One project dating from East Kent days was however not immediately competitive. In 1856 the Sittingbourne & Sheerness Company was incorporated to build a branch from the paper-making town of Sittingbourne to Queenborough and the dockyard town of Sheerness in the Isle of Sheppey. Opened on 19 July 1860, it was worked by the Chatham and was vested in it six years later. On 15 May 1876 a short branch was opened from Queenborough to a new pier, from which the Zeeland SS Company operated a steamer service to Flushing. This was a breach of the spirit, though not of the letter, of the 1865 Continental Traffic Agreement (see page 47). The South Eastern had no legal redress. Instead it carried out a flank attack, supporting the building by the Hundred of Hoo Company (incorporated in 1879) of a line from Hoo Junction on the North Kent to Port Victoria on the Isle of Grain opposite Queenborough. The nominally independent Company was soon taken over. The South Eastern itself obtained powers for a deep-water pier, to be called Port Victoria, perhaps because Queenborough was named after an-

other Queen, Philippa, wife of Edward III. Watkin described the
pier as the beginning of a great port, but a more percipient shareholder considered it as taking traffic away from themselves.

On 2 June 1862 another nominally independent concern, the
Sevenoaks Railway, opened a 9-mile branch from the Chatham's
main line at what is now called Swanley southwards through
Otford to Bat and Ball on the outskirts of Sevenoaks: in the same
year a branch extension (opened on 1 June 1874) was authorized
from Otford to Maidstone East, the name of the Chatham satellite being changed to the Sevenoaks, Maidstone & Tunbridge.
The attack had come into the open. By guaranteeing connections
and through booking, the South Eastern succeeded in making
the intruder use its station at Sevenoaks and thus staved off the
threat of southward extension; but ripples of the threat extended
as far into the South Eastern pond as the remote High Weald, for
in 1864 it obtained powers for a defensive branch from Paddock
Wood to Cranbrook.

If the excursion so far into the rural seclusion of West Kent
brought little profit, the 18¾-mile extension from Maidstone to
Ashford, opened on 1 July 1884, brought even less. But warfare
seemed to be renewed with added bitterness after the failure of
any attempt at fusion.

Smarting under the attack, the South Eastern made one of its
few major blunders, securing powers in 1881 for a most expensive
independent access to Chatham, opened from Strood to Rochester
Common on 20 July 1891 and to Chatham Central on 1 March
1892. In the same session an independent Elham Valley Light
Railway was authorized to build a line from Canterbury to
Shorncliffe. Taken over by the South Eastern, which was concerned with keeping the Chatham at arm's length from Folkestone, in 1884, its line opened from Shorncliffe to Barham on 4
July 1887 and the rest on 1 July 1889.

For its part, the Chatham's final foolishness was to foster the
nominally independent Gravesend Railway, incorporated in 1881,
to build a 5-mile branch from the Chatham line at Fawkham
Junction to Gravesend. Opened on 10 May 1886, the route
offered little competition to those longer established and no
return on the £250,000 investment.

Among the long list of lines, so many of them uneconomic, promoted by the SER and the Chatham, the line between Dover and Deal is outstanding in that it was a joint enterprise built during an armistice, a joint committee being set up by an Act of 1874. The line was opened on 15 June 1881.

After 1881, when so many competing lines were promoted, the rate of new construction slowed considerably through the exhaustion of the parties and the growing likelihood of eventual amalgamation.

1861-99: POLITICAL HISTORY

The arrival of the Chatham at Dover in 1861 touched off a period of internecine competition for the valuable Continental traffic. This resulted in the 1863 Continental Traffic Agreement between the two Companies. A short trial convinced the parties of its practical value and a definitive Agreement was drawn up and signed on 7 October 1865, powers to do so being conferred by the LCDR's Act of 5 July.

In the definitive Agreement the heads of the 1863 document were repeated. All Continental traffic between London and ports between Hastings and Margate inclusive and all local traffic between London and Folkestone and Dover was to be pooled. Gross receipts were to be paid into a common fund and reallocated. Initially the Chatham's share was to be 32 per cent, but this was to be increased annually until 1872 when parity would be reached.

There were two important additions in the new Agreement. One set up a joint committee of six for the purpose of 'managing, superintending and developing the traffic of the two companies', thus recognizing, even at this early date, the ultimate necessity of fusion. The other permitted either Company to make a claim for an allowance to cover working expenses should it carry in any one year a greater proportion of the total traffic than its stipulated proportion of gross receipts. Competition was thereby encouraged to rage as fiercely as before (though there would be no rate-cutting campaigns), culminating perhaps in the 'Club Trains' of 1889-1893, when the few passengers making use of them were virtually fought over by the rival conductors, who incidentally were brothers.

Though it worked well on the whole and remained in force until 1899, the Continental Traffic Agreement led to much friction, not only over Queenborough, but also over Folkestone. Local traffic between London and Folkestone was pooled, so a first-class row developed when the SER, piqued by the loss of the Queenborough campaign, attempted to circumvent this.

The SER had opened two stations on the approach to Folkestone, on 1 November 1863 Shorncliffe & Sandgate (Shorncliffe Camp from November 1874) and on 1 September 1884 Cheriton Arch. Lord Radnor developed his estates to the west of Old Folkestone and the centre of the town began to move westward to the Leas and the Sandgate Road, the area immortalized in *Kipps*. Cheriton Arch became Radnor Park in September 1886 and Folkestone Central, by now an appropriate title, on 1 June 1895.

The SER now held that these stations, engulfed in the new town, 'were not Folkestone' and therefore not affected by the Agreement. Receipts were withheld from the pool. Matters came to a head when in February 1881 the SER replaced Shorncliffe Camp with a new and enlarged station 150 yards to the east (Shorncliffe from 1926 and Folkestone West from 1962). This was provided with a better service and cheaper fares than the other Folkestone stations.

This suited the passengers, for the town's westward spread was rendering the Harbour, then provided with an ordinary service, as inconvenient as the Junction had already become. But it did not suit the Chatham. In 1887 it initiated a prolonged legal battle to recover its share of the receipts withheld from the pool. Eventually it was awarded £85,000, but it was widely rumoured that the cost of litigation was of the order of £250,000.

Meanwhile, the Chatham had failed financially in 1866. Its contractors engaged on new works had been paid by the dubious means of allocating to them debentures at no less than 75 per cent discount. Eventually a *debit* balance on premiums and discounts of £6·6 million piled up. Then, on 30 June 1866, blocks of these debentures fell due and the Company was unable to meet its obligations. Forbes and Johnson, the secretary, were appointed receivers and managers on 12 July 1866 and set the task of reorganization. In 1867 and 1869 Arrangement Acts were passed granting a ten-year moratorium and exceptional powers for raising new capital. By 1871, under the energetic guidance of Forbes, receipts were rising and expenses falling. The Chatham was once more solvent, but it never paid a dividend on its ordinary stock.

In 1868, when the Chatham fortunes were at their lowest, a Bill was presented for the united working, under joint management but separate capital accounts, of the LSWR, the Brighton and the SER, with powers for the Chatham to join. This passed the Commons, but upon the Lords limiting the rates and fares to be charged to the comparatively low level ruling on the Brighton, the SER backed out against all advice.

The next attempt came with an Agreement dated 23 March 1875 between the South Eastern and the Chatham which provided for common working and a division of receipts. This failed after Forbes refused to take a dispute over Continental traffic to arbitration. Forbes's private file is however still in existence and this contains a brief 'history' of the fusion agreements. According to this, the Agreement fell through merely because the South Eastern Board refused to confirm it.

The next year a similar approach broke down on Forbes's persuading his wishful-thinking shareholders of the vulnerability of the SER's position. Once again the Forbes version attributes the breakdown to South Eastern intransigence. In 1878 a fusion Bill was deposited but (according to the 'Forbes History') the Chatham retired after the shareholders considered the SER to be unduly favoured by it.

By now all parties were paying lip service to the desirability of fusion, but all were in fact afraid of the consequences. *Herapath's Journal* reveals that as early as August 1868 Watkin admitted that joint working would save some £100,000 a year and that 'co-operation would bring large benefits to the public'. But his visionary schemes of through Manchester–Paris coaches via his group of lines and the Channel Tunnel blinded him to the real benefits of co-operation nearer home. Forbes in 1877 said, 'We think it a reasonable calculation that the two companies put together would . . . increase the net profit.' But his incurable optimism as to the eventual viability of the Chatham led him to delay in order to gain more favourable terms. The South Eastern shareholders saw their dividends, which they were at least receiving regularly, in danger, while they and the Chatham proprietors feared Parliament would force them to pass on some benefits of fusion to the users. Finally the general public feared that was exactly what Parliament would fail to do. Judging by a number of Watkinian pontifications they certainly could not look for immediate benefits in that direction.

Only this can explain the spate of proposals for fusion coming forward during the 'eighties and 'nineties from frightened share-holders and opposed by all, the shareholders included. Space is lacking for a full account, but this went on while profits declined and sources of capital dried up. Failure to improve the London approaches led to intolerable delays in the service and in 1890 the Board of Trade reported that only 67 per cent of the SER trains and 58 per cent of the Chatham arrived less than three minutes late while 88 per cent of the Great Eastern Railway trains arrived on time. The *Economist* in 1899 was saying categorically, 'the services of these two railways are the worst of any serving the Metropolis'.

But some progress was being made. In July 1894 the Chatham obtained an Act authorizing it to negotiate with the SER on all traffic apart from that covered by the Continental Agreement. Fares were made uniform on 1 January 1895, and the traffic to the Kent Coast resorts pooled. In 1894 Watkin retired through illness and relations rapidly improved. Furthermore it was now obvious that the Chatham would be unable to raise any further capital until after fusion. Finally, the SER's credit was declining. In the period 1878–87 the SER's net income rose by 18 per cent and the Chatham's by 78 per cent. Forbes was now able to get better terms and the South Eastern more inclined to acquiesce. Thus events were rapidly moving towards the great day which came on 1 August 1899, when the South Eastern and London, Chatham & Dover (Working Union) Act received the Royal Assent. The two Companies had in fact been working as one since 1 January that year. Part of the preamble of the Act is worth quoting:

> . . . with a view to avoiding undue competition and unnecessary expense and delays and other inconveniences arising from diversity of interests and to turning to the best account the respective powers and resources of the Two Companies . . . with a view also to the improvement and extension of the service between England and the Continent it is expedient and will be for the public advantage that . . . the undertakings of the Two Companies should be used worked managed maintained and improved . . . as one undertaking . . .

THIRD PERIOD: THE SE & CR MANAGING COMMITTEE

By the terms of the Act the two Companies retained their separate existence, but for operating purposes their lines were to be managed as a single railway by the South Eastern & Chatham Railway Companies Managing Committee of nine members, under a chairman who was also the SER chairman and a deputy who was the Chatham chairman. The net revenue was to be pooled (except Eastbourne traffic, see page 93) and divided 59 per cent to the SER and 41 per cent to the LCDR. The SE & CR was not a company but only a convenient abbreviation of the Committee's title. It had no capital account, any new capital being raised by the Companies in the same proportions.

The success of the Managing Committee was undoubted. It inherited financial impoverishment, inadequate track and station facilities and antiquated rolling stock. These it started to improve, being aided in its task by one unexpected consequence of the 'feud'. Kent and East Surrey, now becoming the repositories of an expanding London, were so seamed by a network of apparently redundant branches that their railway system could cope with unprecedented increases in traffic and resist all attempts to knock it out by bombing in a manner no logically-planned system could ever have done. A correspondent in the *Railway Magazine* once calculated that there were 128 routes between London Bridge and Deal, none of which involved a reversal. Of all the uneconomic competing lines two only, the Elham Valley and the Crystal Palace High Level, have been completely swept into oblivion.

The Committee's first task was to speed up the improvements to the London approaches. By 18 June 1905 quadrupling of the South Eastern line had been completed as far as Orpington. Powers were also obtained to link the two main lines south of Chislehurst, where that of the South Eastern passed over that of the Chatham, by four single-line spurs, those between Bickley and Orpington Junction being opened in September 1902 and those between Chislehurst and St Mary Cray Junction on 19 June 1904. On 1 July that year the LCDR suburban services were extended to Orpington. In 1919, on their restoration after the war, the Continental services were concentrated on Victoria, but ran normally over the spurs and on via Tonbridge. A large number of stations were rebuilt and the present Dover Marine started.

H. S. Wainwright and R. E. L. Maunsell, the successive mechanical superintendents, built many new locomotives and coaches to replace the antiquities which rumbled in even the expresses. Services were thus vastly improved until, at Grouping, the boat trains at least could compare favourably with anything in the country.

But the Managing Committee was not to be allowed time to undo all the harm. Only fifteen years after fusion came World War I and its aftermath, while Government prevented some of the hoped for economies. The unfinished work and a full measure of public opprobrium were passed on to the Southern.

THANET

The first trains to reach Thanet were those of the South Eastern in 1844 (see page 37), but the distance between Margate Sands and London Bridge was 101¾ miles, as opposed to the 64 taken by the crow. At Ramsgate Town a reversal was necessary, the junction being at the very end of the short platforms, which thus could never be lengthened. Later, a spur was put in to allow through running between London and Margate, but it was little used by regular trains.

The monopoly of the South Eastern was eventually broken, in spite of all efforts to maintain it, by the completion of the Herne Bay & Faversham Railway (see page 45). This line, which later became part of the East Kent and thus of the LCDR, reached not only Herne Bay, but Margate and Ramsgate, the shorter route to London being opened throughout on 5 October 1863.

The Faversham and Ramsgate line ultimately became more important than the Chatham's original main line to Dover, which latter was left with the scantiest of through services to London prior to electrification. In spite of the low relief of the North Kent coast, the Ramsgate line still has the typical Chatham saw-tooth profile with gable summits achieved at 1 in 80–100. The worst is Blacksole, just east of Herne Bay. The line finished by descending through a 1,630-yard tunnel at 1 in 75 to Ramsgate Harbour, a four-platformed terminus covered with a large arched roof and on the very seashore.

Though a terminus station was built at Margate, it was never used, the through station of Margate West being ready in time for the opening. It lay at right angles to, and almost immediately above, the South Eastern's terminus, Margate Sands, a connecting link being provided in after years. The two SER and two LCDR stations at Margate and Ramsgate were all small and inconvenient and all were swept away in the Southern Railway's reorganization of the Thanet lines.

On 2 July 1926 a connecting line, only 1⅜ miles long, was brought into use. But, joining as it did the ex-SER line just short of Ramsgate Town with the ex-LCDR line at the landward entrance to Ramsgate Harbour Tunnel, its effects were out of all proportion to its length. Traffic, whether via Chatham or via Ashford, was entirely concentrated on the enlarged and completely rebuilt Margate West (now Margate), on an entirely new station at Ramsgate, and on new locomotive and carriage depots at Ramsgate. The line through the tunnel to Ramsgate Harbour was closed, and so was the SER line from Ramsgate to Margate Sands. However, a new goods depot was built on part of this line. In 1968 imported cars were despatched by the trainload.

This rationalization of the Thanet lines, together with the realignment of a little-used spur at Minster, allowed a complete reorganization of the Kent Coast services, which remained unaltered until electrification in 1959. The basic services ran from Victoria to Ramsgate via Chatham and Margate. A few through trains ran to Dover via Canterbury East, but the normal service was by connecting train from Faversham. The Charing Cross–Dover trains were extended to Margate via Deal, calling at all stations beyond Deal and thus providing the local service as well. A local service, supplemented by a few through trains, was run between Ashford and Margate via Canterbury West, hitherto the only route for through trains using the South Eastern route. In business hours the Chatham line trains were diverted over the Chislehurst loops to Cannon Street, and such was the growth of commuting traffic that in the last years of steam working six trains left Cannon Street for Faversham and beyond between 4.45 and 6.23 p.m. In summer full use was made of the many alternative routes available. Extra trains from Victoria would be sent via Tonbridge and Ashford and through trains from Leicester ran via Bromley South, Maidstone East and Canterbury West.

The order in which down trains left Faversham, sometimes at 5- or 10-minute intervals for hours at a stretch, could not be varied until Margate, 22 miles away, was reached. But thanks to the Southern's liberal use of intermediate block signals, generous time-tabling, and the fact that most trains stopped at all stations, traffic was kept moving in an exemplary fashion even at the height of the season in steam days. The re-signalling and electrification of 1959 obviously brought further improvement.

When Ramsgate's Baltic trade declined at the end of the eighteenth century, the town then took to catering for London visitors coming by sailing 'hoys' and, after 1825, by steamer. By 1841 its permanent population had swollen to 10,919 and in the following decades holiday-makers and day-excursionists came in their tens of thousands by rail. Frith's 'Ramsgate Sands', hung in the 1854 Royal Academy, caused much interest as a social document of the new phenomenon. In 1971 Ramsgate had a population of over 38,000.

In size it has been overtaken by its rival, Margate, in 1971 with over 48,000 people. Margate's firm smooth sands turned the fishing village into a resort for Cockneys and by mid-century rail and steamers were pouring in visitors. Dickens's Tuggses when they came into money turned down a visit here and went to Ramsgate. Margate was 'out' for anyone but tradespeople. Even today Margate accepts anybody with a roaring welcome, while some would say Ramsgate has 'more character'.

Between the great rivals lay the first resort which described itself as 'select', the village of Broadstairs, beloved of Dickens. With only 1,519 inhabitants in 1841, it is now ten times as large, but with its character unchanged. Cliftonville, Westgate and Birchington, suburbs of Margate, strain every nerve to forget the fact. Finally, outside Thanet but part of the same complex, are the towns of Herne Bay and Whitstable and their flanking resort villages.

Ever increasing numbers of cars and coaches choked Thanet Way, archetypal 'arterial road' of the 1930s, at holiday times.

CONTINENTAL EXPRESSES THROUGH THE YEARS—I

(6) *C. Hamilton Ellis's impression of an up 'Mail' of the* SER *about 1850, hauled by two of Crampton's 'Long Boiler' locomotives as it traverses the Weald between Tonbridge and Ashford.*

(7) *A down boat train of the* LCDR *in the mid 1880s between St Mary Cray and Swanley headed by a Martley 2–4–0 of the 'C' or 'Europa' class. Note the method of ballasting.*

(8) *An 'M3' class 4–4–0, the largest express locomotives on the* LCDR, *heads a train of 4- and 6-wheeled stock on a down Continental express near Bickley Junction in 1898. Today the line is quadruple.*

CONTINENTAL EXPRESSES THROUGH THE YEARS—II

(9) *An* SE *&* CR *boat train of 1920, newly reinstated after the first world war, on the last stage of the ascent of the North Downs, the chalk cutting up to Knockholt summit. A Wainwright 'E' class 4–4–0 is the train engine and another Wainwright engine, rebuilt by Maunsell as class 'E1', the pilot. A Wainwright bogie composite brake with the characteristic 'birdcage' lookout is marshalled in front of a string of Pullmans in lake livery.*

(10) *The all-Pullman 'Golden Arrow' of 1956 passes an admiring audience on Ashford station. Note the typical layout of a large* SER *station extensively rebuilt about the turn of the century.*

But even in the 1950s the railway carried thousands of holiday-makers on peak Saturdays. Sixty-two advertised trains then passed on to the Kent Coast line at Faversham, the great majority crowded to the doors, and 32 long-distance and local services reached Ramsgate via Canterbury or Deal. In 1957, 680,000 tickets were collected at Margate alone and on the August Bank Holiday Saturday of 1958 nearly 11,500 at that station.

Ever since the early 1920s the Kent Coast, at least to the west of Birchington, has been popular as a dormitory for London commuters. By 1958 there were 650 season-ticket holders from Herne Bay. Electrification increased this traffic, and the 1964 survey should that 1,584 passengers left Herne Bay and Whitstable between 6 and 9 a.m. in trains which were full by the time they left the latter. There were also numbers of short-distance commuters to the industrial areas of Sittingbourne and the Medway Towns, for local jobs were mainly seasonal. Industry, conspicuous as far as Faversham, peters out there.

FOLKESTONE, DOVER AND DEAL

When the railway arrived at a temporary station (the Foord Viaduct not being ready) on 28 June 1843, Folkestone was an obscure fishing town of 4,144 people, huddled in the mouth of the Foord ravine. It had however attained something of a reputation as a resort during the French wars when it was visited by officers and their wives from the camps at Shorncliffe and Hythe, the latter town then considerably larger than Folkestone. But in 1843 the South Eastern made one of its more astute moves. It bought for £18,000 from the Exchequer Commissioners the almost derelict harbour which Telford had built in 1809. Arrangements were made with the Commercial Steam Packet Company to provide a daily service to Boulogne. This lasted until 1844 when the nominally independent South Eastern & Continental Steam Packet Company was incorporated and took over the service. In 1853 the railway obtained powers to absorb the new Company.

At first facilities were rudimentary, there being only a small basin and, except at high tide, the steamers were unable to berth and mails and passengers were then transferred to rowing boats. Reading between the lines of the chairman's report conditions were indeed chaotic.

The arrangements at the Temporary Station requiring the utmost exertion on the part of the Company's servants—those at the Boat Builders Shed, converted into the South Eastern Pavilion—the unfinished state of the Harbour, and the unavoidable inconveniences attending the first establishment of the Customs Depot—have been submitted to with much consideration and good humour by those who travelled on the line.

The Foord Viaduct was completed and trains extended to the permanent station (Folkestone East) on 18 December 1843. Meanwhile work had begun on the Harbour branch which was opened for goods that year, and for passengers on 1 January 1849. Folkestone East (closed to passengers 6 September 1965) was high above the shore at the back of the town and the Harbour branch trails in with no direct connection with the main line. This is a safety measure as the double track descends at 1 in 30 for three-quarters of a mile to the Harbour station on the mole. Before electrification it was a stirring sight to see the boat trains, usually formed of 10 coaches, 2 Pullmans and 2 vans, mounting the incline in charge of four very vociferous 0-6-0 tank locomotives.

The Harbour station was ready in 1850 and steamers could now berth at most tides. But their increasing size and the growing traffic led to the building of the present mole in 1863. It was extended piecemeal in 1876, 1893 and 1905.

Because there was rail access to the quay at Folkestone and because the Company controlled the steamers in all but name, the South Eastern at first concentrated its business there even after its arrival at Dover on 7 February 1844. But Dover developed fast and Folkestone was outstripped. Cross-Channel passengers at Folkestone Harbour have grown in recent years, from 634,000 in 1957 to 842,000 in 1966 to 1·53 million in 1977. In 1957 some 387,000 tickets were collected at the Central station.

The South Eastern's approach to its Dover Town station was over a timber trestle, but there has since been considerable reclamation behind the sea wall on which the locomotive depot stood from 1929 to 1961. Although it had only a single through platform (on to the Admiralty Pier) and a bay, Dover Town was a very imposing structure. The shattered wreck of Lewis Cubitt's design has recently been swept away to make a car-park. Car-carriers are unloaded in the bay.

The rival Chatham line was opened to its Priory Station on 22 July 1861, naming it after the adjacent monastic buildings now occupied by Dover College. On 1 November an extension through the 684-yard Dover Harbour Tunnel was opened to the Harbour station, of which the main range of buildings still remains as a bonded store, though the platforms have disappeared. The South Eastern trains ran on to the Admiralty Pier in 1860 and on 30 August 1864 the Chatham trains joined them for the first time. On the pier itself there was just room for a double line of rails and two narrow platforms placed in tandem against the rear wall. In rough weather the waves broke over the pier and trans-shipment of passengers and luggage became a nightmare.

In 1862 the Chatham consolidated its position by obtaining the contract for the cross-Channel carriage of mails and soon after it bought the fleet of the previous carriers, Messrs Jenkins & Churchward. The South Eastern concentrated its vessels on Folkestone, but continued to run boat trains to Dover. Local punters would lay bets on which boat train would arrive first and great excitement was shown among the onlookers as the trains appeared, sometimes simultaneously, on either side of the Lord Warden Hotel.

Continuous growth of traffic in the later years of the nineteenth century underlined the need for improving the Admiralty Pier. In the early 1900s the Managing Committee began the present Dover Marine station on reclaimed land inside the Admiralty Pier. It is a spacious two-island structure with an overall roof. Opened for military traffic in 1915, the Marine station came into full use with the restoration of Continental services in 1919.

There were thus three stations in the harbour area and in 1914 Dover Town was closed, all South Eastern local trains being diverted over the Hawkesbury Street curve to the Priory. The number of trains calling at the Harbour station was also gradually reduced until it, too, was closed from 11 July 1927. Some local trains continued to work into and out of the Marine, but growth of traffic there prevented the restoration of this practice after 1945. An hourly service to the Chatham line was instituted in June 1970.

Thus there is now complete segregation of Continental and local traffic, the latter being dealt with by Priory, which was completely rebuilt and modernized by the Southern Railway, which also concentrated the local goods traffic here. The Priory station was always busy with local traffic, but since 1970 Continental passengers also arrive to use the bus connections with the roll-on–roll-off and hovercraft terminals.

The full benefits of the two routes to Dover are felt when the line from Folkestone is closed by landslides, to which it is very subject. Even at the height of the 'feud', when the line under the cliffs was closed from 12 January to 12 March 1877, the South Eastern trains ran to Dover via Beckenham Junction and the Chatham line. Again, a disastrous landslip closed the line from 19 December 1915 to 11 August 1919, yet Dover continued to function as one of the main ports of embarkation for France and there was little effect on the war effort.

'Nor is there in the whole circuit of this famous island any port more convenient, needful or rather of necessity than this Dover', wrote Sir Walter Raleigh to his Queen. In common with the other Cinque ports, coastal currents have entirely choked the medieval port, situated in the estuary of the Dour. But unlike its rivals, the value of Dover was so great that efforts at improvements were made from the early sixteenth to the early nineteenth centuries. They were conspicuously lacking in success. In 1833, with Continental traffic developing fast with the new steamers, 'not even a nutshell could float in or out over the bar'. After a Parliamentary Enquiry in 1836 work was started in 1847 on a harbour of refuge by the building of the Admiralty Pier, completed in 1871. At last the drift of shingle was cut off. In 1895 work was started on the 'Admiralty Harbour' enclosing the whole bay. Completed in 1909, this is the great existing harbour, 600 acres of water sheltered behind three great moles.

The train-ferry dock (1936) was built adjacent to the Marine station. Beyond are the Granville and Wellington docks, where general cargo is dealt with. At the eastern end was the Camber dock, replaced by the first roll-on–roll-off berth opened in 1952. Here also the first hovercraft terminal opened in 1968.

Between 1 February and 1 July 1849, 23,243 passengers were conveyed via Folkestone and Boulogne, 5,124 via Dover and Ostend and 2,600 via Dover and Calais, figures which reveal the fruits of the South Eastern's concentration on Folkestone. But already the natural superiority of Dover was reasserting itself. In

1844 the Post Office, the Stock Exchange, and various newspapers all hired special trains at £25 apiece to bring news to London when the Indian mail arrived at Folkestone after its overland journey from Marseilles. But in 1848, that year of revolutions when crowned heads were falling fast, it was at Dover that *The Times* and the *Herald* both had engines continuously standing by to carry to London the news of Louis Philippe's fall. In 1860 the Folkestone traffic had grown to 96,652 passengers and the Dover-Calais to 76,318 while that to Ostend was only 5,449. By 1887 the Dover traffic had grown to 278,774 passengers and the Folkestone only to 116,657.

In 1880 the first 'fixed' service was introduced – all services being 'fixed' by 1882. Hitherto they had all been 'tidal', the times varying daily according to the state of the tide. Passenger traffic, interrupted only by the first world war when millions of troops were conveyed, grew steadily and in 1939 1·1 million passengers used the port. In spite of air competition post-war figures have been even higher. In 1953 they were 1·2 million, in 1960 2·7 million, in 1966 3·9 million and in 1978 8·5 million. Dover has become the busiest passenger port in Britain, if not the world.

In 1928 a car ferry was started, taking 6,000 vehicles, and in 1931 the Southern placed the *Autocarrier* in service. By 1939 31,000 vehicles were dealt with and this figure grew to 220,000 in 1956 and 655,000 in 1966. In 1963 1·3 million tons of cargo was handled, most of the high value goods going on the train ferries which carried some 60,000 wagons, inwards traffic being chiefly fruit, vegetables, wine and glassware, and outwards machinery and wool. In addition 19,300 cars were exported and 30,000 imported. To the docks came imports of timber, pit-props and wood pulp from Europe and road metal, ballast, cement and coal coastwise. Much of this traffic was then distributed by rail.

The importance of Dover Harbour and the Southern Region to each other is attested by the fact that three out of eight members of the Harbour Board are Railways Board representatives. In 1960 British Railways maintained a fleet of some 35 vessels based on Dover. But since then there have been great changes (page 214) in fleet and port here and at Folkestone.

The Dover & Deal Joint line, opened on 15 June 1881, was 8½ miles long and ran from Buckland Junction, a mile north of

Dover Priory, to an end-on junction at Deal station with the South Eastern's branch from Minster, to be mentioned below. Access from the LCDR was provided by a short curve from Kearsney station to Kearsney Loop Junction. This was built and owned by the Chatham, and opened on 1 July 1882. This scheme was completed by a jointly owned 16-chain curve in the Dover Harbour area from Archcliffe Junction to Hawkesbury Street Junction. Platforms were built on this spur as part of Dover Town station and the South Eastern were given running powers through the Priory station from Hawkesbury Street to Buckland Junction.

The line is one of the more spectacular in southern England. From Buckland Junction there is a 2½-mile climb at 1 in 69–71 round a horseshoe curve and back along the side of the valley towards Dover until the portal of Guston Tunnel (1,412 yards) is reached. This brings the track on to the 400-foot-high plateau of the Kentish Downs. Beyond Martin Mill there is an equally steep fall all the way into Deal.

The original Deal branch from Minster on the Ashford–Ramsgate line was opened across the coastal flats, then, as now, a great market-gardening area, on 1 July 1847, Sandwich being the only intermediate station. It was another example of the South Eastern's love of circuitous (and cheaply built) routes on which rates and fares could be charged on a mileage basis. Walmer (now Deal) was 102½ miles from Charing Cross, compared with 85 by the present route via Sevenoaks and Dover. Sandwich, a Cinque port, has long been abandoned by shipping save for an occasional visit by a small coasting vessel with timber; but after the coming of the railway two of the most famous golf courses in Britain were laid out on the sand dunes which choked the life out of its maritime trade. Today the quiet market town is famous for the architectural beauties of its narrow streets. Its station deals with a moderate but steady passenger traffic. In the 1950s there was also an interesting traffic of several wagon-loads a day of flints for the Potteries from a nearby ballast pit. Deal, suffering from the decline in sail, eventually became a modest resort, lacking the rumbustious gaiety of Margate or the fashionable gentility of Folkestone.

A THIRD ROUTE TO DOVER

The humble origin of the alternative route to Dover from Swanley to Ashford lay in the 9-mile single-track branch of the nominally independent Sevenoaks Railway from today's Swanley through Otford to Bat and Ball on Sevenoaks's outskirts. Opening day was 2 June 1862. For the first few weeks there was no station at the junction (described as a place in Sutton-at-Hone parish), the branch trains making their main-line connections at St Mary Cray. When a station was opened, it was called Sevenoaks Junction, but in 1871 was renamed Swanley Junction. It gave its name to the unlovely settlement on the Maidstone road which grew up round it and now numbers several thousand. The stationmaster's house was the oldest in the village. On 16 April 1939 a new station, half a mile to the west, was opened as plain 'Swanley', but the village is still popularly called 'the Junction' to distinguish it from Old Swanley a mile away. Even today Bat and Ball is well on the outskirts of Sevenoaks, the temporary terminus's inconvenient site being due to the opposition of local landlords. The extension to the South Eastern's Sevenoaks Tubs Hill station was opened on 1 August 1869. Notwithstanding this connection, the Sevenoaks line quickly came to be regarded as an appendix to the Swanley Junction–Maidstone route, which diverged from it by a triangular junction three-quarters of a mile south of Otford station. It was served by an infrequent shuttle service from a bay at Otford until electrification in 1935 altered the picture, a service with a 20-minute headway being put on between Sevenoaks Tubs Hill and Holborn via Swanley, completely revolutionizing the travel pattern and social life of the district.

Like the original line, the new branch from Otford to Maidstone was of single track, but by 11 August 1875 the whole system had been doubled. The Sevenoaks Company, which optimistically changed its name to the Sevenoaks, Maidstone & Tunbridge, was vested in the Chatham by an Act of 1879. The $18\frac{3}{4}$-mile extension from Maidstone to Ashford belonged to another satellite, the Maidstone & Ashford, which opened the line to its own elaborate terminus on the western outskirts of Ashford on 1 July 1884. The Company apparently preferred to go to this expense to remain independent than to take advantage of running powers into the

South Eastern Ashford station granted in its Act. A connecting spur was not opened until 1 November 1891. Thereafter trains terminating at the Chatham station also conveyed through carriages for the South Eastern. One of the first acts of the Managing Committee was to close the Chatham terminus to passengers from 1 January 1899: the station now serves as the goods depot for Ashford. In 1966 Lenham became a terminal for car-delivery trains and in 1980 Hothfield one for aggregates.

The 42¼-mile line from Swanley to Ashford has become a useful relief to those via Tonbridge and via Chatham, being used at times of pressure by boat trains and holiday extras. But it is a difficult road, with the usual Chatham saw-tooth profile, including that bane of hard-pressed drivers of overloaded boat trains, the descent from Barming into the Medway Valley at 1 in 135–100, the sharp curve through Maidstone East station, and the 1½-mile Bearsted bank inclined at 1 in 60.

BRANCH LINES

The branch lines remaining to be described can best be divided into three groups. The first consists of those off the Chatham's main line and the North Kent line between Gravesend and Rochester.

The GRAVESEND Railway was opened on 10 May 1886 from Fawkham Junction, half a mile west of Fawkham station between Swanley and Rochester, and Gravesend (West Street). It was 5 miles long and of double track. A 7-chain extension led on to West Street Pier. The nominally independent Company was vested in the Chatham in 1883.

As in many of its ventures, the Chatham was too late. From Victoria to Gravesend was 27½ miles over a more difficult route than the South Eastern's 24 miles from Charing Cross. Besides, the South Eastern's North Kent was not the only competitor, for the London, Tilbury & Southend offered through fares (still obtainable) at cheap rates from Fenchurch Street via the Tilbury Ferry. Again, although the LCDR opened a station adjoining the Rosherville Gardens, this pleasure resort was nearing the end of its career and was closed finally in 1910. Boat trains were run on to the pier in connection with Batavier Line sailings to Rotterdam, but after the war these were switched to Tilbury. In 1936 the boat train consisted of a three-coach non-corridor set and a single corridor 'swinger' (the term in general use for a coach not marshalled in a set) usually jogging behind a Class 'C' 0-6-0. Passenger traffic on the branch was therefore light and in later years almost entirely local. Electrification on the main line in 1939 failed to increase traffic on the branch, which was closed to passengers on 3 August 1953. Gravesend West remained open for goods until the line was cut back, on 24 March 1968, to Southfleet, where a railhead for coal was established.

As already said, the HUNDRED OF HOO line was planned by a nominally independent company quickly taken over by the South Eastern as the latter's bid to outflank the Chatham at Queenborough on the Isle of Sheppey. The 11 miles of single track from Hoo Junction on the North Kent across the lonely Hoo peninsula and the Isle of Grain were opened in 1882: to Sharnal Street on 1 April and to Port Victoria (opposite Queenborough) on 11 September. From Port Victoria pier a ferry connected with the Dutch steamers at Queenborough. It was 42 miles from Charing Cross to Queenborough against the Chatham's 52 from Victoria, but because of the ferry link it never flourished. In 1901 the ferry ceased and in 1916, because of decay, the Port Victoria pier for which Watkin had forecast great things was closed.

In the years after the first world war industrial activity kept freight receipts high. On 14 May 1932 a double line from Stoke Junction to a spot known as ALLHALLOWS-ON-SEA, 1¾ miles away, was opened and most of the trains diverted there. The Southern had great hopes of Allhallows as a resort, but Thames mud proved less attractive than East Kent sands. Even so, 6,500 people visited the lonely spot during the remainder of 1932. Port Victoria was swallowed up in the Grain oil-refinery opened in 1951. Passenger services ceased on 4 December 1961 and the Allhallows branch closed. But otherwise freight traffic has grown considerably. In 1961 pioneering block cement trains were started between Cliffe and Uddingston (Glasgow) and by 1967 five oil trains left Grain daily. More recently trains of sea-dredged aggregates have gone into service.

From Strood the East Kent's curve led up to the site of the present ROCHESTER station. At first this had been the only link the East Kent had with the outside world, but after the opening of the LCDR line to Victoria in 1858 the service dwindled until the curve was abandoned save by a daily freight train. The feud thus brought no benefits to the Medway towns and civic intervention was needed to bring the warring parties to their senses. In 1876 Alderman Toomer, Mayor of Rochester, brought the matter before the Railway Commissioners. It then transpired that the SER had already proposed to run through coaches into Chatham, but the LCDR had refused to co-operate. Three Orders, the last carrying penalties of £60 a day against the LCDR and £15 against the SER if it was not forthwith obeyed, were issued by the Railway Commissioners before the through service was started in 1877. Henceforth the spur was known as the 'Toomer Loop' and its successor still bears the name in popular parlance.

The South Eastern's CHATHAM CENTRAL branch, opened from Strood to Rochester on 20 July 1891 and to Chatham Central on 1 March 1892, was built parallel to the Toomer Loop, over a new bridge across the Medway to a terminus so peripheral to Chatham it was actually in Rochester, the 'Central' being even more ironical than usual. Fusion soon put an end to the white elephant and Rochester Common and Chatham Central were closed on 1 October 1911. The last few chains of the mile-long branch were dismantled, but the new Medway Bridge was thenceforward used, instead of the original Toomer Loop, as a connection between Strood and Rochester. A further stretch gives access to Chatham Sidings, now the principal goods depot of the Medway Towns. In 1927 the LCDR line at the foot of Sole Street Bank was realigned to ease the curve and all traffic now passes over the newer bridge. The older one has now come to be used as a road.

The SHEERNESS branch was opened on 19 July 1860 as a 7-mile single line from a triangular junction half a mile west of Sittingbourne station. As already mentioned, the independent Company was vested in the Chatham in 1866. The original lifting section of the King's Ferry Bridge across the Swale was replaced in 1904 by a rolling lift span of the Scherzer type, the first of its kind in this country. Owing to its weakness, which severely limited the weight of trains, and also its proneness to damage by passing ships, this was replaced in 1960 by a new vertical-lift structure alongside. The new bridge was first used by road traffic on 29 February and by trains on 10 April. On 1 June 1883 a half-mile extension was opened from the Dockyard terminus to a more conveniently-sited one, now called Sheerness-on-Sea. Passenger trains soon by-passed the original station, which became a goods depot. Connections were provided with the dock lines (the naval port became a commercial one about 1960) and the new steel plant. But Sheerness has also developed as a resort, and while it is the bus centre for the island, it largely depends on rail communication with the mainland. In connection with the 1959 electrification the branch has therefore been doubled to Swale Halt. Queenborough Pier, once the start of the steamer service to Flushing, has long been dismantled.

Queenborough was also junction for the 8¾-mile SHEPPEY Light Railway, opened to Leysdown on 1 August 1901. Leysdown developed in the 1930s as a straggling resort of bungalows and bus-bodies; but, never remunerative and almost devoid of goods traffic, the line was entirely closed from 4 December 1950.

Of the second group of branch lines, those leaving the main South Eastern line, the nearest to London is the 4¾ miles of single track running below the scarp of the North Downs from Dunton Green to Westerham. Promoted by the WESTERHAM VALLEY Company, incorporated in 1876, it was opened on 7 July 1881 and was vested in the South Eastern in the same year. It pursued a placid, almost self-contained existence, its commuter traffic (80–100 in recent years) staving off closure until the line was closed completely on 30 October 1961.

The South Eastern's first branch was that from what is now Paddock Wood to MAIDSTONE (now the West Station), sanctioned in 1843 and opened on 25 September 1844. Two years later the track was doubled. From Paddock Wood the branch follows the banks of the Medway for most of the way to the county town of Kent. The area is beloved of anglers, who have long furnished a steady source of week-end traffic. Maidstone now has a population of 65,000 and besides its administrative and market functions it engages in brewing, paper-making, engineering and confectionery making. In 1853 an Act was obtained to extend the line down the Medway Valley to meet the North Kent at STROOD. The 10¾-mile link was opened on 18 June 1856 and since then a large cement and paper industry has grown up along the banks of the lower Medway.

Within the triangle Tonbridge–Ashford–Hastings there was a

large area of country devoid of rail communication, partly because of its dissected terrain and lack of large towns. After several
abortive proposals from 1844 onwards, the SER, fearful of the
threat implied in the Sevenoaks, Maidstone & Tunbridge Company, came to the aid of local promotors. In 1864 the SER obtained powers for a branch from Paddock Wood to Cranbrook
and a nominally independent Weald of Kent Company was incorporated to extend the line to Tenterden. But the financial collapse of the Chatham in 1866 led to a cooling of South Eastern
enthusiasm and nothing was done. So the matter rested until, in
1877, the privately-promoted Cranbrook and Paddock Wood
Company, appropriately displaying a bunch of hops on its seal,
was incorporated to revive the scheme. Capital was slow in coming
forward and construction even slower. In 1882 the Company
obtained powers for an extension to HAWKHURST, but it
was not until 1 October 1892 that the line was opened to Hope
Mill (Goudhurst from December 1892) and on 4 September 1893
the whole $11\frac{1}{2}$ miles to Hawkhurst went into service, worked, of
course, by the South Eastern. Various abortive proposals were
made to extend the branch, whose dead-end nature robbed it
of much utility. The guardless pull-and-push trains still panted up
the heavy gradients through endless hop gardens and incon-
veniently-sited stations until 12 June 1961, when the branch was
closed. A million pot plants a year were railed at Hawkhurst.

The $3\frac{1}{2}$ miles of double track from a junction on the main line
where Sandling station now is, through Hythe to SANDGATE,
were opened on 9 October 1874. In 1876 powers were obtained for
a 3-mile extension to Folkestone Harbour. Had it been built the
harbour incline would have been by-passed and boat trains would
now run directly to the Harbour station. Both Hythe and Sandgate stations were high above and remote from the towns they
purported to serve and plans to connect them with the Folkestone,
Hythe & Sandgate horse tramway came to nothing. The line
from Hythe to Sandgate was closed from 1 April 1931 and a bus
garage built on the site of Sandgate station. After years of diminishing traffic and ever fewer trains, the line to Hythe was closed
from 3 December 1951 and Hythe station has completely disappeared. An enterprising bus operator used to meet all trains
at Sandling and convey passengers to all parts of Hythe.

The ELHAM VALLEY line opened northwards as far as Barham on 4 July 1887 and throughout on 1 July 1889, was 16⅛ miles long and ran from Harbledown Junction, 1½ miles south of Canterbury West, to Cheriton Junction, 1⅛ miles west of Shorncliffe. For some years the line was operated as part of a 'circle' route through Folkestone, Canterbury and Minster. Passenger traffic was always light, and in later years suffered heavily from bus competition along the parallel road, though agricultural traffic used to be heavy. Singled during the first world war, partly closed to passengers in the second, the branch was finally closed to passengers from 16 June and altogether from 10 October 1947.

And now to Romney Marsh for the third group of branches. In 1881 the nominally independent Lydd Railway obtained powers to build a line from Appledore, on the Ashford-Hastings route, to DUNGENESS. Next year it obtained authority for a three-mile branch from a junction south of Lydd to NEW ROMNEY. This was not the first scheme for the area. In 1873 the Rye and Denge-ness Railway & Pier Company had been incorporated to build a railway and a pier at Dungeness, where the largest of ships can approach very close to the shingle headland. The powers passed in 1875 to the SER who dreamed of a great port, but took no practical steps. On 7 December 1881 the Lydd Company's line was opened for goods throughout to Dungeness and to Lydd for passengers. Passenger trains began working on to Dungeness on 1 April 1883 and the New Romney branch was opened on 19 June 1884. The two branches were operated by a single train connecting with the Ashford-Hastings trains at Appledore. From Lydd it would go up to New Romney and back again before visiting Dungeness, or vice versa. From Dungeness came a traffic in flints despatched from the shingle banks to the Potteries. Boats also came from Rye collecting and flints were railed from Rye Harbour. Between the wars there was much building of summer bungalows between Dungeness and New Romney. The New Romney branch was therefore re-sited (opened 4 July 1937) nearer the coast and two new halts provided, at Lydd-on-Sea and Greatstone-on-Sea. Passenger trains then ceased to call at Dungeness (closed completely May 1953). On 6 March 1967 the line was closed to passengers, but remains as a siding to mile post 74 to serve the atomic power stations.

OTHER RAILWAYS

All the so-called independent lines so far mentioned were operated by one of the two principal companies. There were, however, several genuinely independent lines with their own rolling stock and management.

In spite of the 1864 proposal for a branch from Cranbrook, Tenterden did not see its first passenger train until 2 April 1900, when the Rother Valley (Light) Railway, incorporated in 1896 but soon brought under the new provisions of the Light Railways Act of the same year, was opened from Robertsbridge. Goods traffic had begun on 29 March. The completion to Tenterden Town was opened on 15 April 1903. In that year a Light Railway Order authorized an extension from Tenterden Town to Headcorn, $9\frac{1}{2}$ miles. Another Order the following year changed the name to the KENT & EAST SUSSEX Light Railway. The extension was opened on 15 May 1905, but proved to be a liability, being run at a loss after 1924, whereas the Rother Valley section made small profits until 1930. In 1932 the Company went into Receivership and the line was operated by W. H. Austen, successor to Lieut-Colonel Stephens, as one of the group of semi-derelict light railways he managed from his Tonbridge office. By this time the line was more of a resort for rail fans than of any economic importance. Nevertheless it became part of British Railways in 1948 and services were considerably increased. But its inevitable fate arrived with the withdrawal of passenger trains and of the goods service north of Tenterden from 4 January 1954, but the original Rother Valley section remained open for goods until 12 June 1961. Passenger trains were run to Bodiam at hopping time until 1959. Fortunately, preservationists were eventually able to re-open the line to Wittersham Road in 1977 (see page 219). In 1841 both Tenterden and Cranbrook were among the largest towns in Kent, but because of the late arrival of their railways they stagnated completely. The motor age has brought them much prosperity but small population growth.

A boring in connection with the Channel Tunnel scheme finally proved what geologists had been predicting, that coal lay at depth below the chalk of East Kent. Speculative capital was attracted in the early years of the present century and a number of bores were put down. Many were failures, but in 1960 four pits survived:

Chislet, Snowdown, Betteshanger and Tilmanstone, producing some 1½ million tons a year. Block trains were run to Dover Town gasworks and most of the rest went to gasworks, power stations, cement plants and domestic users throughout Kent, though more coal was consumed in the county than was produced. Much of the coal traffic was concentrated on Minster yard, where 1,200 coal wagons were dealt with weekly, in striking contrast with the other main traffic despatched from the station, strawberries by passenger train. Chislet colliery (closed 1970) adjoined the Ashford–Ramsgate line east of Sturry, and Snowdown the Faversham–Dover line north of Shepherd's Well. BETTESHANGER required a 1¾-mile branch, in effect a siding trailing from the down line north of Deal. (Recent changes in the area are dealt with on page 209).

If the coalfield was to be further developed, railways were needed in the wedge of country between the Canterbury–Minster and Canterbury–Dover lines. A Light Railway Order was obtained in 1911, capital coming from interests developing the field. Portions of the 10¼-mile EAST KENT (Light) Railway were opened to coal traffic in the following year; public traffic (passenger and goods) commenced on 16 October 1916. Several pits, among them Wingham and Tilmanstone, were connected and a reasonable traffic began to pass.

After the war the company owning Tilmanstone became interested in using Richborough port for coal exports. This had been developed on the estuary of the Stour below Sandwich for military traffic, particularly by train ferry. In 1925 a 2¼-mile branch had been opened from Eastry to Sandwich Road and in August 1928 this was connected with RICHBOROUGH. But coal exports did not develop and general traffic was very light. The exiguous passenger service (in 1928 two trains each way on Saturdays) to Sandwich Road was withdrawn from 1 November 1928. But freight traffic continued to be worked down the near-derelict line as required, the passenger coach on the mixed train being left at Eastry. In 1925 a mile-long extension from Wingham Colliery to a place precisely nowhere, Canterbury Road, had opened.

Of all the pits reached by the East Kent Light Railway, only Tilmanstone was successful, though Wingham was worked for some years and one or two became brickworks. The closing of

Wingham was a bad blow and in 1935 only 838 passengers and
9,000 tons of minerals and general freight were carried. But
240,796 tons of coal were carried out of Tilmanstone over the 1¾
miles from Eythorne to Shepherd's Well. The railway, managed by
Lieut-Colonel Stephens, struggled on to become nationalized in
1948. The withdrawal of passenger services soon followed, the
last train running on 30 October 1948. All general freight traffic
ceased soon after and the main line has been torn up beyond
Eythorne. Coal traffic still requires several trains a day between
Tilmanstone Colliery and Shepherd's Well.

Richborough experienced an unexpected revival. The port
installations continued to moulder undisturbed, even through the
1939 war, but afterwards,'though without rail connections, they
were converted into an industrial estate, to help provide permanent employment for Thanet in particular and East Kent in
general. Large quantities of goods were despatched from Margate. In 1959, over 13,000 cases of hot-water bottles were railed
to destinations all over the country by a well-known multiple
store. A large power station was opened in 1962. Up to 3,000
tons of coal were burnt daily, railed from the four Kentish pits
in block trains hauled by electro-diesel locos. Later however it
was converted to oil, which is railed from Grain.

The fate of Kent's surviving independent line has been far
happier, but then in conception, character and operating conditions it is so different from any other railway mentioned in this
book, that it would indeed be churlish to say other than that its
lot is no more than it deserves. For mile after mile across the
spacious, apparently limitless levels of Romney Marsh pound its
'Pacific' locomotives, paint and brasswork gleaming, heading long
trains of bogie coaches, packed with passengers, surely the epi-
tome, in these days of electric and diesel traction and centralized
uniformity, of a steam-hauled express on an independent railway.
A visitor from Outer Space, for it is difficult to imagine anyone
from this world not knowing of the ROMNEY, HYTHE &
DYMCHURCH Light Railway, might be forgiven for being
surprised when stopping at a level-crossing for one of these expresses to find they were running on tracks of 15-inch gauge and
that the locomotives were no taller than the bonnet of his car.

But there is truth in the words of the general manager addressed

some years ago in pained surprise to a lady passenger speaking of
'toy railways' – 'but madam, this is a real railway.' The Romney,
Hythe & Dymchurch Light Railway was incorporated by a Light
Railway Order of 1926 which empowered the construction of a
double line of 1-foot 3-inch gauge railway 8 miles long between
Hythe and New Romney, where the headquarters and workshops
of the line were established. The moving spirit behind the scheme
was a racing motorist, Captain J. P. Howey, a man of sufficient
means to indulge his other interest, the driving of locomotives.

The double-track line across the dead level of Romney Marshes
was opened on 26 July 1927 and soon became a great tourist
attraction. A 7-mile extension was opened from New Romney to
Dungeness Lighthouse in the summer of 1929. During the war
the railway was commandeered by the military and much damage
was done to the permanent way. Public traffic ceased from 30
June 1940, but the line between Hythe and New Romney was
restored and reopened with due ceremony on 2 March 1946. The
Dungeness extension reopened on 21 March 1947. The railway
was a very real addition to the area's amenities. In 1971 350,000
passengers were carried. The majority were holiday-makers
travelling 'for the ride'. But the trains fulfilled a need for a
populous area rather ill-served by public transport. In 1978 a
contract to carry schoolchildren to New Romney was obtained
against bus competition.

Finally, the RYE & CAMBER, just outside Kent but a feeder
to the South Eastern's Hastings line, has naturally fallen for consideration in this chapter. Lieut-Colonel (then Mr) Stephens was
engineer to the Rye & Camber Tramways Company, incorporated in 1895 with a capital of £2,800, which opened its 2-mile-
long 3-foot gauge line from a primitive terminus below the walls
of Rye to Camber Golf Links (which also served the village of
Rye Harbour by means of a ferry) on 13 July 1895. The ½-mile
extension to Camber Sands came into use on 13 July 1908. The
Company owned 2 steam engines and 2 coaches, but in later years
a petrol locomotive was used. Winter services ceased in 1925, but
in spite of bus competition the line was still in operation at the
outbreak of war in 1939. The army later requisitioned the railway and duly returned it to its owners after the war. But it was
not considered worth restoring it for public services.

CHAPTER IV

Sussex and the Brighton Line

(INCLUDING SOUTH SURREY)

THE MAIN LINE

The first proposal for a route connecting London with the fabulous resort of Brighton came from William James, whom we have already encountered at Canterbury. In 1823 he published a pamphlet advocating the building of two horse-operated lines, one from Waterloo Bridge to Brighton and Shoreham and the other from Portsmouth to Chatham, crossing the former near East Grinstead. Nothing came of this, but in 1825 a company retained Sir John Rennie to make a survey from London to Bristol via Brighton. The London–Brighton section was resurveyed in 1833 and plans deposited. There matters hung fire until 1835 when the scheme re-entered the Parliamentary field with no less than five other runners. To gain a clear picture, the six projects are listed below:

1. *Rennie's* project for a direct line from Kennington Common straight across the grain of the Weald to a Brighton terminus on the hillside above the Pavilion. It was only 47½ miles but entailed heavy earthworks.

2. *Robert Stephenson's* project, which was to be the chief rival. It ran from a joint terminus with the London & Southampton via Leatherhead and the Mole Gap, skirted the High Weald in the Horsham area and crossed the South Downs by the Adur Gap. It was much longer than Rennie's, but very much less costly. It was later covered by a series of lines which made it possible to reach Brighton from Waterloo, though with at least two changes, in 61½ miles.

3. *Cundy's* scheme, very similar to Stephenson's.

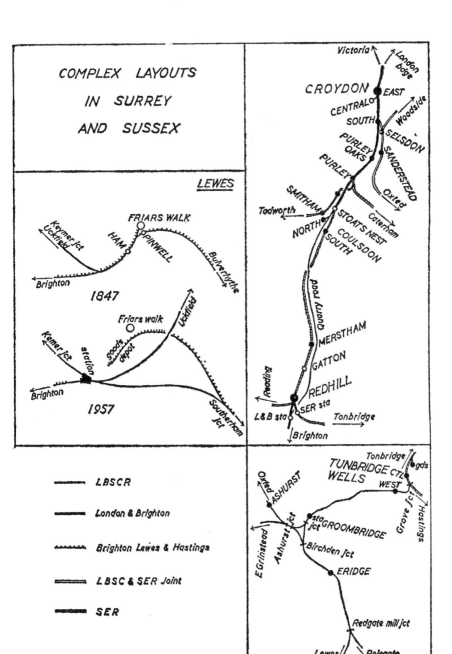

COMPLEX LAYOUTS
IN SURREY
AND SUSSEX

LEWES

FRIARS WALK
HAM
SPINWELL
Keymer Jct
Uckfield
Bulverhythe
Brighton
1847

Friars walk
goods depot
Uckfield
Kemer Jct
station
Brighton
Southerham Jct
1957

——— LBSCR
━━━ London & Brighton
⋯⋯⋯ Brighton Lewes & Hastings
═══ LBSC & SER Joint
▬▬▬ SER

Victoria
London bdge
CROYDON EAST
CENTRAL
SOUTH
Woodside
PURLEY OAKS
SELSDON
SANDERSTEAD
PURLEY
Oxted
SMITHAM
Caterham
Tadworth
STOATS NEST
NORTH
COULSDON
SOUTH
Quarry road
MERSTHAM
GATTON
REDHILL
Reading
SER sta
L&B sta
Tonbridge
Brighton

Tonbridge
TUNBRIDGE CTL
WELLS
gds
Oxted
ASHURST
WEST
Grove Jct
Hastings
sta jct
GROOMBRIDGE
E Grinstead
Ashurst Jct
Birchden Jct
ERIDGE
Redgate mill jct
Lewes
Polegate

4. *Gibbs's* route, 58½ miles, approximated to Rennie's as far as what is now Redhill but ran thence through the Adur Gap.

5. *Vignoles's* project, 54 miles long yet involving heavy engineering works. It was never a serious competitor.

6. *Palmer's* route, later adopted by the South Eastern Railway, ran from a junction with that line south of Oxted to Lewes and thence to Brighton.

It can be seen that the conflict was between the principle of a 'direct' route and the so-called 'natural routes', which would be easier and therefore cheaper to build. Only Rennie's and Stephenson's projects were ever really seriously considered in 1835, and both of those failed to satisfy the Parliamentary Committees. They reappeared in the 1836 session and again the struggle was mainly between them, though those of Gibbs and Cundy were also under consideration. There was some hard hitting. Cundy accused Stephenson of stealing his plans; Rennie's counsel said that Stephenson preferred Shoreham to Brighton and coals to passengers; and Sergeant Merewether waxed lyrical on the impossibility of crossing the Downs by the 'direct' route. Stephenson's Bill was passed by the Commons but rejected by the Lords.

The next year, 1837, all the 1836 contestants came back for another round, joined this time by the South Eastern. Captain R. Alderson, R.E., was called upon to report as to the most suitable. Though well disposed to Stephenson's, he finally found in favour of Rennie's, which had meanwhile been resurveyed. However, the rivals had already sunk their differences and apportioned the authorized share issue among themselves. Stephenson's company got almost as good terms as Rennie's. Rennie complained that his plans had been submitted behind his back to Stephenson – 'whom I do not consider a proper judge of these plans' – and disappeared from the scene.

The London & Brighton Railway was incorporated by an Act of 15 July 1837 to build a line from a junction with the London & Croydon 'at or near Selhurst Farm' (south of Norwood Junction station) to Brighton, with branches from there to Shoreham and to Newhaven via Lewes. The authorized capital was £180,000 in £50 shares, and the Company was compelled to purchase the whole of the moribund Croydon, Merstham & Godstone Railway, part of whose site was to be used south of Coulsdon.

The engineer was John Urpeth Rastrick, who had been previously connected with railways. But this was his first major railway undertaking, and also his swan song. Great was the excitement on 12 July 1838 when the first sod was cut north of Merstham Tunnel, the start of the deep cutting there. Soon over 3,500 men and 57 horses were at work.

By 1840 this number had grown to 6,206 men and 960 horses, now aided by five locomotives. The 1841 Census emphasizes the large-scale employment of labour on these early projects, giving a hint of the revolutionary effect the railway building must have had on the peaceful rural communities. The population of the quiet village of Balcombe, in the midst of the High Weald and roughly two-thirds of the way from London to Brighton, was returned as 1,542, a figure which included 550 labourers and their families. Further towards Brighton, the native population of the parish of Keymer was 916, added to which were 450 temporary immigrants. Some labour trouble occurred during the construction of Merstham Tunnel, on the London side of Redhill. The men complained that there was no supply of beer nearer than Woodmansterne, at least two miles away, and threatened to strike. Boys were being paid $\frac{1}{2}d.$ a journey to fetch the vital liquid.

Because materials could be landed there, the branch from Brighton to Shoreham harbour was given priority and was opened on 12 May 1840. By then good progress was being made on the main line's major engineering works. The Ouse Viaduct was ready in March 1841, and Merstham and Balcombe Tunnels almost simultaneously. On 28 June 1841 inspectors made an experimental journey to Haywards Heath, a station in the open country three miles east of the old town of Cuckfield. Next month 300 more men were taken on to complete the section before 12 July. On that day a service began between London Bridge and Haywards Heath ($37\frac{3}{4}$ miles). A service of four weekday trains each way was provided. The down ones took two hours for the journey (18·9 m.p.h.) and the gap to Brighton was covered by coach in a further two hours. On Sunday there were two services each way and an additional train to and from Horley. Fares from London to Haywards Heath were 10s. first and 7s. 6d. second class, and to Brighton 15s. and 11s. respectively. Seats on the coaches were bookable the day before travel, at London Bridge or at eleven recognized coach offices in the City or West End.

The ceremonial opening to Brighton took place on Tuesday 21 September, public traffic beginning the same day.

The line was boldly planned and well laid out, striking almost directly southward, across the grain of the Weald. The result was a switchback profile with three gable summits, but careful planning, five tunnels and numerous earthworks resulted in surprisingly moderate gradients, 1 in 264 for the most part, and an absence of curves. High speeds and heavy trains have always been possible. In steam days this made for some excitement as the down grades were taken at high speeds to enable the summits to be 'rushed'. With the coming of electricity speeds do not vary perceptibly up hill or down dale and the average traveller may well be forgiven for assuming the line to be almost level.

From Norwood there is a 7-mile rise at 1 in 264 towards the Merstham Gap in the crest of the North Downs. Use is made of the deep dry valley in which South Croydon and Purley are laid out. Beyond Coulsdon South (15½ miles from London Bridge) there is a long cutting through the chalk before Merstham Tunnel (1,831 yards) is reached. Then follows 7¼ miles of down grade, again at 1 in 264, over the Vale of Holmesdale, through the gap in the Greensand ridge in which Redhill town later grew up, and out on to the level Weald Clay Plain. Shortly before Horley the line begins its 7½-mile climb, at the usual 1 in 264, to the next summit at Balcombe Tunnel (1,141 yards). The descent is 8½ miles long, which brings the line to a point just short of Wivelsfield station (40½ miles from London Bridge). Between Balcombe and Haywards Heath the wide Ouse Valley is crossed by the 37-arched Ouse Viaduct, with a maximum height of 100 feet. One final gable summit occupies the remaining 11½ miles, by which the line negotiates the South Downs. The crest is pierced by the Clayton Tunnel, 2,259 yards long and up to 270 feet below the surface. In the early years it was lit by gas, to 'induce a feeling of confidence and cheerfulness' in the passengers and to enable the drivers 'to see the road throughout as well almost as in broad day'. For this purpose the gasworks, which later supplied the town, were built at Hassocks.

As we saw at the end of Chapter II, the countryside through which the new line ran was then very sparsely peopled. Lundie's *The Railway Excursionist's Hand-Book to Brighton* (1851) says, 'on the Brighton line you see no human habitations save a few cottages'. Redhill and Haywards Heath, now large and thriving towns and centres of populous districts, were non-existent, while Hassocks and Horley are equally railway creations. Today continuous building extends as far as Coulsdon South, but in those early days there was so little traffic that trains only stopped when required at any of the stations between Croydon and Redhill. By 1957 16 trains an hour called at Purley in the off-peak and 16 up trains between 8.0 and 9.0 a.m. while 32,000 season tickets alone were sold; but the original station, known as Godstone Road (Godstone is 7 miles from there), was closed from 1 October 1847 and not reopened until 1856. Stoat's Nest, on a site at the sidings between the present Purley and Coulsdon North stations, was used to serve Epsom racecourse, 8 miles away, until the line from West Croydon was extended to Epsom in 1847. It was apparently well patronized, for our hardy ancestors would have thought nothing of such a walk as preliminary and aftermath of an important social event.

Merstham, sited for the benefit of Gatton Park house, was on the section which passed to the South Eastern in 1842. They closed it immediately, but were forced by the owner of the house to reopen it until the new station, three-quarters of a mile to the north and more convenient for the village, was ready.

At Redhill the situation of the stations was even worse. The two Brighton stations, Merstham and Reigate, were well on either side of the junction with the South Eastern, whose own station, also Reigate, was to the east of the divergence. The two Reigates were linked by a muddy, ill-lit lane, and as connections were anyway bad the interchange traffic was discouraged as much as possible. Complaints were loud; a letter to the *Railway Times* of 26 November 1842 says that while the South Eastern was in a reasonably convenient position, the Brighton stations were sited in the wrong places to suit Lord Somers and Lord Monson respectively.

The Brighton in later years became vested with a certain glamour which was the result of its locomotive history. The little umber engines, lined in yellow and black, rather obscure the considerable meanness of the Company with its long tale of public disservice. It was from the South Eastern that the initiative came for a station north of the junction at Redhill. The Brighton eventually agreed and in 1844 a station went into service on the present site. It was rebuilt in 1858 when the present range of buildings on the down side were provided. Until 1923 it was owned and operated by the South Eastern on such partisan lines that the Brighton services suffered chronically.

From its inception the main-line service revealed features which have characterized it ever since, namely provision for the commuting City business man and for the excursionist. The service provided from 21 September 1841 consisted of 6 trains a day each way, stopping at all stations and taking $2\frac{1}{2}$ hours (20·2 m.p.h.). But there was also a first-class only express in the up direction, calling at Croydon only, which left at 8.30 a.m. and reached London Bridge at 10.15 (35·7 m.p.h.). Single fares were 14s. 6d. first and 9s. 6d. second. On 21 September, it is recorded, the 10.45 a.m. up train was made up of 19 coaches, 5 carriages on trucks and horse boxes with 5 horses. The cavalcade was drawn by 2 locomotives and carried 146 passengers.

From 1 November down trains left at 8.45 (a), 10.45 (b) a.m. and 12.45, 1.45 (a), 3.45 (b), 5.45 (a) p.m., while the up trains left at 8.0 (a), 9.30 (b), 10.45 (b), 11.45 a.m. and 1.45 (a), 5.45 (a) p.m. Those marked (a) were first- and second-class all-stations trains and those marked (b) were first class only, calling at the four principal stations, New Cross, Croydon, Redhill and Haywards Heath & Cuckfield. The 12.45 down and 11.45 up were goods trains conveying second-class carriages. Third-class passengers were relegated to the 9.0 p.m. goods trains until, in 1843, anticipating Gladstone's Act, they were allowed on three slow trains each way, very generous provision for those days.

Continual growth of traffic has led to many changes. Except for the few erected to the design of the Company's architect, David Mocatta, the stations were mean in the extreme: short, low wooden platforms and small huts. But all have been swept into oblivion save for a few Mocatta relics, Balcombe station, the downside buildings at Three Bridges and some cottages, once Horley Station, being the chief remains of his elegant little gothic buildings.

In 1846 the situation north of Croydon was rationalized by the amalgamation of the London & Croydon with the London & Brighton. Both the South Eastern and the Brighton had made offers, the Brighton being the more anxious since the South Eastern had obtained a lease of the Greenwich. At the amalgamation, the Brighton took the opportunity to rename itself, though the alteration had nothing to do with Croydon: the new Company formed on 27 July 1846 was the London, Brighton & South Coast Railway. It was still, however, 'The Brighton' to the public. The Croydon was well represented on the new Board and this, as we shall see, had considerable repercussions (page 118).

After the opening of the line to London Victoria in 1860, extra platforms were provided at East Croydon. These were treated as a separate station, called New Croydon, and the South Eastern was rigidly excluded. The extension was needed partly because the Brighton's main-line trains almost invariably carried London Bridge and Victoria portions, divided or joined at East Croydon, where shunting movements mounted. The two Croydon stations were not amalgamated until the present three islands were built in 1897–98, and even then separate booking accounts were kept until 1924. East Croydon is a spacious station – of necessity, for by 1931 1·3 million passengers were booked and 20,000 seasons issued.

In passing, in 1864 the London, Brighton & South Coast, or LBSCR, obtained powers for a short branch, 29 chains, from East Croydon, under Park Lane, to Croydon Central. Opened on 1 January 1868, it met with little success, and was closed from 1 December 1871. However, at the instigation of the Town Council, it was reopened on 1 June 1886 but finally closed from 1 September 1890. Apart from one up Brighton working, the service consisted entirely of London & North Western and Great Eastern trains to and from Willesden and Liverpool Street respectively. The Town Hall was built on the site of Croydon Central and for some 45 years an engineers' depot was maintained on the inner part of the branch. But since 1960 some of the impressive public buildings of the re-developed Croydon have been erected on the site of this yard.

Redhill remained a constant source of irritation, for in spite of all agreements, and in spite of the majority of the trains belonging to the LBSCR, the South Eastern always ensured priority for its own. On one occasion the latter put a slow train from London Bridge one minute earlier than a Brighton express, apparently from sheer devilment. As late as 1889 a dispute led to arbitration by Henry Oakley of the Great Northern, who increased the contribution of the LBSCR for the upkeep of the Stoat's Nest–Redhill section, as its traffic so greatly exceeded that of the South Eastern. When, therefore, it became apparent during the 1890s that widening of its main line was imperative, the Brighton determined to avoid Redhill completely. Quadrupling had been carried out from London Bridge as far as South Croydon in 1864 and it was extended to a point a quarter of a mile north of Coulsdon South (opened 1889) by 5 November 1899. Two new stations were opened on that date, Purley Oaks and Stoat's Nest. The latter was not on the original site but to the south where the four tracks ended. After a number of changes of name it finally became Coulsdon North on 1 August 1923.

From Coulsdon North, the terminus of the suburban services until 1981, a pair of tracks on a separate location, which avoided Merstham and Redhill and exclusive to the LBSCR, were provided for 6½ miles to Earlswood Junction. These, invariably known as the 'Quarry Line', involved considerable earthworks, including the 2,113-yard Merstham (Quarry Line) Tunnel and the deep cuttings approaching it from the north. In these the Quarry Line crosses over the original line from the west to the east side at the site of Star Lane Box. There is also the 649-yard Redhill Tunnel under Redstone Hill and the Tonbridge line. Where the new line traversed the grounds of Cane Hill Mental Hospital, on the steep sides of a narrow valley, in the bottom of which were the SER and the road, a shallow cutting was roofed over for 431 yards and the top-soil reinstated. The Cane Hill Covered Way was opened out in 1954 to save maintenance costs. No objection was raised as there was no longer a smoke problem. The Quarry Line was opened to goods traffic on 8 November 1899 and to expresses on 1 April 1900. It has no stations.

Quadrupling was completed by stages to Balcombe Tunnel Box at the northern end of the tunnel, 32½ miles from Victoria, by 1912. The very heavy earthworks involved have prevented any extension, though powers to widen throughout were obtained in 1903.

BRIGHTON

As already stated, the ceremonial and public opening of the London-Brighton route was on 21 September 1841. Trains had been reaching Brighton from Shoreham since 12 May 1840, but it was the opening of the main line, which was so to alter the resort, that was greeted with the greatest enthusiasm. Thousands of cheering citizens assembled in lineside fields to welcome the first trains. The favoured were allowed into 'the cool and shady colonnades of the station-house' and the 'light, wide-spreading sheds which receive the trains', where massed bands and choirs were waiting to add their contribution to the cacophony.

Demonstrations were not confined to Brighton. The *Brighton Herald* remarked:

> Up to Clayton the country poured forth its inhabitants. Hurst and Ditchling sent out their populations, in holiday array, to meet the train at Hassocks station; and Patcham, Withdean and Preston, all lent their quota to make up one general sum of joy.

Before we are tempted to smile over-indulgently at these scenes, it is as well to pause and try to recapture what exactly the coming of this revolutionary form of transport meant to the people of the time. It cannot be thought of in such contemporary terms as the opening of a new trunk road, or of the inauguration of a new air route. These are not revolutions, but merely another stage forward. That far-off September day, however, was the dawn of a new economic and social era for the whole of Sussex, though of course for Brighton in particular.

What must have been the thoughts of the town's aristocratic clientèle when the first excursion train arrived, on Easter Monday 1844? The train must have been an astonishing sight, for it left London Bridge with 45 carriages (probably no more than open wagons with wooden seats) drawn by four engines. At New Cross six more carriages and another engine were added, and yet six more carriages and another engine at Croydon. This improbable procession arrived eventually at 1.30 p.m., having covered the 50½ miles in four and a half hours.

By 1845, first-class season-ticket rates were already being

quoted from Brighton to London: £12 monthly, £25 quarterly and £50 annually. In that year a second-class excursion was being run on Sundays at a fare of 5s. Cheap excursion fares must have produced results, for the *Illustrated London News* of 6 June 1846 stated that the 8.0 a.m. excursion to Brighton 'on Monday last' had been made up of 44 carriages carrying 4,000 passengers.

Thus began the long association between Brighton and its railway. Between 1841 and 1871 the permanent population grew from 46,000 to 99,000. Queen Victoria refused to revisit the town and the aristocratic patrons gave way to the middle and working classes. Brighton faithfully reflected the social scene of the new age and has continued to do so.

. The station which has witnessed so many changing scenes is one of the largest on the Southern. It was designed by David Mocatta and remains essentially unaltered, though the concourse and platforms behind have been successively enlarged. The exterior is however almost lost behind clumsy later appendages. An early guide-book of 1840 remarks that the two-storey Italian-style buildings 'which cost £12,000, resemble the palace of a prince'. Measom's *Guide* regretted to observe the station was 'quite in the Northern suburbs', a sufficient commentary on the post-railway growth of Brighton, for today it is more conveniently central than the general run of provincial stations.

Rennie's site is remarkable – an artificial terrace of material blasted out of the hill behind. It has always been difficult. Originally the junction with the West Coast line lay outside the station, but platform lengthening has brought the point of divergence within the great overall roof. Within the V formed by the main and West Coast lines lay a chalk hill which was removed for the erection of the locomotive depot in the early 1860s. Prior to this the engines had stood in the open on part of the site of the locomotive works. These were opened in 1852 when they were transferred from New Cross Gate and closed in 1956. They were built partly on arches over the steep hillside – as also are the later enlargements to the adjacent station. Under the arches is a goods station reached by a precipitous gradient.

Cramped though the station is today, it is spacious compared with conditions in early days. In *A Frenchman sees the English in the Fifties* (1850s) we read: 'I remember one Sunday, outside

Brighton, three collectors taking the tickets of 2,000 passengers waiting unprotected in the boiling sun between a rock and a brick wall.' There are now ten platforms under a three-bay roof, two bays curving upwards in spectacular arches. There are in effect three groups of platforms, 1–3 being used by West Coast trains, 4–7 by main-line ones and 8–10 by those using the East Coast or Lewes line. The latter represent the latest additions of the 1880s. Though the hum of electric trains leaving at the rate of 14 to the hour was the dominant noise in the large and constantly crowded concourse, the bark of steam was still heard on regular local trains in 1964. Through trains, in very considerable numbers in the summer, ran as far afield as Plymouth, Cardiff and to industrial cities of the Midlands. 4,033,000 tickets were collected in 1957 and 40,456 seasons issued.

The LBSCR's monopoly at Brighton was not entirely unchallenged. In 1864 the Chatham deposited a Bill for a line from Beckenham and in 1866 returned to the fray in conjunction with the South Eastern. Ten years later a similar scheme, ostensibly independent of these companies, was mooted. Again, in 1883 W. J. Vennal approached the Town Council with a direct London & Brighton scheme. The Council supported the proposal, but Parliament did not. In 1901 came the London & Brighton Electric Railway project, which envisaged no intermediate stations and multiple-unit trains travelling at 90 m.p.h. But this and a modified scheme which came forward the next year received insufficient support and a somewhat chastened LBSCR was left thereafter in undisputed possession.

Brighton had one purely suburban branch, 1 mile 32 chains from the East Coast line to KEMP TOWN, opened on 2 August 1869. Its brief length involved a 14-arch viaduct and a 1,024-yard tunnel. Tram and bus competition led to the withdrawal of passenger services from the circuitous route from 2 January 1933. Kemp Town remained as a goods depot until 14 June 1971, but Lewes Road, the only intermediate station, became a pickle factory. The Cliftonville Spur, allowing through running from the main to the West Coast line, was opened on 1 July 1879.

New Year's Day 1933, when the full electric service was inaugurated from London, might be considered an outstanding date in Brighton's history. The full story of electrification must be delayed, but before leaving Brighton we may mention the oldest electric railway still at work in Britain, the creation of Magnus Volk, a one-time electrical engineer to Brighton Corporation. His name is still linked with the line, popularly if not officially termed 'Volk's Electric Railway'. Volk began by obtaining a lease from the Corporation for the quarter-mile section along the foreshore from the Aquarium to the Chain Pier. The 2-foot $8\frac{1}{2}$-inch line was formally opened on 3 August 1883 and carried 30,000 people in its first six months. It was then closed, reconstructed on the third rail system and extended three-quarters of a mile to Banjo Groyne. It was reopened on 4 April 1884, while the short extension to Blackrock came into use on 21 February 1901. In 1940 the Corporation took over the $1\frac{1}{2}$ miles, which had by then carried some 30 million passengers. Traffic in 1952 amounted to 775,000 passengers, but before the opening of Madeira Drive to buses the annual totals had approached the million mark.

THE 'EAST COAST' LINE

A branch eastward from Brighton to Lewes was authorized as early as the original London & Brighton Act of 1837, but powers lapsed and construction was left to the independent Brighton, Lewes & Hastings Railway, a Company incorporated in 1844 to build a $32\frac{1}{2}$-mile line from Brighton to Bulverhythe ($2\frac{1}{4}$ miles west of Hastings) via Lewes. The next year powers were obtained for a $9\frac{1}{4}$-mile cut-off from Lewes to Keymer ($3\frac{1}{4}$ miles south of Haywards Heath) on the main London–Brighton line. This cut-off would shorten the distance from London to Lewes and stations beyond by nearly 9 miles. In 1845, the Brighton, Lewes & Hastings Company was bought by the Brighton, at a premium of £7 per share.

The Brighton–Lewes section was opened as a double line on 8 June 1846 to a temporary terminal in Friars Walk. The single track extension to Bulverhythe followed on 27 June 1846.

Construction presented no particular difficulties except between Brighton and Lewes. Just outside the former station the valley, on the sides and floor of which the town is built, is crossed by the 330-yard London Road Viaduct on 27 brick arches, the highest of which is 67 feet. Immediately beyond London Road station (opened 1 October 1877) is the tunnel of that name and then the line climbs up through the Downs to Falmer (now with a subway to the University and busier than ever) and after negotiating the 490-yard tunnel descends the $3\frac{1}{2}$ mile Falmer Bank at 1 in 88. Between Lewes and Polegate the line runs along the vale beneath the Downs and thereafter crosses the Pevensey Levels.

The Keymer–Lewes line was opened for passengers on 1 October 1847. A station was opened at Keymer Junction with platforms on the Lewes line only on 1 January 1862, but was closed from 1 November 1883. The present station, north of the junction on the London–Brighton line, was opened in 1886 and renamed Wivelsfield ten years later.

Lewes's permanent station, a terminus with a handsome façade demolished in 1970, was opened on 28 August 1846. The junction with the Bulverhythe extension was 200 yards to the south of the terminus and faced Brighton. Accordingly, platforms locally known as Pinwell, but in effect part of Friars Walk, were erected on the St Leonards side of the junction. From 1846 to 1848 there was also a shelterless platform, Ham or Southover, between the junction of the Brighton and Keymer lines and Friars Walk–Pinwell. In spite of the admitted inconvenience of the arrangements, nothing was done until a new station, almost on the present site in the V of the Brighton and Keymer lines, was built and opened on 1 November 1857. Pinwell and Friars Walk were then closed. Pinwell had been little used, through trains mostly reversing out of or into Friars Walk.

The final rail route to Lewes, from Tunbridge Wells, was opened in 1868, and on 17 June 1889 the present layout was completed by a scheme involving the easing of the curves approaching the 1857 station from both Keymer and Brighton. East of the station the Eastbourne line was re-sited, leaving the original Brighton, Lewes & Hastings line as a loop to the north, used for access to the goods station (in Friars Walk until closure on 5 May 1969).

Lewes, the county town of East Sussex, is aligned along its medieval High Street which pitches steeply down to the Ouse. But by the nineteenth century it was in full decay as a port. At the mouth of the Ouse, however, was the small port of NEW-HAVEN. In spite of improvements it was but a poor one, but the Brighton, Lewes & Hastings Company thought it had considerable potentialities and on 18 June 1846 had obtained powers for a 6-mile branch from Southerham Junction, 1⅛ miles east of Lewes. It was opened to passengers on 8 December 1847 to what was confidently expected to become a great port, the 'Liverpool of the South' according to a guide-book of 1852. The packet service was soon transferred from Shoreham, but the service remained tidal, for we read in a contribution to a discussion on a paper by G. W. Buckwell to the Institute of Marine Engineers, 1891, that, 'the harbour of Newhaven was a mere creek with only two or three feet on the bar at low water.' The Newhaven Harbour Company was created in 1878 under Brighton auspices. Moles were built, together with a quay for packets and quayside station. The freight tramway (closed in 1963) on the right bank of the river was built in connection with these improvements. Fixed sailings began on 1 April 1889, the steamers having become railway property in 1867. The Harbour Company was vested in the Southern Railway in 1926.

The quays lie on the left bank of the River, the East Quay for passengers, the Railway Quay for cross-Channel cargo, and the North Quay for general cargo. In 1928 323,392 tons of cargo and 258,762 passengers were dealt with. One thousand tons a year of flints from the shore were then being railed to the Potteries, though the once prosperous oyster fisheries had disappeared. Since 1947 cross-Channel cargo has considerably increased and so have coastwise imports of oil. Newhaven has lost some of its importance as a packet port (in 1963 302,000 passengers passed through it), though the drive-on car-ferry of 1964 and the Stirling 'motorail' service increased traffic. (See also page 214.)

The extension to Seaford, 2½ miles away, was opened on 1 June 1864. Originally single, it was doubled in 1905 when the present Seaford station, with one platform and a bay, was opened. Bishopstone, the only intermediate station, was said to produce the least revenue of any Brighton station until replaced by a new station half a mile south on 26 September 1938. Seaford had a population of 16,226 in 1971, but its growth has probably been hampered by its shingle beach and lack of sand. Thirty-six passenger trains were scheduled on the Seaford–Lewes line on weekdays during the summer of 1959 and only 5 fewer on Sundays. There were also the boat specials starting at Newhaven.

EASTBOURNE was placed on the railway map on 14 May 1849 by a branch from Polegate, roughly halfway between Brighton and Hastings. The same day a branch was opened from Polegate north to Hailsham, a market town with a population of 1,586 (1841) which in some respects was more important than Eastbourne, though the latter's population had already grown to 3,015. Only a short time before, Eastbourne had been a mere group of buildings around the church and the Lamb Inn, and even in 1849 the site of Grand Parade was a stretch of low, grassy cliff. In 1961 its population was 60,897, ten times as great as that of Hailsham.

Eastbourne's original station was little more than a hut. In 1960 it was in use as a builder's stores behind the goods station, being moved there when the second station was built in 1866. This in turn gave way to the present 'Brighton Baroque' façade in 1886. The spacious concourse and four long platforms were rebuilt in 1935 in connection with electrification. In 1957, 1,492,000 tickets were collected at the station. Originally the branch was worked by a shuttle service connecting with the main line trains at Polegate. The triangular junction between the branch and the Brighton–Hastings line was completed by the opening of a curve between Willingdon and Stone Cross Junctions on 1 August 1871; thereafter some of the Brighton–Hastings trains worked into and out of Eastbourne. The only intermediate station between Polegate and Eastbourne, Hampden Park (Willingdon until 1 July 1903), was opened on 1 January 1888. In the summer of 1958 a half-hourly service ran between Hastings and Brighton via Eastbourne, there were 16 expresses from Hastings to London via Eastbourne and Keymer and 24 steam trains left for the 'Cuckoo' line (page 94). There were also through workings of locomotive-hauled stock to the Midlands and a weekly motorail to Glasgow.

THE BRIGHTON COMPANY

Now is the most convenient time to pause from the area by area survey of Sussex to consider the character of the Brighton Company. Its full title, the London, Brighton & South Coast, aptly described its main interests. Apart from the London suburban business, these were the carriage of traffic between London and the resorts along the coast from Hastings to Portsmouth – the chief of these resorts has always been Brighton – and between the resorts themselves. The Company's history is thus that of the development of the routes and services in the triangle between the Tonbridge–Hastings line of the South Eastern and the Guildford–Havant route of the London & South Western. The area was filled in with a network of branches, not particularly remunerative, but which safeguarded the approach of any rival to the Eldorado of the south coast resorts which the Brighton now looked upon as its own.

Its defensive campaign of construction was backed up by its aggressive relations with its neighbours. But these quarrels lacked the epic quality of the Kentish Feud, being more the bad-tempered growlings of a dog with a particularly juicy bone. Their history becomes tedious, enlivened only now and again by incidents such as the battles of Hastings and Havant and the Caterham troubles. As was usual it was the customer who suffered most from all this. Indeed, as far as services were concerned during the 1860–1900 period the Brighton was little better than its Kentish neighbours.

Probably stimulated by a financial crisis, in 1847 the Brighton and the South Eastern decided upon a comprehensive agreement between themselves. It was signed on 12 November and ratified in full legal form on 10 July 1848. Not only did this agreement influence the development of the Companies until the early 'sixties, but it is also typical of the undercurrent setting towards combination and co-operation which ran beneath the quarrels, and which from 1851 onwards threw up from time to time proposals for amalgamation. Had these been successful a 'Southern Railway' would have come into being long before 1923.

The main heads of the agreement can be thus summarized:

1. The Greenwich and the Bricklayers Arms lines to be freed of tolls to the LBSCR, except for any traffic conveyed by it in the future to and from any place east or north of a line Corbett's Lane–Redhill–Hastings (the first section the main railway to Redhill, the second an arbitrary line drawn on a map).

2. The Corbett's Lane–Croydon section to be freed of tolls to the SER except for traffic conveyed by it in the future to and from any place south of the Reading, Guildford & Reigate Railway

and to the west and south of the arbitrary line mentioned above.

3. The SER could take up and set down at any station between London Bridge and East Croydon traffic to and from SER and Reading, Guildford & Reigate Railway stations. In return the Brighton was given full rights at Redhill (SER).

4. The SER to complete the Bopeep–Hastings line 'within reasonable time'.

At face value the agreement was purely one relating to tolls, but in fact it was a settlement of spheres of influence, on which Parliament and populace would have frowned. It led to much trouble in its interpretation, but probably postponed overt hostilities.

The biggest battle, when the fighting did break into the open, was over Caterham. In June 1854 the Caterham Railway was incorporated to build a branch from Godstone Road (Purley) on the joint South Eastern and Brighton London–Redhill route, south-eastward up a deep and narrow valley in the chalk to the then obscure village of Caterham, just on the point of becoming a dormitory suburb. There was trouble from the start, for while the line was clearly in South Eastern territory, not only did that Company have no right to stop at Godstone Road (on the Brighton-owned section of the joint route), but the station had been closed since 1847 anyway. This last fact was the Brighton's trump card, since for 'reasons of public safety' the station could not be reopened.

The branch was declared ready for traffic on 21 September 1855. But both the Brighton and the South Eastern were unwilling to allow the other to lease or work the line, so a series of delays postponed the opening. After obtaining 'an engine and two or three carriages' from the Brighton, the Caterham Company finally inaugurated its service on 4 August 1856. Public traffic began next day.

Caterham Junction, as Godstone Road became in November 1856, was reopened. But the delaying tactics of the LBSCR led to it being sued by the Caterham Company in the Court of Common Pleas. In revenge the Brighton stirred up trouble over the hire of the rolling stock. Other financial troubles followed and in July 1859 the bankrupt small Company was taken over by the South

Eastern, after the breakdown of protracted negotiations with the Brighton.

But the troubles of passengers were by no means over. Following the breakdown of the 1848 agreement, and with trouble over Eastbourne, relations between the South Eastern and the Brighton were at their worst in 1862. The Brighton forbade the use of East Croydon station to the South Eastern, insisting that all passengers off the Caterham branch travelling to Croydon should hold LBSCR tickets. The trains were timed to leave the Junction before branch passengers could possibly re-book. Worse, attempts were made forcibly to prevent passengers entering South Eastern main line trains at Caterham Junction. This went on until a flood of letters to *The Times* and thunderous leading articles from that journal, then at the height of its power, forced even the Brighton to give way and the subsequent history of the Caterham was calm. The line was doubled in 1897 and traffic grew steadily.

The 1848 agreement was invoked on a number of other occasions. In 1859, for example, there were sharp, if short, exchanges over a spur, less than half a mile long, leading up from Norwood Junction to the Farnborough Extension of the West End of London & Crystal Palace Railway. By an agreement of 7 July the Brighton got its spur, though it was never much used and closed in 1966: in return the South Eastern eventually got full rights at Caterham Junction, thus settling that dispute.

To show how fair minded it had been and how it had been let down by Brighton intransigence, the South Eastern published the whole correspondence on the treaty since 1848. The book is fascinating reading. The letters pass from one side of London Bridge to the other, rising at times to an undiplomatic acrimony. But otherwise they resemble the Notes exchanged between rival governments, explaining how each has kept faithfully to the non-agression treaty while the other has broken it in letter and spirit, thereby justifying the sender in breaking the treaty and declaring war. Once or twice the Brighton directors came across in person to the South Eastern lambs, who included Samuel Smiles of *Self-Help* fame, secretary of the Company from 1855 to 1866.

Before finally leaving Caterham Junction (today's Purley) a second branch of much later origin must be mentioned. The nominally independent Chipstead Valley Railway left the Caterham line a few chains south-east of the Junction and passed under the main line to follow the valley to Tadworth. The Tattenham Corner extension was authorized some years after the rest. Opening dates were: to Kingswood on 2 November 1897, to Tadworth on 1 July 1900 and to Tattenham Corner on 4 June 1901, by which time the track had been doubled. Commuting traffic is now the mainstay of the branch, of course, but vast numbers passed over it to the Epsom races, 40,000 to the Derby of 1951.

The Caterham and Tattenham Corner branches were worked by the South Eastern and later by the Managing Committee, which had a shed at Purley. Though naturally they became part of the London Central Division after Grouping, to this day trains start from the Low Level (formerly South Eastern) at London Bridge at peak hours, and at other times run through to Charing Cross, the only Central section services to do so.

TUNBRIDGE WELLS, OUTPOST IN THE DEFENCE OF BRIGHTON

Remaining developments in the inland area east of the main Brighton line are readily explicable in the light of the LBSCR's determination to prevent South Eastern encroachments once the 1848 treaty had been abandoned. In this Tunbridge Wells played the part of a Verdun to Brighton's Paris.

On 9 July 1855 a single-track branch was opened from the main Brighton line at Three Bridges to the prosperous market town of East Grinstead. The independent Company was soon purchased by the LBSCR, it clearly being in the latter's territory.

On 18 October 1858 a branch was opened from Lewes (in fact Uckfield Junction, 1½ miles to the north on the Keymer cut-off) up the Ouse Valley to the market town of Uckfield. Again the LBSCR quickly bought the independent Company.

East Grinstead and Uckfield are respectively 13 and 15½ miles from Tunbridge Wells, and the LBSCR hastened to support local companies promoted to close these gaps. The Brighton, Uckfield & Tunbridge Wells Company was incorporated in 1861, and the East Grinstead, Groombridge & Tunbridge Wells the next year. The two routes joined at Groombridge, the line from there to Tunbridge Wells being part of the former.

The East Grinstead, Groombridge & Tunbridge Wells opened its single line on 1 October 1866, when the original station at East Grinstead was superseded by a through one at the Eastbourne Road bridge, 200 yards to the east. The route competed with the South Eastern until the latter's Sevenoaks cut-off was ready, it being 28¾ miles from Redhill via Three Bridges and 24¾ via Tonbridge. The LBSCR advertised it as the 'Pleasant Route'.

The Uckfield line was opened on 3 August 1868 and involved a long climb in both directions up to the gable summit on which Crowborough, the principal intermediate station, is sited. Here the railway has created on the healthy sandstone heights an amorphous suburban settlement, neither town, village nor country, of a type peculiar to this outer suburban belt of London. Beloved by company directors and retired officers of the Armed Services, their pleasant villas and golf-courses extend over a very wide area.

Both of these lines to Tunbridge Wells were absorbed by the LBSCR before opening: the approach to Brighton was secure. On 1 October 1868, soon after the extension of the Lewes–Uckfield route to Tunbridge Wells, a new 3½-mile line was built to provide independent access to Lewes, Uckfield Junction on the Keymer cut-off being closed. The new line left the original at Hamsey and joined the 'East Coast' Brighton–Hastings route immediately east of Lewes station.

But if the approach to Brighton was now secure, it was otherwise with that to Eastbourne. In the 1864 Session the London, Chatham & Dover had deposited a Bill for a Beckenham–Brighton line, a threat the Brighton did not take too seriously. But the South Eastern had also deposited one for a line to Eastbourne, a more real threat. As a counter to these moves, in 1864 the Brighton obtained powers for an Ouse Valley Railway, to leave the main line at Balcombe and strike south-east to reach Hailsham via Uckfield. This would have shortened the route to Eastbourne, but would have been hopelessly unremunerative. In any case the Brighton persuaded the South Eastern to withdraw on condition a spur was provided between the two stations at Tunbridge Wells.

Next year authority was obtained for an extension of the Ouse Valley to St Leonards and for a Brighton-inspired Surrey & Sussex Junction Railway from Croydon to Tunbridge Wells via Oxted. The South Eastern was incensed at what it considered a breach of the previous year's agreement, if not of the now defunct one of 1848. But the Brighton blandly replied that it was only shortening its routes just as the SER was seeking to do by its Sevenoaks cut-off. As a consequence, the South Eastern lion temporarily lay down with the Chatham lamb and in 1866 successfully promoted a Bill for a joint London, Lewes & Brighton line.

1866 was a year of bank failures and financial crisis, many railway schemes in all parts of Britain being abandoned. Work had already started on the Ouse Valley and on the Surrey & Sussex Junction but was suspended, and only the Surrey & Sussex scheme came to fruition. The London, Lewes & Brighton was not started.

On the Surrey & Sussex construction was in full swing. Jacomb-Hood, the Brighton engineer, who was actively connected with the Company for fifty-six years, records on 6 August 1866 a 'serious riot at Edenbridge against the Belgians brought over by Messrs. Waring to assist in the Surrey & Sussex Railway works'. But the Brighton, having meanwhile purchased the Surrey & Sussex, now sought to abandon its liability. Powers to do so were refused and the Brighton preferred to invoke the penalty section for non-completion, of £32,500, rather than lay out a further million or so. Thus the works were abandoned just the same – permanently, the Brighton hoped.

The quiescence of financial exhaustion now descended upon the East Sussex battlefield until 1873, when local enterprise promoted a Bill for a 3-foot-gauge line from Hailsham (the terminus of the standard gauge branch from Polegate on the Brighton–Hastings line) to Tunbridge Wells. This came under the wing of the South Eastern and grew into a Tunbridge Wells & Eastbourne scheme, fortunately for posterity of standard gauge. But capital was short and delays ensued until finally in 1876 the Brighton intervened, obtaining an Act to take over the powers on payment of £8,534, and build a line from Hailsham to Eridge, on the Lewes–Uckfield–Groombridge–Tunbridge Wells route. The South Eastern accepted the situation in return for a share in the Eastbourne receipts. Thus the South Eastern obtained some of the prize money without the effort of competing for it, apart from a brief interlude between April 1884 and December 1885 when it exercised its rights of running Charing Cross–Eastbourne trains via Hailsham.

The 17½ miles of single track were opened between Hailsham and Heathfield on 5 April 1880 and on to Eridge on 1 September. Meanwhile a new Polegate station had been built about ⅜ of a mile further east and the Hailsham line diverted to allow through running to Eastbourne instead of Lewes. These alterations were completed on 3 October 1881. For the last 1¼ miles into Eridge the single track of the Heathfield line closely paralleled that of the Uckfield line. When the latter was doubled in 1894 the Uckfield line became the up road and the Heathfield line the down between Eridge and a new signal box and junction at Redgate Mill, the signal box now marking the end of the Heathfield or 'Cuckoo' line.

The Brighton was eventually forced to open fully the short spur between its Tunbridge Wells West station and Grove Junction, just south of the SER's Central station. A Brighton goods train ran from about 1867, but the limited passenger service was delayed until 1 February 1876. In 1894 only 5 passenger and a single freight train used it in the down direction from the Central. In Southern days its use gradually increased. In 1924 there were 9 down passenger trains and in 1952, 13. But in 1956 the service was greatly increased and in 1958 there were 29 passenger trains and 1 goods each way, making the line one of the busiest single-track sections in the country. But use has again declined.

The fiercer quarrels between the Brighton and South Eastern were now dying down. In 1878 a line from South Croydon Junction (just south of the station) to East Grinstead was authorized and part of this was to be a joint enterprise. It was to run via Oxted and make use of the uncompleted earthworks of the Surrey & Sussex Junction. At Crowhurst, south of Oxted, provision was made for a connecting spur up to the SER's Redhill–Tonbridge line and facing the latter place. At East Grinstead an end-on junction was to be made with the Lewes & East Grinstead. The section from South Croydon Junction to Crowhurst East Junction was to be jointly owned and that south of Crowhurst North Junction solely by the Brighton. The whole line was opened on 10 March 1884.

On 1 August 1882 this route was extended southwards from East Grinstead through Horsted Keynes to Culver Junction, 3¾ miles north of Lewes on the Lewes–Uckfield–Groombridge–Tunbridge Wells route. This new branch later became known as 'the

(11) *Ramsgate Town station of the* SER *about 1910. The short low platforms and primitive accommodation were necessitated by the divergence of the lines to Ashford (left) and Margate Sands (right) at the platform ends. The site of the present station lies behind the signal box.*

(12) *Ramsgate Sands in 1925 were as popular as always. The Harbour station of the* LCDR *is conveniently situated for the heavy holiday traffic with which it is obviously dealing. View from above the tunnel.*

(13) *The massive façade of Margate Station, built by the Southern in 1926 to replace Margate West. A typical Southern modernization, functional, impressive, and convenient.*

CONTRASTS IN STATION STYLES—I

(14) *An* SER *roadside station of 1842. This view of Pluckley, taken in 1954, shows the simple single-storey building, the lack of platform shelter, the staggered platforms, and the crossing used by passengers on this busy main line until 1961.*

(15) *Teynham, near Faversham, though built for the opening of the East Kent Railway in 1858, is typical of the severely plain* LCDR *stations, as is the large goods shed beyond. The* EKR *was, of course, the direct ancestor of the Chatham.*

CONTRASTS IN STATION STYLES—II

(16) *Lewes, 1881. The second permanent station, which superseded Friar's Walk, was built at the junction of the Brighton and Keymer lines; the present station, dating from 1884, is almost on the same site. Note the copper-chimneyed Stroudley locomotives and the* LBSCR *route-indicating headcodes.*

(17) *An old signal box is embedded in the 'contemporary' style Gatwick Airport station opened in 1958 on the quadruple-tracked section of the line to Brighton. The station serves the airport terminal buildings (left).*

CONTRASTS IN STATION STYLES—III

(18) *Redhill, 1838. David Mocatta's original drawing of his proposed Reigate station for the London & Brighton echoes the Age of Elegance soon to be submerged under Victorian commercialism. Drawing in the possession of the Royal Institute of British Architects.*

(19) *The Redhill Junction station of the* SER, *north of the junction, had superseded both the original Reigate stations of the* SER *and the* L & B. *This photograph, looking north, was taken about 1865 and shows platform canopies covering running roads as well.*

(20) *The station in post-electrification days, from the same viewpoint as* (19), *in 1935. Note the gradual increase in platform accommodation over the years.*

Bluebell and Primrose'. On 3 September 1883 a 3-mile line was opened from Horsted Keynes to Copyhold Junction on the main line north of Haywards Heath. Physical connection was however at Haywards Heath, crossovers not being put in at Copyhold until 1931.

In 1881 the nominally independent Oxted & Groombridge Company was incorporated to build a 12½-mile line along the remainder of the Surrey & Sussex Junction's abandoned works. It ran from Hurst Green Junction on the Oxted and East Grinstead line to Ashurst Junction on the East Grinstead and Tunbridge Wells. It was opened as far as Edenbridge, the most important intermediate station, on 2 January 1888 and on to Ashurst Junction on 1 October.

Finally, the Brighton had obtained powers in 1878 for a single line spur between Ashurst and Birchden Junctions to avoid Groombridge and allow through running between London and the Uckfield and Heathfield lines. It was soon completed, but for years lay unused, except as a locomotive graveyard.

DEVELOPMENT OF TRAFFIC

The group of lines east of the main line to Brighton has suffered varying fortunes. The joint LBSC and SER section between South Croydon and Oxted gradually became more important as outer suburban traffic developed about the turn of the century. Most of the LBSCR trains ran to and from Tunbridge Wells, but through trains meandered down to Brighton by an 'Inner Circle' via East Grinstead, Horsted Keynes and either Haywards Heath or Lewes, or, in later years, by the 'Outer Circle' via Edenbridge and Uckfield or to Eastbourne via the 'Cuckoo' (Heathfield) line.

But the joint line was of less value to the SER, though a service was started between London and Tonbridge via the Crowhurst spur. This gradually dwindled until the sole survivor, the unbalanced 7.26 a.m. (S.X.) from Edenbridge to London Bridge, ran for the last time on 27 May 1955. At times of pressure or in emergencies it provided a useful alternative to the Sevenoaks route until the spur was closed on 25 October 1965.

Through trains on the 'Outer Circle' (Croydon–Oxted–Edenbridge–Groombridge–Uckfield–Lewes–Brighton) were always in the minority, the route being worked for the most part in two sections, trains running between London and Tunbridge Wells and between Brighton and Tunbridge Wells. But connections were almost universally made at Groombridge, resulting in a constant interchange traffic at what would otherwise be no more than an ordinary roadside station. However, housing development at Crowborough, between Groombridge and Uckfield, led to the need for some through trains, so the 71-chain Ashurst–Birchden spur was doubled and opened on 7 June 1914. The through London to Brighton trains which used this spur usually carried Eastbourne carriages which were detached at Eridge and then proceeded down the 'Cuckoo' line.

The fate of the 'Inner Circle' has been different. With the rapid growth of the East Grinstead area since 1930, the line thither from Croydon and Oxted has become steadily more important. Evening peak hour trains leaving Oxted for East Grinstead carry a considerably heavier passenger complement than do those via Edenbridge to Groombridge, and they are by no means empty, Edenbridge now having some light engineering and being a centre for overspill population from London. Oxted too now has some industry. A visit to Lingfield on a race day in 1959 found it very busy (special trains awaiting their return workings being berthed at East Grinstead). It is also a railhead for bananas.

Electrification of the Oxted line has been planned for a long time and is still intended but, as an emergency measure to deal with the rapidly increasing traffic, 19 three-car diesel-electric sets were put into service between March and December 1962 and over the next year diesel locomotives took over almost all the remaining duties. These figures show traffic trends in the late 1950s.

	Ordinary tickets		Season tickets	
	1955	*1957*	*1955*	*1957*
Sanderstead	50,451	59,260	8,198	9,604
Riddlesdown	32,476	35,810	4,456	5,456
Woldingham	22,987	26,727	1,386	1,984
Oxted	129,105	168,792	8,436	10,941
Hurst Green Halt	104,162	127,270	1,705	2,319
East Grinstead	86,485	139,981	2,459	5,774
Forest Row	17,497	28,117	657	892
Edenbridge Town	43,854	50,399	2,253	2,904
Hever	8,650	8,294	259	457

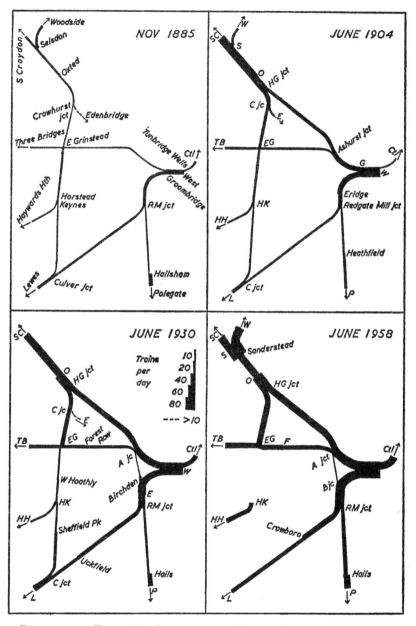

Passenger traffic on the Oxted group of lines. Number of passenger trains each way on ordinary weekdays.

At East Grinstead the 'Inner Circle' runs at right angles under the town's original line from Three Bridges to Tunbridge Wells. A new station, with high and low level platforms, was opened at the intersection in 1882. The old station was not finally closed until October 1883, certain trains continuing to use it instead of the high level. A double track spur led up from St Margaret's Junction on the Oxted line to the high level platforms, while there was another, single-track connection from the south avoiding the station. Both spurs faced Tunbridge Wells. The former was regularly used by passenger trains, but the latter only for the exchange of wagons and coaches and latterly for access to the low-level coalyard. It closed in 1967.

The continuation of the 'Inner Circle' from East Grinstead via Horsted Keynes was much used by excursion trains before the London–Brighton main line was quadrupled to Balcombe. But with the electrification of the Horsted Keynes–Haywards Heath line, passengers from the former place nearly all used the main London–Brighton route, and most of those trains which had continued south of East Grinstead were now diverted to that town's high level station and so on to Tunbridge Wells. South of Horsted Keynes the 'Bluebell & Primrose' line served no centre of population and traffic was very light. It pursued a placid life until British Railways decided to divert the remaining trains to Tunbridge Wells: the line south of St Margaret's Junction at East Grinstead was closed completely, though until 1960 the St Margaret's–Horsted Keynes section was placed on a care and maintenance basis because of its value as an alternative route. Passenger services were advertised to cease from 13 June 1955, but due to a strike the last train of the old service ran on 28 May. But a clause in the agreement between the Brighton and the Lewes & East Grinstead Company guaranteed certain stations four trains a day, and thus enabled local residents to force the reopening to passengers from 7 August 1956 – though the inconvenient service was stopped only at the stations mentioned in the agreement. Special Parliamentary dispensation allowed the line to close again from 17 March 1958, but the Bluebell Society bought the section between Horsted Keynes and Sheffield Park (see page 219). From 28 October 1963 the electric service to Horsted Keynes ceased, leaving a 'siding' from Copyhold to the aggregate depot at Ardingly.

By 1970 all the freight depots had closed, while the once important milk traffic had long since transferred to road. In the 1920s a thousand tickets would be collected on Bank Holidays from anglers at Barcombe Mills, and after 1945 commuters and local passengers increased, encouraged by frequent services and competitive fares. But the Beeching Report led to a reversal of the attempts to foster traffic. In 1964 the interval service timetable of 1955–6 was recast, partly reflecting changes in traffic flow, but also making it inconvenient to use lines proposed for closure. On 14 June 1965 the 'Cuckoo' was closed to passengers north of Hailsham. Goods trains ran as far as Heathfield until 26 April 1968 when a bridge was damaged, while Hailsham was closed completely on 9 September 1968. The Three Bridges–East Grinstead–Ashurst Junction line was closed to passengers (and goods east of Rowfant oil depot) on 2 January 1967. Closure of the 'Outer Circle' south of Hurst Green was refused except for Uckfield–Lewes. The Traffic Commissioners refused to licence the replacement buses but, the Ouse bridge being unsafe, British Rail hired buses from 24 February 1969, the section officially remaining 'open' until 5 May 1969.

THE WEST COAST LINE

Public traffic on the Brighton–Shoreham line began on 12 May 1840, 1,750 passengers were carried. The line was fed by connecting coaches from Kemp Town, while coal soon came to Brighton from Shoreham instead of being landed on the open beach.

Powers for the extension westwards to Chichester and Portsmouth were obtained by the Brighton & Chichester Company in 1844 and 1845, but the concern was sold to the Brighton in 1845. Opening dates were:

    Shoreham–Worthing, 24 November 1845
    Worthing–Lyminster, 16 March 1846
    Lyminster–Chichester, 8 June 1846
    Chichester–Havant, 15 March 1847
    Havant–Portsmouth, 14 June 1847.

Though at first worked as a single line, it was in fact double from Brighton to Lyminster. Westward to Chichester it was at first single, but doubled in 1857. The history of the intermediate stations is so complex, it has been summarized in the table below. The last few miles from Havant to Portsmouth are not in this chapter's area.

INTERMEDIATE STATIONS AND HALTS
WEST COAST LINE

Miles from Brighton	Original name	Opened	Closed	See note
1	Holland Road Halt	3 Sept. 1905	7 May 1956	
1	Hove	12 May 1840	1 Mar. 1880	
1½	Cliftonville	1 Oct. 1865	—	1
2	Dyke Junction Halt	3 Sept. 1905	—	2
3	Portslade	12 May 1840	—	3
3½	Fishergate Halt	3 Sept. 1905	—	
4½	Southwick	12 May 1840	—	
5¼	Kingston	12 May 1840	1 April 1879	4
6	Shoreham	12 May 1840	—	5
6¾	Bungalow Town Halt	1 Oct. 1910	15 July 1940	6
8¼	Lancing	24 Nov. 1845	—	
9¾	Ham Bridge Halt	3 Sept. 1905	—	7
10½	Worthing	24 Nov. 1845	—	8
11½	West Worthing	4 Nov. 1889	—	
12¼	Durrington-on-Sea	4 July 1937	—	
13	Goring	16 Mar. 1846	—	9
15½	Angmering	16 Mar. 1846	—	
18	Littlehampton	16 Mar. 1846	1 Sept. 1863	10
18	Lyminster Halt	1 Aug. 1907	Sept. 1914*	
19¾	Arundel	8 June 1846	—	11
21	Yapton	8 June 1846	1 June 1864	12
22½	Barnham	1 June 1864	—	
23¾	Bognor	8 June 1846	1 June 1864	13
26	Drayton	8 June 1846	1 June 1930	
28¾	Chichester	8 June 1846	—	
30¾	Fishbourne Halt	1 April 1906	—	
31½	Bosham	15 Mar. 1847	—	
33½	Nutbourne Halt	1 April 1906	—	
34¾	Southbourne Halt	1 April 1906	—	
35¾	Emsworth	15 Mar. 1847	—	
37	Denville Halt	Nov. 1907*	—	14
37½	Havant	15 Mar. 1847	—	

NOTES

1. Renamed West Brighton, 1 July 1879; Hove and West Brighton, 1 Oct 1894; Hove, 1 July 1895.
2. Renamed Aldrington Halt, 17 June 1932.
3. Closed July 1847,* reopened Oct. 1857* (possibly on slightly different site). Renamed Portslade and West Hove, April 1927.

4. Renamed Kingston-on-Sea, Dec. 1870.*
5. Renamed Shoreham Harbour, July 1906,* Shoreham-by-Sea, Oct. 1906.*
6. Closed 1 Jan. 1933, reopened 1 July 1935 as Shoreham Airport, closed 15 July 1940.
7. Renamed East Worthing Halt, 23 May 1949.
8. Renamed Worthing Central, 5 July 1936.
9. Renamed Goring-by-Sea, 6 July 1908.
10. Renamed Arundel and Littlehampton, May 1850.*
11. Renamed Ford, May 1850;* Ford Junction, 1 June 1864; Ford (Sussex), 9 July 1923.
12. Closed Oct. 1847,* reopened June 1849,* finally closed 1 June 1864.
13. Renamed Woodgate for Bognor, Oct. 1846;* Bognor, Oct. 1847;* Woodgate for Bognor, Jan. 1853.*
14. Renamed Warblington Halt, Dec. 1907.*

* First or last appearance in *Bradshaw* timetable.

When it was opened the line served few places of any importance. Hove was described by Measom's Guide to the LBSCR of 1853 as 'a village . . . now a mere western continuation of Brighton', a description the modern Hove would resent. Though physically joined with Brighton, Hove had a vigorous municipal life of its own until the 1974 local government re-organization. The port of Shoreham, with 5,765 people in 1841, the recently established resort of Worthing, popularized by Queen Caroline, with 4,702, and the cathedral city and county town of Chichester, with 8,512, alone exceeded 3,000. Lyminster was considered the most important station. It has long since been closed and its site is in an unusually isolated stretch of country.

Growth of these towns and some of the intervening villages was fairly rapid during the nineteenth century and by the turn of the century their populations had been doubled and trebled. Hove and Worthing stations were rebuilt a number of times to cope with increased traffic, but in LBSCR days the latter town was never satisfied with its indirect route. Pressure from this quarter was instrumental in the building of the Cliftonville curve, by-passing Brighton, and there were numerous proposals, all abortive, for a direct line from Horsham. By the 1900s local traffic had become very heavy and numerous halts were opened. Today there are 22 intermediate stations and halts between Brighton and Havant with an average distance of 1¾ miles apart.

This, together with parallel and feeder bus services, led to a rapid expansion of the smaller places in the inter-war years, an expansion which has been renewed with increased vigour after 1950. What is virtually a continuously built-up zone extends from Brighton to west of Bognor. In 1840 Shoreham had an important coasting trade, but the rail link with Brighton did not lead to any great increase. The LBSCR preferred to haul coal from Deptford Wharf: in 1848 38,000 tons reached Brighton by rail, and 21,000 by sea through Shoreham and by rail from Kingston Wharf where rails had been laid on to the quayside. By 1938 the imports through Shoreham had risen to 630,000 tons, but more than half was consumed on the quayside in the gas and electricity works. In the same year 370,000 tons reached Brighton by rail from all sources. In 1952 imports to Shoreham totalled over a million tons, of coal, stone and oil. Exports were mainly cement from Upper Beeding works in the Adur Gap. Port traffic has increased but is road-hauled (see page 215).

A very important market garden and horticultural industry has grown up on the coastal plain around Worthing. Much of the produce is grown under glass and, unlike any other type of agriculture, this can compete with housing in the fierce competition for land. Transport and marketing is done by the Worthing & District Growers' Association and cordial relations have long been the rule between this body and the railway authorities. Special covered loading facilities were provided at the main forwarding stations, those between Angmering and Lancing. The passenger vans were made up into special trains which ran daily to London Bridge. 263,000 items a year came from Chichester alone in 1958.

Starting in 1908, the Brighton began to transfer (from Brighton itself) its carriage and wagon works to Lancing; the move was completed in 1912. The works were closed in 1965, the site becoming an industrial estate in this rapidly expanding area of light industry. But none of the products now go by rail.

West of Worthing the line runs inland, connection with the seaside being made by a series of branches. Between Chichester and Havant, however, the main route is only a little inland from the heads of several creeks of Chichester harbour, its shores lined with yachting centres. The eastern end of the coastal plain, from Ford to Havant, is rich agricultural land. In 1955 Bosham was forwarding some 7,000 tons of sugar beet annually together with 5,000 pads (large baskets) of watercress and quantities of parsley and nursery trees. Inwards traffic consisted of coal and yachting stores. 80 passenger trains called daily. Bosham was typical of the West Coast line where passenger traffic has been encouraged by good services. In 1968 there were five trains an hour east of Angmering and three west of Barnham. There have been subsequent modifications, described on page 209.

Leaving the Mid-Sussex system to be described later, the first of the branches concerning us is the only inland one – the 3½ miles of single track from Dyke Junction, west of Hove, up to the popular beauty spot of DEVIL'S DYKE. The line climbed up the Downs by gradients of 1 in 40–41, rising a total of 400 feet. Opened on 1 September 1887 and worked by the Brighton, it once carried a heavy traffic at holiday times, but was closed after the last train on 31 December 1938. Freight was always negligible.

The 2⅝ miles, originally single, from a trailing junction at Ford to LITTLEHAMPTON were opened on 17 August 1863. The present layout east of Ford, which allows through running from Worthing and Horsham, dates from 1 January 1887. In 1861 Litttlehampton, with 2,350 inhabitants, had a regular trade with the Channel Islands and Honfleur. As it grew as a resort, however, it declined as a port until traffic ceased in 1939. In 1961 the town numbered 15,647 persons, its selectness as a resort depending on the rigid control by the ground landlord, the Duke of Norfolk.

The single-track BOGNOR branch was opened on 1 June 1864, from a new station called Barnham Junction. The track was doubled by 1911; Bognor's present station dates from 1902. Bognor began life as Hothampton, being laid out by a London merchant of the name of Hotham. It has grown steadily, along with neighbouring villages, and in 1971 numbered 28,000. In 1929 it acquired the suffix Regis after George V convalesced there, the latest Royal patron of this coast. 635,889 tickets were collected at the station in 1957.

The independent HAYLING Railways Company was incorporated in 1860 to build 4½ miles of single line from Havant to Hayling Island. It was not fully opened until 17 July 1867 and was worked by the contractor. The Brighton took over from 1 January 1872, the temporary arrangement being converted to a lease of £2,000 a year from mid-1874. Weight restrictions over the Langston Viaduct limited motive power to the famous 'Terrier' 0-6-0 tanks. It was completely closed on 4 November 1963, though a preservation society hoped to reopen it. In August 1961 32,176 tickets were collected at Hayling, but only 2,072 in the March.

The HUNDRED OF MANHOOD & SELSEY Tramways was a much less successful venture. Built without Parliamentary powers its line ran for 7¾ miles from its own station at Chichester to Selsey, and was opened on 27 August 1897. The extension to Selsey Beach followed on 1 August 1898. The line was worked in the most primitive manner; eventually it was managed from Tonbridge as one of the Lieut-Colonel Stephens 'group'. It was closed from 19 January 1935, the Company being wound up three years later.

THE MID-SUSSEX LINE

With the completion of the Brighton–Portsmouth 'West Coast' line in 1847, the LBSCR offered a London–Portsmouth route totalling 95¼ miles. Needless to say, with the opening of the London & South Western Railway's Portsmouth Direct in 1859, it ceased to be competitive. Thus the Brighton was led to develop a cut-off route, 87 miles long, via Horsham, a route usually known as the Mid-Sussex line.

The Mid-Sussex developed in a most haphazard fashion, the various links becoming part of a main line more by accident than design. If there was any purpose behind them, it was to bar the LSWR's entry into West Sussex. The first Brighton line actually to penetrate into the West Sussex Weald was the 8½-mile branch from Three Bridges to Horsham, the principal market town of the area, and destined also to become the chief railway centre. The line was authorized in 1845 and opened on 14 February 1848.

The next development was the formation of the Epsom & Leatherhead Railway in 1856 to extend the London & Croydon Railway's route, which had reached Epsom Town in 1847. The Epsom & Leatherhead was to forestall a South Western creation, the Wimbledon & Dorking, which would allow the South Western to penetrate towards Horsham. When the Wimbledon & Dorking was opened from a junction where Raynes Park now stands, near

Wimbledon, to Epsom, the Epsom & Leatherhead became a joint LBSCR and LSWR route. It was opened with an LSWR service on 1 February 1859 and LBSCR trains commenced on 8 August.

On 10 August 1857 the Mid-Sussex Railway was incorporated with powers to build a line 17½ miles long from Horsham to Coultershaw Mill, near Petworth, a small market town below the South Downs. Then on 12 July in the next Session, the Brighton obtained an Act for a 17-mile line from a junction with the Mid-Sussex at Itchingfield, 3 miles south of Horsham, to the West Coast line at Shoreham. In this it was spurred on by an abortive Shoreham, Horsham & Dorking proposal, nominally independent, but suspected of being in league with the LSWR. Yet another flank in the defence of Brighton had been secured.

Two gaps remained to complete the Mid-Sussex route: Hardham Junction near Pulborough, a few miles short of Petworth, south through Arundel to Arundel Junction east of Ford on the West Coast main line; and Leatherhead to Horsham. The LBSCR obtained powers to close the former in 1860, and 1862 an independent Horsham, Dorking & Leatherhead Company was incorporated to link Horsham with a junction with the South Eastern's Redhill–Guildford–Reading branch at Boxhill (now Deepdene). Powers for the remaining 4½ miles to Leatherhead were obtained next year by the LBSCR itself. By its Act of 29 July 1864 the LBSCR absorbed all the quasi-independent companies.

The Mid-Sussex opened its single line from Horsham to Petworth on 10 October 1859. Doubling to Hardham was completed in time for the opening of the Hardham-Arundel Junction section on 3 August 1863. The line up from Shoreham was opened as far as Partridge Green (near West Grinstead) on 1 July 1861 and on to Itchingfield Junction, just short of Horsham, on 16 September. It was doubled between 1877 and 1879.

For some years all traffic via the Mid-Sussex route had to pass along the area's first branch from Three Bridges to Horsham, only slow progress being made with the line from Leatherhead. Not until 11 March 1867 was this opened to Dorking, completion to Horsham – and completion of the Mid-Sussex route – following on 1 May. The connecting spur to the SER at Boxhill was never used.

The Mid-Sussex line abounds in curves and short banks, but is saved from any serious climbs or heavy earthworks by crossing the North and South Downs through the Mole and Arun Gaps, and it avoids the High Weald altogether. The LSWR station at Leatherhead was closed 9 July 1927, Epsom Town was closed from 3 March 1929, and the present station was erected more or less on the site of the South Western's. Horsham station was entirely rebuilt for electrification in 1938, the present two-island structure replacing a ramshackle warren full of bays, holes and corners into and out of which popped like rabbits the ubiquitous 'motor trains' of 'balloon' stock propelled by diminutive tanks.

Christ's Hospital, 2½ miles south, was not opened until 1902, when it was anticipated that there would be large housing developments. The junction for Guildford and Shoreham, its 7 platforms and lavish buildings made it incongruously massive. But in 1973 it was reduced to two nearly shelterless platforms.

The countryside followed both by the main north-south Mid-Sussex route and its subsidiaries was lonely, and though there has been much development since, the area south of Dorking is still less closely settled than other parts of Sussex. Horsham was, and is, the only large centre. The route has always been used mainly by through trains to Portsmouth and Bognor, most of which travelled via Dorking until 1978. Local traffic has grown since electrification, particularly on the Three Bridges–Horsham section, where Crawley and Ifield stations serve Crawley New Town.

It remains to describe the branches from the Mid-Sussex. The 4-mile branch from Sutton to EPSOM DOWNS was built by the Banstead & Epsom Downs Company, incorporated in 1862 and bought by the Brighton two years later. It was opened on 22 May 1865 and at first local traffic was light. Even in the early years of the present century a rail motor, which must have looked incongruous in the 8-platform terminus, sufficed to deal with it. Today suburban traffic is heavy and trains frequent. Epsom racecourse was now directly served by two stations, Epsom Downs and Tattenham Corner.

The HORSHAM & GUILDFORD DIRECT Railway Company, a grandiose name for a not very important scheme, was incorporated in 1860 and the 15½ miles of single line ran from Stammerham Junction (the site of Christ's Hospital) to

Peasmarsh Junction on the LSWR, 1¾ miles south of Guildford. After negotiating with both the LSWR and the LBSCR, the Company eventually sold its uncompleted works to the latter in 1864. It was opened on 2 October 1865 and pursued an uneventful, bucolic existence until closure on 14 June 1965. Fuller's Earth was railed from Baynards.

The Itchingfield Junction–Shoreham line lacked the heavy through traffic of the Mid-Sussex and on 7 March 1966 was completely closed except for access to Beeding Cement Works.

The original Mid-Sussex Company ended rather in the air at Petworth and in August 1859 a Mid-Sussex & Midhurst Junction was incorporated, with the intention of pushing on to PETERS-FIELD. However the line was sold to the Brighton and as that Company wished to honour a territorial agreement with the South Western, the latter was left to complete the link. The Petworth-Midhurst section was opened on 15 October 1866 and worked by the Brighton from the start. The Brighton and South Western stations at Midhurst were not very far apart and on 17 December 1866 the two Companies opened an 11-chain connection for the interchange of goods.

A CHICHESTER & MIDHURST Company had only begun building a 12-mile single line over the Downs when it collapsed, its powers later being transferred to the LBSCR, which completed and opened the work on 11 July 1881. Singleton, equipped with two island platforms, became the station for Goodwood races. Otherwise it had little value but was regarded with great pride locally. At Midhurst the junction with the new line faced Petworth, and so a new station nearly half a mile east of the LSWR station, and a mile by road, had to be opened. Complaints were laid before the Railway Commissioners. But nothing was done until 12 July 1925 when all traffic was concentrated on the second LBSCR station, unfortunately inconveniently situated for the town.

Lacking a steady inter-urban traffic, passenger services ceased between Midhurst and Chichester from 7 July 1935 and the through trains from Pulborough were diverted to Petersfield. They ceased altogether from 7 February 1955. The Chichester–Lavant section was retained for sugarbeet railings and later for aggregates. Freight trains ran from Pulborough to Midhurst until 1964 and to Petworth until 1966.

CHAPTER V

East Hampshire and North Surrey

BEGINNINGS OF THE SOUTH WESTERN

The London and South Western Railway, unlike the others in Southern England, was by any standards in the front rank of pre-1923 companies. Its 966 route miles open to traffic in 1911 made it one of the longest, while traffic density was higher than average.

Among its many achievements was the establishment of a virtual monopoly over a wide area which included most of Hampshire and parts of neighbouring counties, particularly West Surrey. It was an area of special importance as it included Portsmouth, Southampton and Bournemouth. But as a county Hampshire has centrifugal tendencies, and consequently the pattern of railway development is less coherent than in the other areas studied. The nearest approach to a central theme is the efforts of the South Western to establish and maintain its monopoly.

These efforts led to constant warfare on two fronts. On the eastern it was with the Brighton, but the chief battles were fought out on the northern flank with the GWR, always regarded as the arch-enemy. As we shall see in the next chapter the long campaign was waged for the most part in the 'no man's land' between the West of England main lines of the contestants, but repercussions of the main battles and minor skirmishes occurred over a much wider area.

Developments in and around Portsmouth, Southampton and Bournemouth form the three most important *motifs* to the story. Each was an important traffic centre, Portsmouth being the main gateway to the Isle of Wight, Southampton one of the major ports of the country, and Bournemouth one of the largest seaside resorts. Their spheres of influence were wide: Guildford played its part

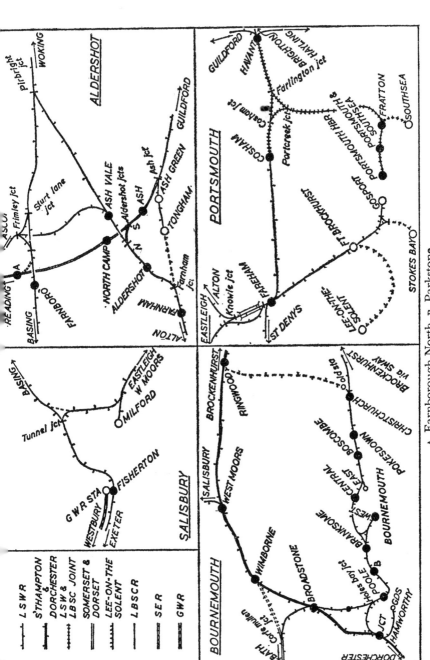

A, Farnborough North. B, Parkstone.

ALDERSHOT

WOKING
Pirbright Jct
READING
BASING
Frimley Jct
Sturt Lane Jct
FARNBORO
A
ASH VALE
Aldershot Jcts
ASH
N S
ASH GREEN
GUILDFORD
Ash Jct
TONGHAM
NORTH CAMP
ALDERSHOT
FARNHAM
Farnham Jct
ALTON

PORTSMOUTH

GUILDFORD
HAVANT
BRIGHTON
HAYLING
Farlington Jct
Cosham Jct
COSHAM
Portcreek Jct
PORTSMOUTH & SOUTHSEA
FRATTON
SOUTHSEA
PORTSMOUTH HBR &
GOSPORT
FT BROCKHURST
STOKES BAY
FAREHAM
Knowle Jct
ALTON
EASTLEIGH
ST DENYS
LEE-ON-THE-SOLENT

SALISBURY

BASING
Tunnel Jct
EASTLEIGH W MOORS
MILFORD
FISHERTON
GWR STA
WESTBURY
EXETER

BOURNEMOUTH

BROCKENHURST
RINGWOOD
BROCKENHURST via SWAY
CHRISTCHURCH
POKESDOWN
BOSCOMBE
SALISBURY
WESTMOORS
BOURNEMOUTH CENTRAL
EAST
WEST
BRANKSOME
WIMBORNE
BROADSTONE
POOLE
Holes Bay Jct
B
OGDS
JCT
HAMWORTHY
BATH
Corfe Mullen Jct
DORCHESTER

L S W R
S'THAMPTON & DORCHESTER
L S W & LB SC JOINT
SOMERSET & DORSET
LEE-ON-THE-SOLENT
L B S C R
S E R
G W R

in the story of Portsmouth, while Basingstoke and Salisbury were bastions in the defence of Southampton.

There is another *motif,* for in 1855 the War Office established a depot at Aldershot and subsequent military developments in the area led to much railway development. Again, the major traffic centres of Hampshire, though linked principally with London, generated cross-currents of through traffic to and from the Midlands. As these grew so did the ambitions of the GWR. The strategists of Waterloo had the delicate dual task of keeping the enemy from the gate and at the same time promoting interchange traffic through his territory. Thus was the South Western drawn into the Battle of the Gauges and thus was it affected by the quarrels of Paddington and Euston over the Oxford, Worcester & Wolverhampton. Finally, Hampshire functioned as a corridor, for through it would have to pass the main line of the LSWR's westward drive.

THE LONDON & SOUTHAMPTON

The South Western's trunk line originated in a proposal for a ship canal from Spithead to London, for which Francis Giles was retained to make the survey. When the impossibility of the scheme became obvious, thoughts turned to railways. The first practical step was not, however, taken until 1831 (the year after the Liverpool & Manchester's opening). On 26 February a meeting was held at the house of A. R. Dottin, M.P. for Southampton and later a director of the London & Greenwich. Sufficient money was promised to allow the appointment of Giles as engineer.

On 6 April there was a public meeting at Southampton at which the Southampton, London & Branch Railway & Dock Company was formed. The title is revealing: the initiative was coming from Southampton and the railway and the docks were regarded as complementary, as they were until nationalization. The branch referred to a Basingstoke–Bristol scheme.

Evidence of traffic potential, even in the underdeveloped and sparsely peopled Hampshire of the day, was considerable. But the common sense of the promoters deserted them in calculating expenses. To earn a total income of £181,241, working expenses were not going to exceed £61,241, no more than £1 per week

per locomotive being allowed for motive power. The chairman made the extraordinary statement that 'two locomotive
engines making two trips a day each would suffice for passengers . . . and three engines would be adequate for the transport
of goods'.

In all this the promoters were undoubtedly led astray, not only
by the natural optimism of company floating, but by the general
ignorance of railway operation. Giles was also to blame. He was
a good engineer, but lacked a business sense. His prestige had also
been lowered by a wild miscalculation which resulted in his
attacking Stephenson upon the grounds of the impossibility of
crossing Chat Moss, on the Liverpool & Manchester.

The promoters held back to await the fate of the London &
Birmingham Bill, which was eventually passed in 1833. Meanwhile the docks side had been dropped completely and the Bristol
scheme held in abeyance. The Bill therefore went forward at the
next session as the London & Southampton Railway. Support had
been widely canvassed and evidence in favour was given before
the Committee by the Lords of the Admiralty, the Quartermaster-
General of the Army and by fishing and agricultural interests.
The Act received the Royal Assent on 25 July 1834. Its passage
had cost only £31,000, a very modest sum compared with the
£150,000 of the Brighton Act.

At the first meeting of the Company, held on 24 October 1834,
Giles reported that work had begun. Next February it was decided
to present a Bill for the Bristol line, the GWR Bill not having yet
been passed. But after a 46-day enquiry, the latter gained the
victory, to the mortification of the Southampton Company, which
thenceforward reserved its special enmity for the GWR. For its part
Paddington rubbed salt in the wound by obtaining powers for a
Thingley–Melksham and Trowbridge line across the only possible
line of advance towards Bath. A statement that the loss of revenue
to the London & Southampton 'would not amount to one or two
per cent' was pure face-saving.

Though construction had begun, all was not well. Progress was
slow and costs were rising, iron rails jumping from £7 18s. 6d. a
ton to £14. It became quite obvious that Giles's estimates were
wildly optimistic and powers for capital increases had to be obtained. Furthermore in 1836 the Southampton Docks Company

was incorporated. It also retained Giles, who thenceforward gave less time to the railway than he should. Public confidence was undermined and it became difficult to obtain calls on shares. Stephenson, no doubt to pay Giles off for the Chat Moss incident, announced that 'the whole wealth and strength of the Company would be for ever buried in the cutting through St. George's Hill, Weybridge' a prediction fortunately as far wide of the mark as Giles's had been over Chat Moss. The coaching interests, too, were active in stirring up opposition. From this time dates the famous remark that the London & Southampton 'would be used only for the conveyance of parsons and prawns, the one from Winchester, the other from Southampton'. In short, in the words of a shareholder 'to be connected with the Southampton Railway is to make the choice of being considered a fool or a rogue'.

Fortunately the situation was restored by the recruitment of two great personalities in the early history of railways, Joseph Locke and W. J. Chaplin. Locke was appointed engineer upon the resignation of Giles in 1837. His first act was to clear out numerous small and inefficient contractors. One, however, was considered 'very able and responsible' and was given all the unfinished work as far as the Wey Navigation, Byfleet. He was Thomas Brassey, of whom more will be heard anon. From now on work went ahead rapidly.

Chaplin, the other recruit, was a large road carrier, owning 64 coaches and 1,500 horses. In 1834 he had been called upon by the Southampton promoters to supply them with figures of possible traffics. As a result he became convinced of the great future awaiting the new form of transport – to such an extent that he sold his road interests and put the money into the London & Southampton. Always active, he became chairman of the LSWR in 1843 and piloted it through the difficult years following the Mania. With Locke as engineer and with the faith and integrity of Chaplin among the directors, the tide was turned. The London terminus of the railway was at Nine Elms (near Waterloo).

On 19 May 1838 an official party travelled to Woking Common (23 miles from London), where a cold collation awaited them. Speed was retarded on the return journey by a headwind and the situation was not improved by the number of gentlemen riding on the carriage roofs, no doubt mellowed by the cold collation. Public traffic began on 21 May. A service of 5 trains a day each way (4 on Sundays) was provided, and there were connecting buses from all over the City and West End. At the stations passengers were booked over open counters, a practice which lasted until the conventional *guichets* were introduced in 1847. The tickets were slips of paper with the destination printed on them. Intending passengers were given a handbill setting out the Company's regulations. These included one that passengers were not to alight without the assistance of a servant of the Company, and another that on approaching a habitation or crossing the guard would blow his whistle (surely a reflection on the sparsely inhabited route). The whole procedure was a curious blend of former coaching practice and subsequent air travel.

For the Derby, which took place a few days after opening, an excursion to Kingston (Surbiton) was announced. The response caught the Company completely unawares, for early in the morning a vast crowd, estimated at about 5,000, were found milling about in front of the gates of Nine Elms. Several trains were got away, but the crowd increased and eventually invaded the station. The police had to be summoned to restore order. Perhaps because Sir John Easthope, a well-known figure in racing circles, was chairman, the Company was by no means discouraged and a few weeks later advertised excursions in connection with Ascot, an even further walk from Kingston. Thus, from the very start, the tradition of handling large race-going crowds grew up, a tradition which has persisted to this day. Waterloo lost the Epsom traffic but served Sandown Park and Kempton Park as well as Ascot.

On 24 September 1838, the railway was extended to Shapley Heath (Winchfield), 38½ miles from Nine Elms. It was now long enough for people travelling from all over Southern England to transfer to it, and one can picture the lively scene at Shapley Heath as coaches brought passengers and luggage for the new means of transport. As in the West Country, the coaching business flourished during the short-lived partnership with the railway; but soon, of course, the coaches were left with merely the unremunerative territory. As for the railway, by February 1839 receipts totalled £42,158 2s. 9d. and operating expenses

£24,788 9s. 7d. and nearly 8,000 passengers a week carried. This was a most satisfactory position and gloomy prognostications had already been refuted.

On 10 June 1839 came the formal opening of the Shapley Heath–Basingstoke and Southampton–Winchester sections, 8 miles and 12½ miles respectively. Another year passed before the works on the most difficult intervening section were ready, excitement rising the while. The long-awaited day was 11 May 1840.

The directors and 'bands of music' left Nine Elms at 8.0 a.m. and arrived at Southampton, amid a twenty-one gun salute, at 11.0. On their return, Brassey had a cold collation laid on for them at his camp at Warren Farm near Andover Road Station (Micheldever). The festal air of the train crews aroused some apprehension among passengers, but the only casualty was a dog decapitated by a train, while Northam crossing gates were run through in an excess of *joie de vivre*.

The Southampton line is a fitting monument to its builders – a high-speed route from end to end which carries traffic infinitely greater than that envisaged by the most sanguine of the promoters. In spite of the need to climb to 430 feet at Litchfield, in order to cross the chalk plateau, gradients were kept to a minimum. There are long steady climbs, but never at over 1 in 250. There are no severe curves and but six short tunnels.

The line has been quadrupled all the way to Battledown (50 miles from Waterloo), the actual point of divergence of the West of England line, though the junction is at Worting. The widening has been on a most spacious scale and there are but three flat junctions. Unfortunately one of these, with the Portsmouth Direct line at Woking, is the busiest of all.

The original intermediate stations were 13, while a further 15 have been added over the years. Only two, Wandsworth (later Clapham Common), and Bramshot Halt (serving a golf club), have been closed. It is noteworthy that Micheldever is still the only intermediate station in the 18¼ miles between Basingstoke and Winchester. Modernization has swept away most of the early stations, which were severely plain, almost featureless two-storey brick buildings. Characteristically, Micheldever remains unaltered.

But generally low architectural standards did not prevent the London & Southampton retaining Sir William Tite, designer of the Royal Exchange, for the termini. These he planned with great effect, adopting a simple classical style which reminds us that the Age of Elegance did in fact survive into the Railway Age. The *façade* of Southampton Terminus survives intact and is one of the glories of British station architecture. The sadly battered *façade* of Nine Elms survived, buried in the goods depot (closed 29 July 1968), until the latter gave way to the new Covent Garden.

In 1846 the Company had reputedly the fastest trains in the world with its 110-minute schedule to Southampton, 42·9 m.p.h. On one occasion the Gooch 2-2-2 'Elk' did the up journey in 93 minutes, 50·3 m.p.h. The coaching stock was reasonable for the standards of the time. The firsts had 3 compartments each seating 6, while the seconds had wooden seats and open sides. Luggage was carried on the roofs of the first and in boots in the second. Guards and brakesmen were seated at the roof ends.

The thirds were apparently removable bodies mounted on the chassis of goods wagons, which gave rise to the epigram 'in some of the trucks was the swinish multitude, in others a multitude of swine'. At first they were attached to goods trains, but the public, and who can blame them, tended to fight shy of this form of conveyance, especially after a bad accident on the GWR at Sonning. The chairman, making a virtue of necessity, said in 1842:

> The Goods Trains were not so secure from danger as the passenger trains and therefore we have adopted a third class conveyance by an early morning train, which gives the industrious poor not only a greater sense of security, but also encouragement for early rising.

In 1841 a train was hired by an enterprising person who was organizing an excursion, and the Company began running its own excursions to satisfy a growing demand for cheap rail travel. But not everyone was yet converted. The Duke of Wellington lived at Stratfield Saye, 7 miles from Basingstoke, and in 1842 the chairman said 'Although a special train was always in readiness for His Grace, this has not been taken advantage of by him'. The next year however the Queen patronized the Company for the first time, and she was attended by the Duke. With justifiable pride the chairman reported they were both 'highly pleased with our mode of conveyance'. The accolade of social respectability had been bestowed.

Initially goods wagons were attached to the last passenger trains in the day, but freight trains were run when the extension to Basingstoke was opened. Traffic, however, did not develop satisfactorily, as the railway would not accept goods from ordinary consignors, but only from certain carriers. Sir Sam Fay, from whose work *A Royal Road* so many details of early operation have been culled, paints a vivid picture of these trains. At first they were conducted by three 'juvenile delinquents' but these were later replaced by a guard. There were no brake van and no brakes, the guard riding in a wagon known as the 'Noah's Ark', which conveyed small packages for roadside stations. The wagons, 12 feet long, had dead buffers and springless drawgear. To start a train the guard scotched the last wagon and the engine backed up to slacken the couplings. Two of these equipages were run each way, mercifully under cover of night.

Trouble was experienced in recruiting staff in those early days when there was a general lack of experience. Easthope was alleged to have recruited all the staff from Leicester, of which he was M.P. and in 1852 he was forced to resign. Meanwhile a fiery Irishman, one Davies, was recruited from 'A Northern Line'. He brought with him a number of porters to help train the ignorant Southerners. After a violent quarrel however he was relegated to station agent, Weybridge. Men of all classes were taken on at first, a station-master might be a gentleman, a former stage coach proprietor, shopkeeper or farmer.

THE PORTSMOUTH DIRECT

Portsmouth was an early objective. Powers for a branch to Gosport, on the opposite side of the harbour, were obtained on 4 June 1839, the junction with the London–Southampton line being at Bishopstoke (today's Eastleigh). In deference to the citizens of Portsmouth, by the same Act of 4 June 1839 the London & Southampton changed its name to London & South Western Railway. Apparently, unlike the Brighton and the South Eastern, the Company felt that politeness cost it nothing. But it was the mailed fist in the velvet glove, as the citizens of Portsmouth found out when they presumed to ask for a better connection with London.

The 15¾-mile branch from Bishopstoke (Eastleigh) to Gosport was opened on 29 November 1841. Owing to the tunnel at Fareham being considered unsafe, it was closed after four days and not reopened until 7 February 1842. The route was devious; it was 89½ miles from Waterloo to Gosport, and the ferry crossing at the end naturally did not satisfy Portsmouth. Agitation mounted for more direct communication with London.

By 1845 three more lines had been authorized, their termini many miles from Portsmouth but each line aiming at the town.

In 1844 a Guildford Junction Company was authorized to build a 6-mile branch from Woking, then an insignificant village, to the important market town and road centre of Guildford. This was to have been built on Prosser's system, recently demonstrated on Wimbledon Common: flangeless rolling stock wheels ran on flat wooden rails and were kept in position by additional guide wheels. But the South Western, a prospective purchaser of the new Company, insisted on a conventional railway.

The other two embryo routes to Portsmouth were mentioned in the last chapter: the Croydon Company's extension to Epsom, and the Brighton & Chichester (pages 99, 104).

The next step was obviously a series of projects to extend these three routes on to Portsmouth. First in the field was the Direct London & Portsmouth Company, energetically supported by the Croydon, then in an imperialistic mood under the dynamic chairmanship of W. A. Wilkinson. This line was to run from Epsom through Dorking and Godalming and thence very much along the present Guildford–Portsmouth line. Because the Croydon was then experimenting with atmospheric propulsion, the Direct Portsmouth was to adopt the system.

Secondly the Brighton & Chichester, founder of the Brighton's West Coast line, had a Bill for an extension from Chichester. There was also to be a branch to Fareham on the Bishopstoke–Gosport line.

Both these schemes met with the strenuous opposition of the South Western which adopted the not uncommon tactic of loudly and frequently proclaiming there was no real demand for an alternative to the Gosport line. The third project, however, did receive the Company's grudging support, more in self-defence than out of any real desire to shorten a route on which fares were calculated on a mileage basis. This was the Guildford, Chichester & Portsmouth, whose proposed route was via Godalming, Haslemere and Midhurst.

All three Bills passed the Commons, but only the Brighton & Chichester's passed the Lords, receiving the Royal Assent on 8 August 1845. The Brighton and the South Western now signed an agreement, no doubt made possible by the proposed new route being even more circuitous (95 miles) than that via Gosport, though it would at least cut out the ferry. The Chichester–Portsmouth line, together with the Fareham branch, was to become joint property, the two Companies would support the Guildford, Chichester & Portsmouth against the Direct atmospheric line, and finally the South Western would not support any new line east of the Guildford, Chichester & Portsmouth and the Brighton any line west of its main line.

But in July 1846 circumstances were radically altered by the amalgamation of the Brighton and Croydon Companies. Wilkinson became the Brighton's deputy chairman and a number of his supporters obtained seats on the Board. The new Company was persuaded to support the Direct scheme and the agreement with the South Western completely collapsed. Wilkinson unblushingly announced that he had not influenced the Board in any way and added with equal effrontery that the Direct would be as well suited to locomotive traction as to atmospheric, which had by now been proved a failure.

The Direct was duly authorized, subject to its using a 'union' station at Portsmouth (i.e. a station jointly owned by the three companies), from which atmospheric propulsion was excluded. The South Western had to be content with a very truncated plan, an extension from Guildford to Godalming to join the Direct and a line from Fareham (on the Bishopstoke–Gosport branch) round Portsmouth harbour to the union station at Portsmouth.

However, the financial difficulties which brought about the collapse of the Mania prevented work even being started on the Direct line. Thus there was a *rapprochement* between the Brighton and the South Western. The former dropped its Fareham

TOWN AND COUNTRY ON THE LBSCR

(21) *This interior view of Brighton taken about 1938 shows the high arched roof and divergence of the Worthing and London lines within the station itself.*

(22) *Lingfield, dating from 1882, is built in the then fashionable 'Queen Anne' style popularized by Norman Shaw. The extra platform is to deal with race-day crowds, but otherwise this substantial structure is typical of country stations on the* LBSCR.

(23) *Godalming Old station, once the terminus of the line from Woking and now the goods office, survives to give a good idea of the* LSWR *country station of the 1850s. Note the short low platforms, the extension to the right being a later addition.*

(24) *The primitive accommodation of Blechynden station, the most easterly on 'Castleman's Corkscrew' (the Southampton & Dorchester), was still intact in 1920 when this photograph was taken. Since then the Civic Centre has been built over the tunnel.*

branch, while the latter built a line from there to Cosham, from which point the line into Portsmouth became joint property. The London–Portsmouth receipts were pooled, five-eighths to the South Western and three-eighths to the Brighton. In 1852 the pool was enlarged to include the Gosport takings, the proportion becoming two-thirds to one-third.

The final result was that, sensibly enough, there was only a single approach to the island on which Portsmouth stands. But the town was still without its direct line from London, while the pooling agreement took away any incentive to an improved train service.

On 14 June 1847 the line was opened from Chichester to Portsmouth. It was owned by the Brighton as far as Portcreek Junction, where the Fareham line came in, and jointly therefrom, while the Brighton owned the northern side of the triangle. The South Western's Fareham–Portcreek link was opened on 1 October 1848.

Though the economy of having only one line running actually into Portsmouth was welcome enough, the lack of a short route from London angered the citizens. As no improvement was to be looked for from the South Western or the Brighton, the town jumped at the opportunity to help the Portsmouth Railway Company, floated principally through the efforts of Thomas Brassey, the great railway contractor. An Act for a line from Godalming (already reached by a branch from Guildford; see page 127) to Havant, on the Brighton's Chichester–Portsmouth section, received the Royal assent in 1853. It was a 'contractor's line', built as a speculation with the intention of leasing or selling to anyone willing to work it.

This neither the South Western nor the Brighton wanted to do, for by shortening the distance from London to Portsmouth by 20 miles, fares would be reduced. Accordingly an amending Act was obtained in 1854 for a line northward from Godalming to Shalford station on the South Eastern's branch across from Redhill. Later, however, running powers were obtained from Godalming to Peasmarsh Junction and from Havant to Portcreek Junction and on to Portsmouth. Work was then begun on a Peasmarsh–Shalford spur. The remains can still clearly be traced. But before completion the South Eastern virtuously refused to work the Portsmouth Railway, invoking its 1848 agreement with the Brighton.

The South Western, through fear that South Eastern scruples might eventually be overcome, was thus persuaded to lease the new line, including its running powers which had been obtained over Brighton metals from Havant to Portcreek Junction. The Brighton now began to make difficulties. T. E. Harrison, chief engineer of the North Eastern, was called in to arbitrate, but he failed to bring the parties together. The line had been ready twelve months and the South Western grew impatient. It was announced that passenger traffic would begin on New Year's Day 1859 but the South Western advised the Brighton that it would send a goods train through to Portsmouth on Tuesday 28 December 1858.

The events of that day are best described by Sir Sam Fay. When the goods steamed into Havant

> it was manned by upwards of a hundred platelayers and other rough and ready employees of the Company, under the orders of Mr. Scott [Archibald Scott, the Traffic Manager]...The South Western train was not expected until about 10 o'clock, but Mr. Scott took time by the forelock and reached the junction at 7.0 a.m. He found the Brighton people had prepared for a surprise by removing the points, and placing an engine on the crossing during the night. No time was lost in relaying the points and...the Brighton engine was forcibly seized... By this time the rival army had mustered in force and before Mr. Scott could get clear they had lifted a rail on their main line. The South Western goods was then on the crossing, blocking both lines, and in that position Mr. Scott and his force remained for two hours...At one time a serious fight appeared imminent, but at length...Mr. Scott retreated on Guildford.

Passenger traffic on the Portsmouth Railway began as announced, but with bus connections from Havant. Eventually an injunction was obtained restraining the Brighton and through running began on January 24. Then came the usual ruinous fare war, said to have cost the companies about £80,000, before they reverted to the *status quo ante bellum* of the 1852 agreement. The following year, 1860, the Havant–Portcreek section became joint property.

The Portsmouth Direct line, as it is now invariably but incorrectly called, is a most difficult road as it was built on the 'undulating principle' then in vogue. Even so 1·6 million cubic yards of earth were moved and severe curvature tolerated in order to keep the gradients down to even 1 in 80. From Godalming there is an 8½-mile climb, mostly at 1 in 80 to the gable summit at Haslemere, then a long descent nearly to Petersfield, followed by the gable summit at the 485-yard Buriton Tunnel through the South Downs, approached from the south by 2 miles at 1 in 80. Prior to electrification, which revolutionized train working, Haslemere bank had an evil reputation and numerous trains stalled on it. At holiday times a pilot engine was maintained at Haslemere for 'rescue' purposes.

The line was originally single, but was doubled throughout by 1 March 1878. It was always given a very poor service. The working timetable for April 1865 shows only 4 passenger trains leaving Waterloo for Portsmouth via Godalming, together with one goods train from Nine Elms. In South Western days it never had an express service. The junction with the original Godalming line was a few chains north of the terminus, which remained in use by local trains, even though a new and more convenient station was provided on the Direct line. Godalming Old retained its passenger service until Farncombe was opened on 1 May 1897, and was still used as the goods station for the district until 1969.

The countryside through which the Direct line runs, though fertile, has few people by the standards of Southern England. There is no large town between Guildford and Portsmouth and Southsea, 42½ miles. Haslemere, however, one of the amorphous outer London residential settlements, provides much commuter traffic and Liss, junction for the Longmoor Military Railway (page 216), used to deal with some 250,000 passengers a year, mainly soldiers. There was only one other junction station all the way from Godalming to Havant–Petersfield.

Because of the lack of local traffic, many people felt the decision to electrify the 'Direct' was rash, but in 1947 seven and a quarter million passengers were carried, compared with the three million in 1936, the year before electrification. This of course was largely the result of improved services, as many fast trains for Portsmouth leaving Waterloo in an hour on a summer Saturday as in a day in South Western times. But after 1960, the service stagnated, with declining summer traffic. Portsmouth is also served by electric services from Victoria via the Mid-Sussex, and from Brighton, and by diesel-electric services from Southampton and Eastleigh.

PORTSMOUTH AND DISTRICT

In 1841 Portsmouth had 53,941 inhabitants and, across the harbour, Gosport had 13,510. It was a large centre by the standards of the day and had grown along with the naval base during the Napoleonic Wars. With the coming of the railway it continued to grow, for soon after the Navy was mechanized and the complexity of the dockyard work thereby increased. Neighbouring Southsea became a popular seaside resort. By 1861 Portsmouth–Gosport numbered 117,481 inhabitants and Portsmouth, on its island and hemmed in by a fortified zone, was becoming intolerably overcrowded. It was still a commercial port and in 1857 191,046 tons of coastwise cargo and 27,470 tons of foreign cargo were dealt with. Sheep, grain and coal came coastwise, while timber, wine and cattle came in from Spain. A hundred homeward-bound vessels landed mail.

Portsmouth–Gosport is still the Royal Navy's principal base. Its commercial trade, after a long period of stagnation, revived after 1960 (see page 214). The area now has more than 275,000 inhabitants. Portsmouth has long since burst the bonds of its fortified island site, spreading along the coastal plain to the profit of the railway and up on to the slopes of the Downs to that of the buses.

Despite the very poor service at first provided by the Portsmouth Direct, holiday traffic to the Isle of Wight was growing. Portsmouth Town station was a mile from Clarence Pier, whence the steamers sailed for Ryde. To close this gap a horse tramway was opened on 1 May 1865. But that it was unsatisfactory seems to be an understatement. J. M. Richards, reminiscing in 1913, says:

> In 1872 . . . the journey [from London to Ventnor] was rarely accomplished under five to six hours. The scramble at Portsmouth and Ryde for tram accommodation was not an agreeable experience, and with a party of children, nurses with

luggage, perambulators and bath tubs, a man had to be something of an organiser to get through without losing his temper and some of his belongings as well.

Thus did the Victorian middle class sally forth on pleasure bent. Two years previously however an alternative route had become available. As early as 1855 the STOKES BAY Railway & Pier Company had been incorporated to build a line 1½ miles from Gosport to Stokes Bay, only 2½ miles across the Solent from Ryde. The railway and steamer connections started on 6 April 1863. Until the opening of Portsmouth Harbour station in 1876, this was the only route with direct access between train and steamer. Through coaches were run from London and it was advertised, on grounds just made obvious, as 'The Family Route'.

Railway, pier and ferries were leased to the South Western in 1872 and were purchased by it in 1875, but with the competition of the new route which began the next year, the service gradually languished. On the outbreak of the first world war steamers ceased to call, though local services on the branch continued until 1915, the last train running on 31 October.

For a long time the joint Companies serving Portsmouth were barred from extending their line from Portsmouth Town to the harbour but eventually they cut through Service red tape, and the Harbour station, with direct access to the ferries, was opened on 2 October 1876. It quickly became the principal gateway to the Isle of Wight. The steamers passed into railway control in 1880.

Behind the populous coastlands around Portsmouth, northward to Farnham, is a tract of Downland which became a great corn-growing area during the Napoleonic Wars. After a long period of depression it has come into its own again since 1939. It is sparsely peopled with few towns or large villages and consequently it is poorly served with public transport even today. Alton, with 8,688 inhabitants in 1951, is the centre of a hop-growing area and has a large brewery. In times past its products required a special train nightly to Nine Elms. The only other place of any importance is Alresford in the Itchen valley, where watercress was grown and railed in quantity.

Until 1861 this area was penetrated only by the Alton branch. In that year the Alton, Alresford & Winchester Company obtained powers to extend this for 17 miles over the Downs and along the

Itchen Valley to Winchester Junction, on the trunk Southampton
line 2 miles north of Winchester itself. The Company, which had
changed its name to MID-HANTS Railway, opened its line on
2 October 1865: it was worked by the South Western. At Alton
it diverged just before the original terminus, destroyed by fire
in the 1950s, and a new station was provided on the extension.

Nothing further occurred until 1897 when the MEON
VALLEY line, southward from Butts Junction for 22¼ miles to
Knowle Junction near Fareham, was authorized. It was opened
on 1 June 1903 and though laid with only a single track was
built to take two, while the line from Farnham to Butts Junction was doubled in 1901. Butts Junction box was closed in
1937 and thereafter the two lines up from Alton became two
parallel single tracks. The stations on the Meon Valley were
provided with 600-foot platforms, at which the pull and push
trains of later years looked rather forlorn. The line was intended
as a main route to Gosport and Stokes Bay, but though
it was provided with through trains from Waterloo, it did not
develop as hoped. With electrification to Alton in 1937 services on
both the Meon Valley and the Winchester line were cut back at
that point and they ceased to have any pretensions as through
routes. The Winchester line was occasionally used as a relief to
the Basingstoke line, but its usefulness was reduced by the
gradients which have earned it the title of 'over the Alps'.
Privett and West Meon tunnels, both between the stations of
the same names, are 1,058 and 539 yards respectively.

The fate of the two lines offers a curious contrast. The Meon
Valley closed to passengers on 6 February 1955. Freight trains
ran from Alton to Farringdon until 5 August 1968, while the
line between Knowle Junction and Droxford lasted until June
1962. But in 1957 an interval service of diesel-electric trains was
introduced on the Mid-Hants. Closure was proposed for 6 May
1968, but a long battle deferred the date until 5 February 1973
(for later events see page 220).

Butts Junction, south of Alton, was also the start of the
BASINGSTOKE & ALTON Light Railway, built under a
Light Railway Order of 1897 and opened on 1 June 1901. Of
purely local import and serving a sparsely populated agricultural
area, it had an unprofitable career and was closed from 1 January

1917. Somewhat unwillingly, the Southern Railway reopened it on 18 August 1924, but soon closed it again, to passengers on 12 September 1932 and freight on 1 June 1936. The rural Light Railway was never popular in Southern England. On 2 October 1906 a diversion was built round Fareham Tunnel, which always gave trouble (page 117), and doubled in 1906. The original line was singled and could be used only by Meon Valley trains, which could not use the diversion. After 1921 the Eastleigh trains could use both. The diversion was singled in 1962 and abandoned in 1973. The GOSPORT line gradually sank into insignificance. Long distance passengers deserted it for Portsmouth Harbour and local passengers for trams and buses. It was singled in 1934 and, after some years with only two trains a day, was closed to passengers from 8 June 1953. Tite's original station, its specious colonnades wreathed in brambles, was still used for parcels and freight until January 1969 when the line was closed beyond Bedenham sidings.

The remaining line serving Fareham quickly became important and is still growing busier – the Southampton–NETLEY–Fareham route. The Southampton & Netley Railway was incorporated in 1861 to build a line from a new station at Southampton (see page 138) to the Netley Military Hospital. Opening day was 5 March 1866. The local Company was amalgamated with the LSWR in 1865. The extension to Fareham was built by the LSWR and opened on 2 September 1889. Originally single track, the rather sinuous route was doubled throughout in 1910. Local passenger traffic is heavy and the train service correspondingly frequent. An even more intensive service operated by diesel-electric trains was started in 1957. Swanwick is the centre of a market gardening area which specializes in strawberries and other soft fruits. In one week of 1931 one and a quarter million baskets were forwarded. But the goods depots are now closed.

Three minor lines in the Portsmouth area were short, dead-end branches and as such were vulnerable to road competition. The BISHOP'S WALTHAM Railway opened its 3½-mile line from Botley, on the Fareham–Eastleigh line, on 1 June 1863. Passenger services ceased from 2 January 1933, and goods traffic on 30 April 1962.

The small resort of LEE-ON-THE-SOLENT was given rail access by a Company of that name, incorporated in 1890 by a Certificate of the Board of Trade under the Railway Construction Facilities Act, 1864. The Light Railway from Fort Brockhurst, on the Fareham–Gosport line, was opened on 12 May 1894, and worked by a contractor until the South Western took over in 1909. Even in 1908 the expenditure of £1,102 was £400 more than receipts, but the line lingered on until the Southern closed it to passengers from 1 January 1931 and altogether from 28 September 1935. Six men and a dog travelled on the last train. The habit of assisting at closures had not yet caught on.

Equally unfortunate was the 1¼-mile EAST SOUTHSEA branch, which trailed into the main line outside Portsmouth at Fratton. Built by an independent Southsea Company, it was opened on 1 July 1885, and worked by the South Western. The Brighton obtained a joint lease the next year, but soon regretted it, for by 1908 the electrification of the local tramways had dealt it a death blow. The outbreak of the first world war was seized on as an opportunity to abandon the service, probably from 6 August 1914, an action not authorized until 1923.

GUILDFORD

Guildford is an old market town in the gap where the River Wey flows through the North Downs. In recent years it has grown rapidly and has to some extent become a dormitory town for London and an industrial centre. In the ten years to 1961, the population grew by 12 per cent to 53,977.

Because it was the most important town in West Surrey and because of its strategic situation, even though avoided by the London & Southampton, it quickly became a railway centre.

As already seen, its first line was the Guildford Junction Company's from Woking, opened on 5 May 1845 and doubled two years later. In 1846 powers were obtained by the LSWR for a route on to Farnham trailing into the Woking line just north of Guildford station. This branch was opened on 20 August 1849 as far as Ash Junction (for Reading, Guildford and Reigate traffic) and on to Farnham on 8 October. An extension to the market town of Alton was opened on 28 July 1852: for convenience the branch as a whole will be referred to as the Alton line. The extension of the line from Woking on through Shalford Junction to Godalming (Old) was opened on 15 October 1849 and the 'Portsmouth Direct' ten years later.

The LBSCR arrived from Horsham in 1865 (page 106). The last line to be built, that from Hampton Court Junction ($1\frac{1}{2}$ miles west of Surbiton) is still the 'New' Guildford line, though opened on 2 February 1885. In 1880 a Guildford, Kingston & London project was floated for a line from the District Railway at Putney Bridge. Naturally, though the District disclaimed connection with the scheme, the LSWR reacted strongly to the threat, depositing a Bill for a line of its own from Hampton Court Junction and with a branch from Effingham Junction to its station at Leatherhead. The LSWR won the day south of Surbiton (what happened north thereof is told in Vol. III, p. 58) and obtained powers on 22 August 1881.

The 'New' Guildford line was built as double track and has always enjoyed a good service, was electrified early and carries a heavy residential traffic. However it still runs through open country between stations.

Guildford station, with seven through platforms and a bay, as rebuilt by the LSWR is a much better building than the original. But though large, it is awkwardly laid out. At one time notices were displayed advising passengers not to enter any train before ascertaining its destination.

The Reading, Guildford & Reigate Company had been incorporated in 1846 to build $45\frac{3}{4}$ miles of line between Reading and Reigate (Redhill) on the London–Brighton trunk line. On the grounds of its utility as a through link between the Great Western and the Channel ports, the South Eastern willingly supported the project and the Act empowered it to lease the concern at $4\frac{1}{2}$ per cent and half any surplus profits, which never materialized. In 1852 the independent Company was vested in the South Eastern, whose Reading outpost always looked most strange on a pre-Grouping map, though the branch fitted usefully and neatly into the post-1923 scene.

The cross-country route was somewhat complex. Its Reading terminus adjoined the GWR's station; from Reading the line ran south-east to Farnborough, where for some years there was a little-used connecting spur up to the LSWR's main Southampton line, and on to Ash Junction, where it joined the South Western's Alton branch. Running powers were exercised thence over the 5½ miles into Guildford and on over the Godalming extension for two miles through the narrow Wey Gap through the North Downs to Shalford Junction. Here the cross-country concern regained its own metals. Because the Brighton had alleged that the South Eastern's interest in the project was merely a device to reach Dorking and that all the works west thereof would be dropped, Parliament had stipulated that the Reading end must be opened to traffic before the lease to the South Eastern could be effected.

The Redhill–Dorking and the Reading–Farnborough sections were opened simultaneously on 4 July 1849. The extensions of these two sections to Shalford Junction and to Ash Junction came into use on 20 August, when as we have just seen the South Western's Guildford to Ash Junction line was also opened, enabling the South Eastern to run from Reading to Guildford. Through running between Reading and Redhill began on 15 October 1849, the last link to be ready being the LSWR's Guildford–Godalming extension, opened the same day.

At first the Redhill, Guildford & Reigate was useless as a through route, for there was no narrow gauge continuation beyond Reading until 1858 (see page 133). And as a route from London it competed unfavourably at every important point west of Reigate. But though it could offer nothing in the way of speed, the South Eastern undercut fares, and hired vans to collect goods for despatch from as far afield as Farnham and Newbury. But it got no profit from this, and a tariff agreement was reached with the Great Western and the South Western in 1858. Subsequently the line became even more wayward than the general run of South Eastern branches until improvements by the Managing Committee and, in its turn, by the Southern, gave it a local service which was quite respectable. This was threatened by the Beeching Plan, but in the end an interval service of diesel-electric trains was put on. From 1897 through services were established between the Midlands and the Kent and Sussex resorts. In the 1950s six to eight through trains ran each way on summer Saturdays, but there was a subsequent decline. Freight traffic for Dover steadily increased. For recent developments see page 214.

THE MILITARY AREA

In 1855 Queen Victoria opened the new permanent North and South Camp outside the small and remote village of Aldershot, with 875 inhabitants in 1851. It was a good site. The surrounding heaths, with soils too poor for agriculture, made excellent training grounds without unduly disturbing civilian activities, while the Channel Ports could easily be reached by rail in time of trouble.

At first Farnborough on the main line and Tongham on the Alton branch were the nearest stations. But soon Ash, on the South Eastern's Reading branch, became railhead and in 1858 the adjacent North Camp station was opened. This was later rebuilt, reputedly to the designs of General Gordon. It is typical of several in the military area, with very long and deep platforms almost devoid of shelter, which could be used to draw up a battalion prior to entraining or take several hundred horses just offloaded.

So far the South Eastern were having things all their own way, but in 1865 the South Western obtained powers for a line from Pirbright Junction on the main line to Farnham Junction on the Alton branch. This would have the double function of serving Aldershot and of providing a direct route to Farnham and beyond. A spur was provided where the South Eastern was crossed to allow access from Ash to Aldershot. The South Eastern was given running powers into the latter station and in return the South Western received similar facilities between Ash Junction and North Camp. The branch was opened as a double line on 2 May 1870, but the Ash spur did not come into use until nine years later, when the South Eastern started a shuttle service in connection with its Reading trains. The South Western's powers were never invoked.

From now on military traffic, even in peace time, became important to the South Western. For instance, in September 1910, after large scale manœuvres, 25,080 troops, 6,722 horses and 1,174 guns were conveyed in 48 hours, and this at a time of heavy holiday traffic. The ability to cope, often at short notice, with sudden floods of special traffic, military, race or boat, became a strong feature of South Western management and of the Southern's in later years.

With the opening of the direct line from Pirbright Junction through Aldershot to Farnham, even the Guildford–Farnham traffic was steadily diverted up the short piece of the South Eastern between Ash Junction and Ash and so on to the new direct line into Aldershot. Services over the original Alton branch route via Tongham dwindled, and ceased altogether with the electrification of other lines in the neighbourhood on 4 July 1937. The Ash Junction–Tongham section remained open for goods traffic until 1961 to serve a gas works.

A number of schemes for connecting Aldershot with Windsor were promoted, but only the one put forward by the South Western came to fruition. Authorized in 1873, it consisted of a single line from the Aldershot branch at Ash Vale to the South Western's Reading branch at Ascot. Where it passed under the main line at Sturt Lane Junction two connecting spurs were put in from Frimley Junction. The branch was opened for passenger traffic from Ascot to Sturt Lane on 18 March 1878 (1 April for goods) and on to Ash Vale on 2 June 1879. It was later doubled as far as Frimley Junction. The remainder is one of the few electrified single track sections.

A number of large permanent camps were subsequently established in that region, usually remote from any town and served by short branches, a number of which carried public passengers. But buses and army lorries connecting at main line railheads have gradually robbed these services of their utility and they have all disappeared, though the lines sometimes remained open for military specials and freight traffic.

On 11 December 1905 the BORDON garrison situated on the edge of Woolmer Forest was given a rail service with the opening of a 4¼-mile branch from Bentley, between Farnham and Alton. It was authorized by a Light Railway Order of 1902. Military traffic always preponderated on the branch, which was closed to passengers on 16 September 1957 and to all traffic on 4 April 1966. At Borden connection was made with the LONG-MOOR MILITARY RAILWAY (page 216).

Brookwood, west of Woking, was the junction for two specialized branches. The first, 1¼ miles long, led northward to serve the rifle ranges at BISLEY. Authorized by a Provisional Order under the 1870 Tramways Act, the applicants being the

National Rifle Association, it was opened on 14 July 1890. Trains ran only when meetings were held on the ranges, the last running on 19 July 1952. During the first world war the tramway was extended to serve Pirbright, Deepcut and Blackdown camps. In the second world war the line was re-instated to Pirbright only.

Southward was a branch with a different function. With the enormous growth of London, disposal of the dead became a problem before cremation became socially acceptable. In 1852 the LONDON NECROPOLIS Company was incorporated to establish an extensive cemetery at Brookwood. The Act of incorporation empowered the company to contract with the South Western for the conveyance of bodies. The company built the ¾-mile, single-track branch, which opened in December 1854 and which was worked by the LSWR. The 'Necropolis Train' ran from a separate station which was on the down side just outside Waterloo and was twice moved south of Westminster Bridge Road, the second time in 1902, when Waterloo was enlarged. Train and station were bombed in May 1941 and the branch was then closed. Brookwood station was opened in 1864 at the expense of the Necropolis Company.

READING AND WINDSOR

In this area, the no man's land between South Western and Great Western, warfare was long and bitter. East of Reading the battle was joined in the Mania Session of 1846. The GWR projected a line from Ealing to Staines, which failed to comply with Standing Orders, but which stirred up successful opposition to two South Western protégés, the Staines & Richmond Junction and the Windsor, Slough & Staines Atmospheric Companies. Temporary allies of the GWR were the residents along the Great West Road, Eton College, and the Commissioners of Woods and Forests. The victorious Great Western came to terms with the two last and obtained the powers for the Slough–Windsor section itself. Whereupon the two small companies changed their names to Windsor, Staines & South Western (Staines to Wokingham) and Windsor, Staines & South Western (Richmond to Windsor) and obtained their respective Acts in 1847. Meanwhile the South Western had obtained powers for a branch from the Southampton main line at Weybridge to Chertsey (Old).

The Chertsey branch was opened on 14 February 1848. On 22 August the Richmond line was extended to Datchet, across the river from Windsor. The Commissioners of Woods and Forests had opposed closer approach. In the report for the first half of 1848 by the Chairman of the South Western, however, it is remarked that 'Her Majesty having graciously consented to an extension of the Windsor Staines and South Western line from Datchet across the Home Park into Windsor . . .' This polite fiction obscures the fact that the Prince Consort, requiring £80,000 to drain the Home Park and fearing to go to Parliament, persuaded the South Western to pay this sum for access to Windsor. The extension was opened on 1 December 1849.

In 1853 the Staines, Wokingham & Woking Junction Railway Company was incorporated to build a line from Staines to the South Eastern's Reading line at Wokingham, with a branch to Woking diverging at Virginia Water. The Staines–Ascot section was opened on 4 June 1856, but the section thence to Wokingham did not go into service until 9 July, thus depriving the South Eastern of access to Ascot for that year's meeting. Worked from opening by the South Western, the line was leased in 1858 and acquired in 1878. Meanwhile the Woking branch languished in spite of protests from local residents. Finally it developed into an extension of the Chertsey branch to Virginia Water, authorized in 1864 and opened on 1 October 1866.

The effect of these lines was soon to convert this beautiful but agriculturally poor area into a high class residential district. As early as 1870 there were complaints of inconvenience caused to 'City gentlemen' by the absence of trains from Waterloo between 4.45 and 6.35 p.m. This development has continued to this day, Chertsey, Sunningdale and Virginia Water being centres of scattered residential areas of the type already encountered at Crowborough and Haslemere. But in addition East Berkshire is becoming industrialized and Wokingham, Bracknell and other towns now produce furniture, plastics, electronic apparatus, water heaters and aircraft. The railway has shared in these developments.

The GWR was thus effectively held off from the South Western's territory south-east of Reading. But south-westwards of the town the struggle was longer and less successful. Here the South Western was attempting to promote lines northward from Basingstoke in order to develop a through route between Southampton and the industrial cities of the Midlands. In the same connection the Company was taking a close interest in the struggle developing in the Oxford area between the narrow-gauge LNWR and the broad-gauge GWR. In 1845 it produced a scheme for a line from Basingstoke to Didcot. The Great Western replied by supporting a nominally independent Berks & Hants Company, which was really two broad-gauge branches from Reading, one to Basingstoke and one to Newbury. The Advisory Committee of the Board of Trade, under Lord Dalhousie's chairmanship, pronounced in favour of the Berks & Hants, causing the South Western to cut its losses by coming to an agreement with the GWR not to promote penetrating lines into each other's territory. The Didcot line was dropped and the Berks & Hants was duly authorized. The 13½ miles from Southcote Junction, Reading, to a station at Basingstoke adjoining the South Western's was opened on 1 November 1848.

Meanwhile, in 1846 the Gauge Commission had laid its report before Parliament. In it was the following passage: 'That in order to complete the general chain of narrow gauge connections from the North of England to the Southern coast, any suitable measure should be promoted to form a narrow gauge link from Oxford to Reading and thence to Basingstoke'. This was confirmed in the Regulation of Gauge Act of 18 August 1846. But the GWR, though harried by the North Western, waged a fighting retreat and the Banbury–Oxford line was not 'mixed' until 1852. But by the terms of its Act of 31 July 1854 the Great Western was required to lay in the narrow gauge onwards to Basingstoke within eighteen months. Accordingly work went forward and the first narrow-gauge goods train reached Basingstoke from the Midlands on 22 December 1856. The broad gauge was removed from the branch in 1869. GWR local trains used the Southern's station at Basingstoke after its own was closed on 1 January 1932.

The importance of this Reading-Basingstoke cross-country link increased steadily. In 1958, for example, five through freights each way were scheduled on the Reading and Basingstoke line.

Three regular north-bound services left Southampton Docks or Bevois Park yard for Didcot and beyond. The balancing southward services chiefly originated in the Birmingham area. On the passenger side there were daily services from Birkenhead and from Newcastle to Bournemouth. At peak periods they also ran to Portsmouth. On summer Saturdays 14 south-bound trains from places beyond Reading were scheduled through Basingstoke. Most of the local services from Reading continued on to Eastleigh or Southampton.

When the Basingstoke through route was opened, the narrow-gauge tracks led straight from Oxford Road Junction to Reading West Junction, avoiding Reading itself. The South Eastern and the Staines, Wokingham & Woking were still deprived of a through connection. In 1857 therefore both the South Eastern and the Staines, Wokingham & Woking deposited Bills for a connection with the Didcot–Basingstoke mixed-gauge section. The South Eastern's scheme was for independent access from its station to Reading West, which was of course opposed by the G W R. But the Staines, Wokingham and Woking was able to come to an agreement whereby the G W R withdrew opposition to its project for mixed-gauge lines through the Great Western station: the G W R had to be allowed one year to carry out the work itself. The scheme was authorized and the G W R duly accomplished its part. Thus the 64-chain connection between South Eastern and Great Western became the property of the Staines, Wokingham & Woking and later of the South Western. It was opened on 1 December 1858, but its usefulness was limited by the fact that it involved an awkward burrowing junction under the G W R main line to the low level coal sidings beyond. An improved direct connection was brought into use on 17 December 1899. The present connection, known as Reading New Junction, was opened on 26 May 1941.

Though this link has perhaps never attained the strategic importance of the Basingstoke connection, it has been much used for through passenger and freight trains. In 1958 there were twelve scheduled freight trains to, and six from, the Southern Region and traffic between the Midlands and the Continent via Dover steadily increased in the 1960s. Finally, on 5 September 1965 all Southern Region passenger trains were diverted into Reading General, and the S R station closed.

(25) *The view of Guildford above, looking north, was taken about 1850.*
(26) *Taken from a different angle, this view of the 1940s covers the same area as* (25). *Though the rebuilt station is not the most convenient either for staff or for passengers, it is nevertheless a considerable improvement.*

(27) Tite's classical frontage of Southampton Terminus, the twin of Nine Elms, survives unaltered; photographed in 1957.

CHAPTER VI

Southampton and the Isle of Wight

SOUTHAMPTON

From the first, the links between port, town and railway at Southampton have been of mutual benefit. When the railway was opened in 1840 the mudflats within the angle between the Itchen and Test rivers came almost up to the medieval town walls. The only points of embarkation were the Royal Pier, since 1833 the terminal of the Isle of Wight steam packets, and the Town Quay. The 27,523 souls which comprised the 1841 population had spread but little beyond the walls on the landward side. Work on the Outer Dock was however in progress, under the auspices of the Southampton Dock Company, formed in 1836.

On 30 August 1842, even before the official opening, two P&O steamers tied up in the Outer Dock and discharged passengers, mail and cargo into railway vehicles on the quayside. On 18 September 1843 the Far Eastern and West Indian mails were transferred from Falmouth, while liners were calling in increasing numbers. From 1845 regular cross-Channel sailings began, to the Channel Islands and to Le Havre, the South Western taking over the ships in 1860. In 1851 the Inner Dock was completed and in 1857 the Union Line, which amalgamated with the Castle Line in 1899, began Southampton's connection with South Africa in addition to its already well established links with the Far East and South America.

In 1876, 9,984 vessels entered the port; 750,000 tons of imports, among them tea, rubber and cotton, and 591,000 tons of exports, then as now mainly manufactured goods, were handled, together with 357,000 tons of coastwise cargo. Though hit by the transfer of the P & O vessels to London, trade grew steadily and by the turn of the century the Itchen and Test Quays and the Empress Dock had been built to deal with the growth.

In 1892, on the initiative of the general manager, Sir Charles Scotter, the LSWR bought the docks from the Dock Company for £1,360,000: completion date was 1 November. New capital became available for what was, by now, the only port in the British Isles which could be entered at all states of the tide by the

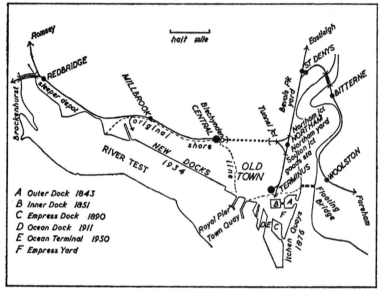

A Outer Dock 1843
B Inner Dock 1851
C Empress Dock 1890
D Ocean Dock 1911
E Ocean Terminal 1950
F Empress Yard

Southampton.

largest vessels afloat. In 1893 the American Line transferred its express service from Liverpool and in 1907 the White Star line followed suit, the Ocean Dock being completed for its large vessels in 1911. Southampton had become the principal ocean passenger port in the country.

The Southern Railway, in its turn, was equally alive to the importance of the port. In 1934 it opened the New Docks, built along the mudflats of the Test. The well-equipped quays, nearly 1½ miles long, have 9 berths – there is also the King George V graving dock – all of which can accommodate the largest ships. By 1939 the port's annual trade was in the region of 2¼ million tons of cargo and ½ million passengers. During the later stages of the war the port was being used to the utmost capacity and in 1944 26 million tons of shipping entered.

After the war came the building of the ocean passenger terminal. It was opened in 1953: in that year 650,000 passengers, just over half of them cross-Channel, passed through the port together with no less than $12\frac{1}{4}$ million tons of cargo. Of this enormous total 10 million tons was accounted for by the petroleum refinery at Fawley. The docks handled $1\frac{1}{4}$ million tons a year and the Town Quay, rail-connected but owned by the Corporation, and the river wharves, 1 million tons, mainly of coastwise cargo including coal and cement. Fruit is an important import, over 3 million packages of citrus being dealt with annually, together with bananas by the shipload. Meat, wool and other high value imports were also handled in large quantities.

The railway's share in the trade of the port remained large until the mid 1960s. Numerous freight trains originated or arrived daily, totalling some 2,900 each way in a year, conveying about 120,000 wagons. On 12 November 1958, for example, twelve freight trains of 523 wagons were despatched in $13\frac{1}{2}$ hours. Ocean liner specials, which owing to the uncertain timing were more difficult to arrange than regular boat trains connecting with Channel packets, were a conspicuous feature on the Waterloo line. In August 1958 94 specials were run, and on one day – Thursday, 28 August – nine of them left Waterloo between 7.5 and 10.35 a.m., a procession which somehow was merged in with the heavy regular traffic. From 14 May 1961 all Channel Islands steamers left from Weymouth, though the boat trains still used the Waterloo line, and in 1964 the BR steamers to Le Havre were withdrawn. (See also page 215.)

All this has been matched by Southampton's population growth: 34,108 in 1851: 145,096 in 1911; and 204,707 in 1961. Apart from the port, Southampton is an important traffic centre in its own right. As well as oil refining and associated heavy chemicals, its industries include shipbuilding and repairing, the manufacture of aircraft, general engineering and flour milling.

Southampton's second railway was the Southampton & Dorchester, to be described in the next chapter. It was opened on 1 June 1847. Like many other early South Western branches, it trailed into the main line. Immediately beyond the junction at

Northam was a tunnel, and at its western portal was sited the small roadside station of Blechynden, then in open country. The tunnel was not ready for the opening, so until 29 July 1847 Blechynden served as a temporary terminus, there being a bus link with the main Southampton terminus station.

Ten years later the Southampton & Dorchester line was doubled, and as part of the same scheme in July 1858 a loop was opened at Northam to allow through running from London. Thus there was a triangular junction to the east of the tunnel. At the same time Blechynden was renamed Southampton West End. On 1 November 1892 a new station, Southampton West, was opened on a site adjoining the old station to the west. In 1931 this was enlarged and now has four through platforms and a down bay. It was again rebuilt in 1968. Romsey and Salisbury trains travel via Millbrook this way as well as those on the ex-Southampton & Dorchester. On 7 July 1935 the new station changed its name from West to Central, an apt commentary on the growth of the town. In 1958, 1·3 million tickets were collected. The Terminus was closed on 5 September 1966.

The 1886 opening of the Southampton & Netley Company's line to Netley Military Hospital, later extended to Fareham to give a through if circuitous Southampton-Portsmouth route, has already been noted. The new route left the original London–Southampton line at a new station at first called Portswood but renamed St Denys in 1876. The trains continued from there into Southampton Terminus, and the indirectness of the route is emphasized by the fact that Woolston station, less than a mile from the Terminus by the Floating Bridge, is over four by rail.

There was but one other local passenger-carrying line in the area, the branch down the western shore of Southampton Water to FAWLEY. It was opened on 20 July 1925 under a Light Railway Order granted as long before as 1903. The district is more conveniently reached by passengers on the ferry between Southampton and Hythe, and workers travelling to Fawley were virtually the only passengers. But oil traffic from the refinery and associated chemical plants led to much increased traffic in block trains, especially since the 1963 agreement with Esso. In 1966 up to 13 freight trains a day left the branch. The exiguous passenger service ceased on 14 February 1966.

CROSS-COUNTRY LINKS

Southampton was too valuable a prize to be left undisputed South Western property, rival routes to it being considered from a very early date. The machinations of the GWR in the Basingstoke area were undoubtedly aimed at the port, and in the Mania year of 1846 a Manchester & Southampton Company was floated. Its route would have been roughly that later followed by the Midland & South Western Junction to Andover from Cheltenham through Swindon. Thence it would have reached a point where the New Docks now are. The project was supported by Southampton, but strenuously opposed by both the South Western and the GWR. The former refused to supply a special train to convey the deposited plans, and the latter offered to 'mix' the Basingstoke–Oxford link as an alternative. This offer, as we have seen, it was slow in carrying out, but it nevertheless sealed the fate of the new Company's Bill.

The project fared no better in the next Session, being rejected on the grounds that the levels were wrong, for which Robert Stephenson got the blame. Profiting from this, the South Western obtained powers for a branch from Redbridge, on the Dorchester line, up to Andover, to be laid along the bed of the canal, dating from 1796 and by now almost derelict. However, in grave financial straits after the collapse of the Mania, the South Western allowed the powers to lapse, which it was later to regret.

With the recovered prosperity a decade later, the GWR deposited a Bill for the extension of its Salisbury branch to Southampton. The South Western's counter was to revive its 1847 project, but both Bills were rejected. The next year, 1858, an independent Andover & Redbridge Company sought powers for a line along the canal. This was strongly supported by the GWR and, to the alarm and distress of the LSWR, a proposal was accepted that the line should be broad gauge, in order to connect at Andover with a GWR branch thence from Pewsey. In vain did the LSWR plead this was a narrow-gauge district, and that at the very least the line should be 'mixed'. On 12 July 1858 the Act received the Royal Assent and construction began.

But work was delayed by lack of capital and in 1861 both companies sought control over the now bankrupt, uncompleted line. The next year, however, saw one of the rather unexpected truces in the bitter struggle. It was agreed that the South Western should take over and an enabling Act was obtained in 1863, back-dating the powers to 14 November 1862. The Act also authorized an extension from Andover Town to the Junction station, on the main line to the West, and deviations in order to link up with the Eastleigh–Salisbury branch so that a single station could be used at Romsey. The line, at one time known as 'the sprat and winkle', was opened with a single track on 6 March 1865. Built along the canal, it abounded in severe curves and derailments were common. In 1885 it was re-aligned and doubled.

Following the abortive attempt for a line right through to Bristol, the Eastleigh (then called Bishopstoke) to Salisbury branch was authorized in 1844. It trailed into the main line to Southampton at Eastleigh and terminated at Milford on the outskirts of Salisbury.

The market town of Romsey, at the crossroads of the Eastleigh–Salisbury and Southampton–Andover lines, has a population of 6,300 and is the only place of any consequence between the Southampton and the West of England trunk lines. The through services from Brighton and Portsmouth to South Wales, Bristol and Plymouth ran via Southampton Central, Redbridge and Romsey and on to Salisbury. This route was followed by the interval service of diesel-electric trains introduced in 1958. Through freight traffic, including coal and oil, is also heavy between Salisbury and Southampton or Eastleigh (travelling either via Redbridge or Chandler's Ford). In 1966 up to 20 freight trains a day were scheduled through Romsey to and from Salisbury. When the local services were dieselized, the trains from Eastleigh were diverted from Salisbury to Andover Junction. This line, which ran beside the pretty river Test with the thatched fishermen's huts, was closed on 7 September 1964 except for the short length to Andover Town goods depot which was not closed until 18 September 1967. Passenger trains were withdrawn from the Eastleigh–Romsey section on 5 May 1969.

Unlike Romsey, the town of Eastleigh, which also has four routes leading to it (including of course the main line to London and to Southampton) is purely a railway creation, a lesser Crewe or Swindon. In 1891 the South Western's carriage shops, and in 1909 the locomotive works, were removed from Nine Elms to flat land on the banks of the Itchen here. Eastleigh was built to house the workers and had a 1961 population of 36,577 (20 per cent up on 1951).

The story of the remaining cross-country links to Southampton is less happy. The MIDLAND & SOUTH WESTERN Junction Railway had its origin in two separate independent Companies. The Swindon, Marlborough & Andover Railway, incorporated in 1873, was opened from Red Post Junction on the South Western's main West Country route (running powers were exercised into Andover) to Grafton on 1 May 1882. On 5 February 1883 it connected through to Swindon. In 1884 it was amalgamated with the Swindon & Cheltenham Extension and became the Midland & South Western Junction.

Its title indicated its main functions, that of a link for through traffic, especially to and from Southampton, between the Midland at Cheltenham and the South Western at Andover. Prospects of local traffic were poor, for it passed through almost deserted uplands with but a few small towns. But in later years it came to serve numerous military camps, which for long provided a steady traffic, swelling to a flood during the two world wars.

But its early years were difficult and in 1892 the services of the most brilliant of the South Western's younger officers, Sam Fay, were obtained as general manager and secretary; he took over as receiver in 1893. In these capacities, until his return to the South Western in 1899, Fay was able to set the Company on its feet. As a result of his good relations with the South Western, the MSWJR started to exercise its running powers into Southampton for goods traffic on 1 November 1892 and regular passenger trains on 1 June 1894. These powers had been obtained in 1882 when the GWR was pressing its support of the Didcot, Newbury & Southampton, and this line offered an alternative route to the Midlands independent of the GWR. Because emigration to the Dominions was at a peak, a weekly boat train was put on in 1893. Through coaches were run between Southampton and Bradford, Leeds and Liverpool and through goods traffic developed. So efficient did the little Company become under Sam Fay, later knighted, that it was quicker to travel to Cheltenham via Waterloo and Andover Junction, changing carriages there, than by a through GWR train from Paddington. Fay became superintendent of the South Western in 1899, and later general manager of the Great Central (Vol. III, p. 143).

In 1923 the line passed to the GWR, although it was a connection between the LMSR and the Southern. The GWR had at last got running powers into Southampton, but too late, for the era of peace and pooling arrangements had begun. Perhaps because of all this, the Midland & South Western Junction declined as a through route between the wars, although the Liverpool through coach survived until 1939. After being worked to saturation during and after the last war, an even more severe decline set in. From 30 June 1958 drastic cuts left a single daily through service and this was soon diverted to Cheltenham St James, severing connection with the ex-Midland line. All passenger services ceased from 11 September 1961 and the line was abandoned between Ludgershall and Savernake.

The Midland & South Western Junction had one branch, built by the War Office under an agreement dated 19 November 1900 – the 2½ miles from Ludgershall to TIDWORTH, one of the large permanent camps established on Salisbury Plain. Military traffic began in July 1901, and public passenger services on 1 October 1902. The latter were withdrawn from 19 September 1955, and from 25 November that year all traffic was operated by the War Department until closure in 1963. Though at the end of the branch, Tidworth was for many years the busiest station on the Midland & South Western Junction, and was in the charge of its highest-ranking stationmaster.

The DIDCOT, NEWBURY & SOUTHAMPTON Junction was another independently promoted line, which came to link Southampton with the Midlands. It was authorized in 1873 to run from the GWR at Didcot to the LSWR 2 miles north of Micheldever; there was also to be a connection with the West of England main line at Whitchurch. At first the promoters thought of it only as a local line, but like the Midland & South Western Junction it traversed country with a very limited traffic potential. Capital was slow to be subscribed, the first sod was not turned until 1879, and the next year powers were sought to abandon the line south of the proposed Whitchurch connection.

At this period the South Western was bitterly unpopular in Southampton: a deputation was therefore sent to promise support to the new venture. It was this which determined the Didcot, Newbury & Southampton to seek an independent approach to the port and develop itself as a through route. To spite the South Western, the GWR gave grudging moral support, but no financial aid. To minimize the threat, the South Western came forward with a proposal to link its West of England main line with its Andover–Southampton route by means of a $7\frac{1}{2}$-mile line from Hurstbourne to Fullerton. With the authorized connection at Whitchurch, this would give the Didcot, Newbury & Southampton direct access to Southampton without the necessity of building any further southward from Whitchurch. Spurred on by the GWR this sensible offer was refused.

Nevertheless in 1882 the LSWR obtained powers for its HURSTBOURNE–FULLERTON line, mainly to stave off Didcot, Newbury & Southampton designs on Bournemouth. The double track branch was opened on 1 June 1885. Passenger traffic was catered for by an exiguous shuttle service and was always very small. The line was singled in 1913 and closed to passengers from 6 July 1931. Goods traffic continued to be worked up from Fullerton to Longparish until 26 May 1956, inclusive.

On 10 August 1882 the Didcot, Newbury & Southampton obtained powers for its direct route into Southampton with a terminus near the Royal Pier. There was also to be a connection at Aldermaston with the GWR to create a Paddington–Southampton route 88 miles long. Worse than that, the next year powers were obtained for a GWR-sponsored Pewsey & Salisbury Company to build a direct London–Southampton link. The threat to its monopoly was so great that the South Western sued for peace. In 1884 a non-aggression agreement with the GWR was signed; meanwhile the citizens of Southampton, who had staged a torchlight procession to celebrate the incorporation of the Didcot, Newbury & Southampton, were not prepared to back up the Company to the extent of subscribing to it. The little concern was thus left in a very difficult position and in 1884 it called in first as director and then as chairman that noted resuscitator of moribund railways, J. Staats Forbes.

Work had already begun in Southampton, where a tree-covered embankment still survives in the valley between Hill Lane and the Polygon, but on Forbes's advice this was stopped. Efforts were concentrated on the Newbury–Whitchurch section, which went forward with painful slowness. The situation was made even worse by the G W R having out-smarted itself. In the 1882 Didcot, Newbury & Southampton Act it had guaranteed not only to work the new line but to divert to that line much of the through traffic passing via Basingstoke. But in 1884 it had signed the non-aggression pact with the South Western. Consequently it was now just as interested as the latter in keeping the Didcot line out of Southampton.

But this small Company was now determined to achieve success. Going against Forbes's advice, it concentrated on a drive to Winchester, dropping work on the connection to Whitchurch. By building a costly line through the bare hills to a back street in Winchester, where a station was opened to public traffic on 4 May 1885, it gained nothing and lost much. No physical connection between the lines at Whitchurch was ever provided. The proprietors, while their line earned next to nothing, now quarrelled over the next move. Some wished to push on to Southampton; but there was no money. Others wished to connect with the L S W R; but the latter's terms were unacceptable. But eventually, the Winchester dead-end being useless, they were forced to accept the crumbs the L S W R now tossed down from its impregnable position. There was to be a junction at Shawford, but no running powers beyond, while the connections from Winchester must be worked by the South Western.

The connection was opened on 1 October 1891 and trains were worked through to Southampton, engines being changed at the Cheesehill (later Chesil) station in Winchester. With increased traffic G W R engines began to be seen in Southampton from 1 October 1910, but by agreement, not by running powers. Though worked by the G W R, the Didcot line remained independent until 1923 when it was absorbed into the working company.

There were some attempts to introduce through passenger trains, but neither as a passenger nor as a freight route could it really compete with that via Basingstoke. In the early 1900s there were through trains from the Great Central via Banbury, and between the wars there were through coaches to Glasgow, but these were attached as far as Didcot to all-stations trains. Who travelled in them across the Berkshire Downs from Sutton Scotney and Burghclere is a mystery. Passenger services were withdrawn from 7 March 1960 and the line completely closed by 1966.

ISLE OF WIGHT

Because of its varied geology, the Isle of Wight epitomizes the scenery of Southern England, though it is only 20 miles east and west by 13 north and south. From the railway viewpoint it is of

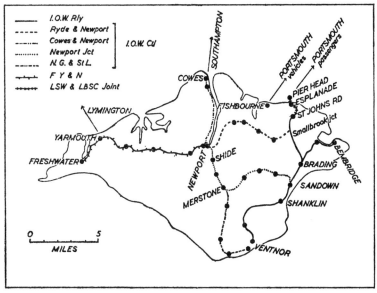

The Isle of Wight.

particular interest for the system of 45¼ route miles was owned and worked by several rival companies, each with its own administration, each struggling for profits from but a few miles of route.

The Island's main concern is with the extensive holiday trade which has developed as a result of its natural beauties, its sandy beaches and its high sunshine figures. This industry is the mainstay, direct and indirect, of its population of some 100,000. The growth of the Island resorts was, however, later than that of many on the mainland and came about only with improved communications with the mainland. Though Ryde was then firmly established, in 1851 Shanklin had but 355 inhabitants, and in the

1870s Sandown could be described as 'an improving village'. The Island is particularly dependent on adequate ferry services, but it is by no means so dependent on its railways. Throughout their rather melancholy history the latter have suffered from grave disadvantages. The companies were small and lacked capital. The smallness of the Island made them very vulnerable to the competition of road and coastal shipping: the first motor-bus service was established in 1905. Finally, there has always been a violent fluctuation, which became worse in later years, between the light winter traffic and the heavy traffic of summer. To cater for the peak period meant capital locked up in idle equipment during the winter, while to reduce equipment to the minimum meant loss of summer revenue. It was this dilemma which caused the closure of such a large proportion of the mileage in the 1950s, not any falling off of traffics, which if spread evenly over the year would be very respectable by branch line standards.

It was only during the period they were owned by the Southern Railway that the lines even approached a prosperous condition. For the most part they have worn an air of genteel decay. Their history makes a fascinating study, but unlike that of the ferries, it does not fit into the main stream of events in Southern England.

Prior to the railway age, the main gateway to the Island was Cowes, its pre-eminence being due to its site on the estuary of the Medina river, which ships could enter and tie up at the wharves. The Cowes packets sailed from Southampton. Inland from Cowes was the town of Newport, which was one of the most important on the Island, numbering some 8,000 souls in 1869. There were also 5,000 more in the adjoining parish of Carisbrooke. The industries of the town included milling, brewing, iron founding, cement and a millwright's factory.

Thus, though there were earlier schemes, the first railway to be built was the 4½ miles of the Cowes & Newport Company. This was authorized on 8 August 1859, and opened to passenger traffic on 16 June 1862; no goods traffic was carried for some time.

In 1860 the Isle of Wight Eastern Section Railway Company was incorporated to build an 11¼-mile line from St John's Road at Ryde to Ventnor, with branches to Brading Quay and Bembridge. Amid scenes of great joy, this was opened as far as Shanklin (which soon began to grow rapidly as a resort) on 23

August 1864. In 1865 the 7¼ miles carried 165,000 passengers and 11,000 tons of goods, a very good start.

The final 4 miles to Ventnor, diverted inland by the Earl of Yarborough through the ¾-mile tunnel under St Boniface Down, went into service on 10 September 1866. In 1863 powers had been obtained for a branch to Newport and accordingly the 'Eastern Section' was dropped from the title of the Company, though only one branch was built; the 2¾ miles from Brading to Bembridge. The construction of the sea wall in connection with land reclamation had cut off the old port of Brading from the sea and Bembridge had developed in its place. The 2-mile extension from Brading Quay was authorized under the Brading Harbour Improvement & Railway Company's Act of 1874 to serve the port. It was also intended to start a train ferry service to Langston on the Havant–Hayling Island branch, and a former Granton–Burntisland vessel, *Carrier*, was purchased. The Bembridge branch was opened on 27 May 1882, and the ferry service duly started, but lasted only until 1888. In 1898 the bankrupt Brading Harbour Company's undertaking was purchased for £16,500 by the Isle of Wight Railway, which had worked it.

As early as 1814 a 1,704-foot long pier had been built out over the mudflats of the Ryde foreshore in order to reach deep water beyond. By 1833 another 1,000 feet had been added. In spite of this, little traffic was attracted from Cowes because of the long walk involved. When the Portsmouth Direct line was opened there was an obvious opportunity for the Pier Company to encourage new traffic, but it was an opportunity it for long let slip. It was proposed that the gap between the Pier Head and St John's Road station should be closed by a tramway, but it was not until 28 August 1864 that a service of horse trams between Pier Head and Esplanade began. The extension to St John's Road was opened on 1 August 1871. But the transfer between steamer and tram and tram and train was inconvenient.

In 1877, therefore, the LSWR and LBSCR jointly obtained authority for a rail link, the line being built on a new pier close alongside the old. It was opened from St John's Road to the Esplanade station on 5 April 1880 and on to the Pier Head on 12 July. The joint owners had no rolling stock on the Island, the new line being used by the Isle of Wight and the Isle of Wight Central.

The extension of trains to Pier Head ruined the Pier Company and its property eventually passed to the Southern Railway – in 1924. The tramway was cut back to serve the pier only, being used by passengers from the steamers not travelling on by train. Petrol cars were provided until closure on 26 January 1969.

As a result of these events Portsmouth became the principal port of entry into the Island. By 1929 2 million people a year were using the railway-owned ferries from Portsmouth and on some Bank Holiday Saturdays nearly 100,000 people, mostly travelling to and from the Island, have used the Portsmouth Direct line. In 1957 3,461,000 people were conveyed by the Portsmouth fleet.

In 1872 the Ryde & Newport Company was incorporated to build a line from Smallbrook Junction, 1½ miles out of St John's Road, to Newport. It was opened on 20 December 1875. The new Company had entered into an agreement with the Cowes & Newport for their respective lines to be worked by a joint committee, a move which would allow some measure of economy. A modified agreement was confirmed by the two Companies' Act of 1877 which also authorized the building by the Ryde & Newport of Medina Wharf, on the river 1½ miles above Cowes. Since its opening the wharf has been the principal point of entry for coal, heavy freight and rolling stock.

The main centres of population were now connected by rail. The remainder of the system, serving the less populous southern and western part of the island, was very much less successful. It was this more recent part which was first closed, while the lines already mentioned remained in service for a longer period.

The Isle of Wight (Newport Junction) Company was incorporated in 1868 to link Newport to Sandown via Merstone. From the start the Company was in financial difficulties, but, after long delays, on 1 February 1875 opened its line from Sandown (on the Ryde–Ventnor route) to Shide, 8½ miles. The inspecting officer had refused to pass the last half mile thence to Pan Lane, Newport, which was to be the temporary terminus. This last section was not ready till 6 October, the same year. Then followed difficulties in raising money for the viaduct on the short connection to a junction with the Ryde & Newport; this was not opened until 1 June 1879. The Company was now bankrupt and its line operated by the Joint Committee of the Cowes & Newport and the Ryde & Newport, under arrangements made by the Receiver.

The three short and poverty-stricken lines were amalgamated on 1 July 1887 as the Isle of Wight Central Railway. Several proposals were put forward for further construction, but the Company made only one addition to its empire, the $5\frac{1}{4}$-mile line from Merstone to Ventnor West. It had been opened as far as St Lawrence by the Newport, Godshill & St Lawrence Company on 20 July 1897, and extended to Ventnor West on 1 June 1900. Though always worked by the Isle of Wight Central, it was not absorbed until the smaller Company went bankrupt in 1913. Thus with its $28\frac{1}{2}$ route miles, the Isle of Wight Central was by far the longest line in the Island.

The remaining concern, the Freshwater, Yarmouth & Newport, was incorporated in 1880 to develop the extreme west of the Island. The Company was assisted by local residents and also by the South Western, which was interested in enlivening its Lymington–Yarmouth boat service.

The new railway was opened for goods on 10 September 1888 and for passengers on 20 July 1889. There was a trailing junction with the Cowes line at Newport just short of the Central Company's station. Since the Central had undertaken to work the addition, the latter had no station of its own. Trains started from the Central's station, the locomotives propelling them for a short distance before starting off for Freshwater. In 1913 the Isle of Wight Central demanded better terms for the services it was providing, a demand which the Freshwater, Yarmouth & Newport was unwilling or unable to meet, deciding to work the line itself (from 1 July 1913). But it found itself excluded from the Central's station and had to build a small corrugated-iron one, which involved a walk for through passengers. It meant obtaining rolling stock, too; and finally bankruptcy. Sam Fay was appointed Receiver and secured some coaches from the Great Central.

On 1 January 1923 the Isle of Wight and the Isle of Wight Central were absorbed into the Southern. The Freshwater Company remained independent until 1 August, for the Southern was reluctant to take over its few assets and many liabilities, though eventually forced to do so. Thus in all the Southern absorbed $45\frac{1}{4}$ route miles, owned by 5 companies, including the LSWR and

LBSCR. All were single save for the 2¾ miles between Ryde Pier Head and Smallbrook Junction.

Eighteen locomotives and 90 coaches were also taken over, together with 26 other coaching vehicles and 584 goods wagons. The Isle of Wight Railway owned 9 engines, 7 of them handsome Beyer Peacock 2-4-0 tanks and 38 coaches. The Central's stud consisted of 7 locomotives, most of which were secondhand, including 4 ex-Brighton 'Terrier' tanks, and 40 coaches. The Freshwater's contribution was 2 locomotives and 12 coaches.

These formed a working museum that fascinated enthusiasts as much as they repelled normal passengers. Another source of complaint were the high fares, levied it was said by the Companies to enable them to run winter services when trains were nearly empty. But whatever the reason for their imposition, the high fares did not lead to large dividends. Until 1914, except for a few early and late services, trains were first and second class only. First-class fares too were as much as 3*d*. a mile and second class 2*d*. a mile, while the heavy tolls levied for the use of Ryde Pier amounted to 10*d*. on a second-class single ticket. On the other hand it was possible in 1913 to obtain a holiday 'runabout' ticket, apparently valid for the whole Island, for 7*s*. 6*d*. a week, second class.

Altogether the Island's railways were bitterly unpopular. At best they were grudgingly accepted as a necessity. Murray's *Handbook* of 1898 says: 'The Island is at least sufficiently – some may think far too much – supplied by railways.' But the rejoicing at the opening of the line to Shanklin had not altogether been misplaced. In the interval there had been an increase of over 50 per cent in the population. Much of this would have been impossible without the trains and less progress by 1914 would almost certainly have meant less development since.

The expanding economy was reflected in the railway traffic: in 1881 0·96 million passenger journeys were made, in 1901 1·5 million and in 1921 1·76 million. In 1922, the last year of independent working, and an exceptionally prosperous one, the Isle of Wight Railway carried 1·4 million passengers (allowing 600 journeys per season ticket holder), or 92,000 per route mile (including the worked Pier Head line). On the Central there were 1·1 million passenger journeys or 38,000 per route mile (also including the worked Pier Head line), and on the Freshwater line there were 217,000 or 18,000 per route mile. The Isle of Wight carried 13,618 tons of merchandise and 44,444 tons of coal and minerals, the Central 3,777 and 158,952 and the Freshwater 1,777 and 10,838 tons respectively. The last figures represent a daily average (Sundays excepted) of 4 wagon-loads of coal and minerals and 6 tons of freight carried by the Freshwater line.

These statistics tell their own story. The Isle of Wight alone normally paid a dividend on its ordinary stock, but not a high one. In 1922, when passenger traffic was 40 per cent up on the previous year, it was 2½ per cent. The Central declared no ordinary dividends until 1913 and only occasionally afterwards. Though a small net profit was made in 1922, no dividends were distributed on the second preference or ordinary stocks. The Freshwater's net receipts in 1922 were £2,135, but this had little effect on the £90,000 *debit* balance.

The Southern however made great and much-needed improvements in the services and between the wars the system appeared to prosper. The Brading–Sandown section was doubled and a number of passing loops laid in elsewhere. It became the practice to close Smallbrook box in winter and work the section thence to St John's Road as two single lines for trains to and from Newport and Ventnor respectively. The four and six-wheeled coaches and all the engines but the 'Terriers' were swept into oblivion and in their place were drafted reasonably comfortable sets of bogie non-corridor coaches with 'O 2' 0-4-4 tanks to haul them.

Train services were radically improved, now being based on Ryde Pier Head, where connections were made with the Portsmouth ferries, which in turn connected with the Waterloo trains. After electrification of the Portsmouth Direct in 1937, these, together with their ferry and island train connections became hourly, with extra services at holiday periods. On peak Saturdays in 1955 five trains an hour left Ryde Pier Head for the Ventnor line and one for the Newport line, while Luggage in Advance was sometimes so great that special trains of box wagons were needed.

Its efforts were reflected in the traffic figures, which showed large increases in spite of road competition: from 1·76 million in 1921 to 2·5 million in 1938 and an estimated 3 million in 1951. But the railways failed to gain anything like their share of the traffic: the buses carried well over 17 million passengers in 1951. This fact, coupled with increasing costs and the decline in the already modest freight figures, go far to explain the unhappy post-war history of the Island's railways. On the other hand, critics of the Transport Commission believed an over-centralized organization was out of touch with local conditions.

Whatever the rights and wrongs of the case, the Merstone–Ventnor section was closed to all traffic on 13 September 1952. On 21 September 1953 the Newport–Freshwater line and the Bembridge branch were closed. The Newport–Sandown line survived until 6 February 1956. The storm of protest induced a pledge by the Transport Commission in 1955 to give five years' notice of closing the Cowes line and seven for the Ventnor line. But this was repudiated in 1964 on the grounds that governmental acceptance of the Beeching Report created new conditions. Ryde–Cowes passenger trains ceased on 21 February 1966, Shanklin–Ventnor closed on 18 April and all freight services ceased on 16 May. The only remaining line, Ryde Pier to Shanklin, was temporarily closed for electrification and reopened on 20 March 1967 using ex-London Tube stock.

A last word on the ferries. The only one not Sealink-owned, the Southampton–Cowes, lost its rail connection after trains ceased to run to the Royal Pier in 1914, though buses were provided from Central. But as the ferries had plenty of space, it became popular for cars. The Portsmouth–Ryde service always handled much the largest passenger and parcels traffic, and was supplemented by a vehicular ferry from Portsmouth (Broad St) to Fishbourne, west of Ryde. The Lymington–Yarmouth service maintains its popularity as it serves the resorts in the western part of the Island. Trains run alongside the ferries at Lymington. Vehicles have been carried for many years, in barges until special vessels were introduced in the 1930s. In 1965 Hovertravel inaugurated a hovercraft service between Ryde and Southsea and in 1976 took over a Seaspeed (BR) service between Cowes and Southampton. In 1979 650,000 passengers were carried on the Ryde–Southsea service, the 7 hovercraft taking 7 minutes for the crossing. For foot passengers hovercraft are now the most popular means of crossing. The only attempt to establish a train-ferry was the short-lived one operated by the *Carrier*. In 1901 and 1913 a railway tunnel under the Solent, connecting the Lymington branch with the Freshwater line, was proposed.

CHAPTER VII

West Hampshire

THE DRIVE TO THE WEST

One of the more epic chapters in South Western history is the Company's drive to the west. It is fully described in Volume I and part of it can be traced in the fascinating history of the *Salisbury and Yeovil Railway* by Louis H. Ruegg, happily now reprinted; but its effect on Hampshire railway developments was considerable and it must be summarized here. As we have already seen, the Company unsuccessfully interested itself in Bristol even before the Railway Mania, and the next move was the modest one of a 22-mile branch from Bishopstoke (now Eastleigh) to Salisbury, authorized in 1844. The branch made a trailing connection with the main line, preventing through running from London, and terminated at Milford, on the outskirts of the city.

On 27 January 1847 *Rhinoceros*, a double-framed 0-6-0, steamed into Milford, amid cheering crowds, with a goods train of 22 wagons. W. J. Chaplin then distributed 16 tons of coal among the poor. It was a symbolic gesture, for one of the chief consequences of the new railways was the great reduction in coal prices in the rural areas of Southern England. This could bring about not only a rise in living standards but also the coming of new factory industries. 'Salisbury might become the Manchester of the South', said a speaker quoted in the *Salisbury & Winchester Journal*. Public passenger traffic commenced on 1 March.

Salisbury was more than an important market and the county town of Wiltshire; it was a natural route centre. It lies at the confluence of a number of valleys carved into the great chalk plateau: the Wylye, which provides a routeway to Westbury on the way to Bristol; the Nadder, leading to Yeovil and the West; and the Bourne up to Andover on the way to London. All these converge on the Avon, which allowed easy access to the Vale of Pewsey to the north and the port of Christchurch to the south.

The Eastleigh–Salisbury line was thus of more than local import, and in 1845 the South Western projected an extension to Yeovil, a branch from Salisbury to Dorchester, and the 'Hookpit deviation' – a cut-off from the Southampton line at what is now Winchester Junction westward to the Salisbury branch at a point in Mottisfont parish.

Meanwhile the Southampton & Dorchester Railway, 60½ miles long, had been promoted under the energetic leadership of a Wimborne solicitor, A. L. Castleman. Presumably to tap any settlements there were and also to save costs, the single track was planned to wind deviously among the low hills and round the heads of estuaries, via Brockenhurst and Wimborne. It thus came to be known as 'Castleman's Corkscrew' or 'the Water Snake'.

Both Castleman and the South Western well knew the Southampton & Dorchester could never thrive on the exiguous local traffic; they saw it as a link in a trunk route to the West. The LSWR was thus anxious to work it, and Castleman to extract the best terms possible. To this end he became positively dictatorial: his should be the only trunk line, and the South Western should not advance 'an inch beyond Salisbury'. The South Western refused to agree and Castleman had turned to a willing GWR.

However, GWR support was not long-lived. The South Western schemes for extensions beyond Salisbury had been counters to the projected broad-gauge Wilts, Somerset & Weymouth line. This latter was favoured by the Board of Trade and the South Western, then in a mood for consolidation, being under Chaplin's cautious guidance, withdrew as part of an 1845 agreement with the GWR. For its part the GWR dropped support of the Southampton & Dorchester. This, of course, meant that Castleman had to come to terms with the LSWR. Construction of the Southampton & Dorchester started on 21 July 1845 and the main line opened on 1 June 1847. The next year the Company was amalgamated with the LSWR and Castleman was given a seat on the Board.

As far as the GWR was concerned the nominally independent Wilts, Somerset & Weymouth project had served its purpose in blocking the South Western's advance. Financial difficulties coupled with lack of interest delayed completion, and only after complaints from the Mayor of Salisbury was the line to that city completed by the opening of the 19½ miles of single track from Warminster. Opening date was 30 June 1856, the Salisbury station being on Fisherton Street.

Thus by 1847 there were two embryonic routes to the west: the sinuous single track of 'Castleman's Corkscrew' and the devious route via Eastleigh to Salisbury. Under its 1845 agreement the South Western had pledged itself to go no further. But in the Mania Session of 1846 two independent Companies deposited Bills for extensions: the Exeter, Yeovil & Dorchester and the London, Salisbury & Yeovil Junction. The GWR too was supporting an extension of its Berks & Hants line from Hungerford.

Because of this last the South Western was persuaded to abrogate the 1845 agreement; the breach was made without undue difficulty, for a party wishing to reverse Chaplin's 'sluggish policy' had grown up among the shareholders. As proof of its support for the nominally independent London, Salisbury & Yeovil Junction extension scheme, the South Western obtained an Act for a direct line from Basingstoke to a junction with the Salisbury branch near Milford. But the Lords rejected all the other Bills and the struggle was postponed. Work had begun on the Basingstoke–Salisbury section but was stopped. By the time it was resumed, civil war had broken out in the South Western. It was becoming clear that two trunk lines were unnecessary, but each scheme (via Salisbury and via Southampton and Dorchester) was strongly upheld by a large section of the shareholders. Meetings became more and more acrimonious. But events overtook the contestants.

In 1847 all three Bills for western lines were deposited, the Berks & Hants extension of the GWR from Hungerford, the Exeter, Yeovil & Dorchester's line from Dorchester, and that of the London, Salisbury & Yeovil Junction from Salisbury. The GWR's was defeated, but the other two were eventually authorized, on 22 July 1848. By then the financial depression following the Mania found the South Western dangerously over-committed in capital expenditure. The shareholders were content to return to the Chaplin policy, and neither of the extensions nor the direct line to Salisbury were proceeded with.

Dividends had fallen sharply. On 18 August 1849 it was announced that 3¼ per cent would be paid for the half year as against 9 per cent for the preceding half-year. Chaplin, with supreme faith, backed the Company to the limit of his credit, but this did not save him from acrimony. On 22 December 1849 a committee of enquiry was set up to investigate allegations of financial sharp practice. From its investigations, however, Chaplin emerged with credit and he piloted the South Western safely through the stormy period until 1853. In 1852 Archibald Scott became traffic manager. His reign lasted thirty-three years and it was he who finally set the South Western on its feet and made possible the subsequent expansion. It is true that the passenger services suffered from creeping paralysis throughout the period, but he quickly reformed the goods side and persuaded the Company to assume the status of Common Carrier. Hitherto it had accepted no traffic from individual traders, but only from certain large carrying firms with whom it had contracts and who thus acted as unnecessary middlemen between traders and railway.

By the early 'fifties the residents along the abandoned Basingstoke & Salisbury line were getting restive and gave notice they would deposit a Bill enabling them to take over the uncompleted works. This stirred the South Western to the extent of opening the line with a single track to Andover on 3 July 1854, and on to Salisbury on 1 May, 1857. Then, as now, Andover Junction was the only station of any importance. It served a market town which has grown from 4,641 in 1841 to 16,974 in 1961 and which grew from 4,641 in 1841 to 16,974 in 1961 and which has had industrial and railhead functions grafted on. Its progress and that of Basingstoke, now an even more important with that of the former market towns of Odiham and Kingsclere. Neither were within easy reach of a railway station, both decayed and even the motor age has failed to re-vivify them, for it was the towns which had grown during the railway age which became bus centres and which had the facilities to attract those with cars. A rail-connected paper mill at Overton – paper for bank-notes has been produced since 1790 – is one of the few signs of industry outside Basingstoke and Andover.

Meanwhile, the internal struggle over the trunk line to the West continued. When the directors went to the General Meeting of 26 October 1852 for approval of their financial support for the proposed Salisbury & Yeovil they were narrowly defeated by the Castleman party. Chaplin resigned and Francis Scott took over. He gave a guarantee to the Parliamentary Select Committee that the line on from Dorchester would be adopted. But on returning to the proprietors with details of the Bill, they repudiated him in his turn by a majority of three votes. In 1854 Chaplin was back in control, the independent Salisbury & Yeovil obtained its Act on 7 August, and the Dorchester route was quietly dropped. This made some difficulty with Parliament over Scott's unfortunate pledge, the breaking of which took a long time to live down.

At Salisbury the line from Basingstoke joined the original Bishopstoke (Eastleigh) route just outside Milford station. Soon after the former's opening on 1 May 1857, powers were obtained for a new station at Fisherton, adjoining that of the GWR, where an end-on junction with the Yeovil Company's line was made. The new station, opened on 2 May 1859 (opening day of the first section of the Salisbury & Yeovil), could be reached from both Basingstoke and Eastleigh by connecting curves, that from the Milford direction being particularly sharp. Passenger trains ceased to use Milford and the original Basingstoke line between Laverstock Junction and Milford Junction was eventually taken out. Milford itself remained as a goods depot until 1967. The GWR had of course its own station and yard adjoining that of the LSWR, and in 1860 it provided a goods transit shed between broad and narrow gauge, used until the Westbury line was narrowed in June 1874. The GWR closed the passenger station on 12 September 1932, but the yard has remained in use.

Salisbury is an important cross-roads station. After the narrowing of the Westbury line, through running began between South Wales and Southampton, coal being the heaviest traffic, though oil is now important. Through passenger trains between Cardiff, Bristol and Portsmouth were introduced in July 1896.

Such is the importance of Salisbury that all passenger trains on the main Waterloo–Exeter line stop at the station of four through platforms and two bays. The two birds of taking water – early in 1964 this line was still steam worked – and dealing with passenger and parcels traffic were killed with one blow. In the past it was also usual to change engines in view of the harder road to the west, but occasionally Templecombe would usurp this function. Thereby hangs one of the most tragic tales of the South Western.

The road from Waterloo all the way to Exeter is well suited to high speeds and with its general renaissance in the 'nineties, the LSWR made full use of this in its competition with the GWR. After 1900 competition for the up passenger traffic from the American liners, which called at Plymouth before docking at Southampton, became severe. From 9 April 1904 a weekly high speed special was run, the way having been prepared by a normal schedule of 195 minutes to Exeter, 20 minutes better than the GWR's best.

On the night of 30 June 1906 the special consisted of 5 eight-wheelers of the light 'Eagle' stock with 43 passengers. At Templecombe L 12 4-4-0, No. 421, backed on for the non-stop run to Waterloo. It was driven by W. J. Robins, a man of experience and a teetotaller. According to the signal box registers he ran down from Dinton to Wilton at 70 m.p.h. and to the consternation of the signalman at Salisbury West box he opened his whistle at the distant and bore shrieking out of the darkness, through the station and down on to the 10-chain left-hand curve immediately beyond – a curve with a rigid permanent limit of 30 m.p.h.

It was over in seconds. 421 canted over to the right and fell through the vans of a train of empty milk churns passing on the adjoining down line on to a goods engine minding its own business in the Bournemouth bay beyond. All the vehicles of the express, save the last van, were reduced to matchwood and more than half the passengers, together with Robins, his fireman and two other railwaymen, were dead. Robins's lapse must remain forever inexplicable. That he was alert is indicated by his whistling. The inspecting officer could only recommend a 15 m.p.h. limit, but in 1908 a stop for all trains was stipulated, in consequence of signalling alterations. This was rescinded when further alterations were carried out in 1929, but in 1947 the speed limit was lowered to 10 m.p.h. The only passenger train which has not called at Salisbury since the accident, was the short-lived post-war *Devon Belle*, which to save congestion changed engines at Wilton.

Salisbury, a city of 33,000 and centre for a very large area, owes much to its railway crossroads. When the crossroads was taking shape, an increase in the movement of produce to the city was promised. But accommodation was limited and local business men feared the new facilities might equally mean that the town could be by-passed. So in 1856 the SALISBURY RAILWAY

PORTSMOUTH AND LONDON
DIRECT
RAILWAY.

The Inhabitants of these Towns and Neighbourhood
are again summoned to the Conflict,—it is for them to
decide between

MONOPOLY & INDEPENDENCE

They are not compelled to take Shares or make any
sacrifice of their Money; but all who wish well to their
Families, to the Trade and Prosperity of the Town,
can, and ought to show by their presence in the
Society's Hall, at Six o Clock, on *Monday Evening
next*. (January the 19th, 1846), their warm interest
in this great question.

MEN OF PORTSMOUTH,

Be at your Posts, show by your Union that neither
the wiles or stratagems of the South Western Mono-
polists, nor the tricks of Nobles or Dukes, can prevent
your demanding and obtaining

A Cheap, Direct, and Independent
LINE OF RAILWAY.

HARRISON, PRINTER, PORTSMOUTH.

(28) *Railway politics in 1846. This handbill, couched in the characteristically vigorous political style of the age, was issued by the company which hoped to build an atmospheric line from Epsom to Portsmouth.*

LOCAL TRAINS IN HAMPSHIRE AND THE ISLE OF WIGHT

(29) *C. Hamilton Ellis's impression of an* LSWR *local train of 1860 vintage. Joseph Beattie's 2–2–2 well tank 'Jupiter' on the Midhurst branch train.*

(30) *One of the infrequent local trains on the Portsmouth Direct line near Liss. A 'Paddlebox' 4–6–0 heads a short train of miscellaneous coaches.*

(31) *An Isle of Wight Railway 2–4–0 T on a train of then elderly 4–wheelers prior to the first world war lends colour to the complaints Islanders were then making.*

(32) *In outer suburbia in 1920. A down local train near Knockholt headed by a Wainwright 'J' class 0–6–4T is formed of Wainwright 'Birdcage' stock.*

(33) SOUTHERN STEAM. *The pre-war 'Bournemouth Belle' passes Battledown hauled by an immaculate green 'King Arthur' 4–6–0, 773 'Sir Lavaine'. The embankment behind carries the up Southampton line up to the flyover crossing of the Salisbury line.*

(34) SOUTHERN ELECTRIC. *A 5-coach set for the 'Brighton Belle' built for the first main line electrification, to Brighton in 1932.*

BRANCH LINE STEAM: THE FINAL PHASE

(35) *The south end of Oxted station in 1960. The pull-and-push trains, widely used throughout the Southern, were to be replaced on this line two years later by diesel-electric units.*

(36) *A BR class '2' 2-6-2T leaves Baynards with a Bulleid 3-corridor set on a Horsham–Guildford train in 1965 shortly before closure. The goods sidings had already been lifted.*

& MARKET HOUSE Company was incorporated to build a new market with 21-chain rail connection from the LSWR's new Fisherton station. The railway portion of the enterprise was in fact only a siding. It was still in use in 1969, though no longer reaching the market house, having been cut back to serve only the warehouses *en route*. The Company remained independent. The line was worked by the South Western under agreement and by the British Railways Board, until closure.

One other branch has to be mentioned – that to serve BULFORD military camp on the rolling chalk plateau of Salisbury Plain. In 1898 the LSWR obtained a Light Railway Order for a line to Amesbury from Newton Tony Junction 2¼ miles west of Grateley on the Basingstoke–Salisbury line, and in 1903 another Order authorized its extension to Bulford. Public traffic on the Grateley–Amesbury section began on 2 June 1902, military traffic having passed since 1 October 1901. The Bulford extension was opened on 1 June 1906. In 1904 the branch was extended parallel with the up main line to Grateley station, and near the original point of divergence a burrowing junction in the Salisbury direction was provided. A passenger and goods service between Salisbury and Amesbury commenced on 8 August 1904. Regular passenger services were withdrawn from 30 June 1952 and goods trains from 4 March 1963.

BOURNEMOUTH

'Castleman's Corkscrew' was given a wide detour inland to serve Ringwood and Wimborne, then two of the most important towns in the area between Southampton and Dorchester. To the south lay poor heathland of little agricultural value, while on the coast were the two small ports of Christchurch and Poole.

Today the two latter towns are at the eastern and western ends of a continuously built-up area with a population of nearly 300,000. This is centred on Bournemouth, which dates only from 1810 and which, when the 'Corkscrew' was opened, was a hamlet and coastguard station with fewer than thirty houses. Nor was its early growth very rapid. While Poole had 6,093 inhabitants in 1841 and 6,718 in 1851, the parish of Holdenhurst, which contained the hamlet of Bournemouth, grew only from 905 to 1,330 in that decade. Even in 1891 its population was but 27,908. But thereafter growth was very rapid. In 1911 the population was 78,674 and in 1931, 116,797. At the census of 1961, 153,965 persons were counted. Its development, typical of most seaside towns, was the result of urban growth, industrialization, and transport developments in the nineteenth century. (See Fig. 1.)

The particular advantages of Bournemouth lay in the very sterility of its soils. Land was plentiful and at first values were very low. The sandy plateau was seamed by narrow ravines or 'chines'. These were planted with pines and villas were built among them by speculators such as W. Tapps Gervis. Decimus Burton was the architect of central Bournemouth and made an excellent job of informally fitting rather ponderous buildings into an informal site. Dr Granville saw in the rising resort 'a real Montpellier' in England. In 1878 it was described as a 'small improving town . . . and bathing place', but the 1871 census did not put it among the seaside resort towns.

Its reputation was then mainly among invalids, but as an English Davos it would never go far. First its pale consumptives must be swamped by healthy holiday makers, and their late arrival was consequent on the late arrival of the railway. But once connected with London and with the Midlands they poured in along with pensioners and catering workers. Day trippers have, however, never been an important resource. At the locomotive depot was a large notice enjoining 'quiet please – residential area'. This seems an adequate summing up of the character of the town. But in 1938 an estimated 2 million visited it and in the 1950s about 10,000 tickets would be collected at the Central Station on a June Saturday and as many more at the West.

In its early days, Bournemouth was reached by bus from Poole (Hamworthy Goods), at the end of a short branch off the Southampton & Dorchester. Christchurch was served by bus from Christchurch Road station, later Holmsley, 8 miles away. But, by the late 1850s, the attention of railway promoters had been attracted to development in the district. In 1859 the Ringwood, Christchurch & Bournemouth Company was incorporated and given powers to build 7¾ miles of single track along the Avon from Ringwood to Christchurch. This was opened on 13 November 1862. At once Christchurch became railhead for Bournemouth.

Then in 1863 an Act was obtained for a 3½-mile extension to Bournemouth, still in the parish of Holdenhurst. This was opened on 14 March 1870 to a terminus which later became the East station: it was a quarter of a mile east of the Central station, and has been swallowed up in the expanding goods depot. The line from Ringwood was worked by the South Western and amalgamated with it on 1 January 1874. It abounded in severe grades and curves, and was subject to a speed limit of 25 m.p.h. But it was the main line to Bournemouth, now 116 miles from Waterloo, and served by through coaches detached from the Southampton & Dorchester's Weymouth trains at Ringwood, where a covered bay platform was evidence of former importance.

The resort's continued steady growth led to a double track cut-off from Lymington Junction, a mile west of Brockenhurst, to a point just west of Christchurch station; a new station there and the doubling of the line on to Bournemouth; and a connecting link between the East and West Stations, the Bournemouth Junction railway. A new through station was provided on this link and was opened on 20 July 1885, replacing the original East station; it was renamed Central on 1 May 1899. The second track in from Christchurch was brought into use on 30 May 1886. Finally the 'Sway line' as the cut-off was called, was opened on 6 March 1888. This brought Bournemouth Central to 107½ miles from Waterloo, and made possible higher speeds and increased traffic capacity. The line between the Central and West stations was opened on the same day as the Sway line.

The story of the western approaches to Bournemouth, and indeed much about the place itself, has been told in Volume I, but we should note that the Broadstone (on the Southampton & Dorchester) to Bournemouth line was opened to Poole on 2 December 1872 and to Bournemouth West on 15 June 1874. Thereafter the Hamworthy branch lost importance.

The Weymouth and Bournemouth portions of through trains were now divided and joined at Brockenhurst, so that the Ringwood–Christchurch line sank to purely local importance. It was closed to all traffic from 30 September 1935. On 1 June 1893 the last links in the present layout at Bournemouth were opened, the Branksome avoiding line and Holes Bay curve, which obviated reversals at the West and at Broadstone respectively for South-

ampton–Dorchester–Weymouth services. Trains were now divided
at the East for the West and Weymouth.

The 'Corkscrew' between Lymington Junction and Hamworthy
now lost all main-line traffic except for Weymouth extras avoiding
Bournemouth. The section between Broadstone and Hamworthy
junction was singled. From 4 May 1964 local passenger services
from Bournemouth West via Wimborne to Brockenhurst were
withdrawn. Wimborne freight depot closed on 13 May 1977.

Before electrification Bournemouth Central had four through
roads and two through platforms, the down one lengthened to
1,760 feet in 1930 so that it could accommodate two trains of 14
coaches. Central is one of the few stations in Southern England
to have an overall roof and has long, red-brick facades. In contrast the buildings of the West, still in their original form when
closed in 1965, were somewhat small and primitive. Platforms
were added piecemeal until there were six in all.

Connection with the Midlands and North, so vital to the development of Bournemouth, came about in a chance and piecemeal fashion, dealt with fully in Volume I. Suffice it to say that
originally the SOMERSET & DORSET Railway terminated
at Wimborne, where passenger trains for Poole and Bournemouth
had to reverse, but that a 2¾-mile cut-off from Corfe Mullen to
Broadstone was opened on 14 December 1885.

Only one effort was ever made to break the South Western's
monopoly at Bournemouth. In 1885 the Didcot, Newbury &
Southampton, backed by the GWR, unsuccessfully attempted a
line from Whitchurch.

Two lines remain to be mentioned. The small port of LYM-
INGTON was reached by a 4-mile, single track branch from
Lymington Junction officially opened on 12 July 1858. Lymington was the terminus of services to the Isle of Wight and the
Lymington Railway Company hoped to develop traffic. But the
line languished as a result of the LSWR concentrating on Portsmouth in competition with the Brighton. Only after the independent Company had been vested in the LSWR in 1878 was the
Lymington pier extension opened – on 1 May 1884, the year the
ferries were also taken over. Connections were thus greatly improved and traffic increased steadily.

The SALISBURY & DORSET JUNCTION Company

was incorporated in 1861 to connect the Salisbury–Romsey line at Alderbury Junction with the Castleman line at the site of West Moors station, east of Wimborne. Opening date for the 19 miles of single line was 20 December 1866. The LSWR worked the concern until absorbing it in 1883. Next year a derailment near Downton focused attention on the dilapidated rolling stock and decayed permanent way. One of the engines was able to keep time only by being driven dangerously downhill, and Constance Hill, daughter of the Rector of Downton, had found numerous keys fallen out of the chairs. It was an unfortunate *exposé* of branch line operation in the South Western's unregenerate middle period. Local passenger traffic was always exiguous and services were infrequent by the standards of Southern England. The route had some pretensions at being a through one to Bournemouth at holiday times, but from 4 May 1964 it was completely closed.

RELATIVE IMPORTANCE OF THROUGH ROUTES IN HAMPSHIRE AND BERKSHIRE
TOTAL THROUGH TRAINS ON WEEKDAYS: AUGUST 1958

Route	Passenger		Freight	Remarks
	Basic	Saturdays (total)		
W.R. to S.R. at Reading	2	10	17+3Q	Trains to and from stations north of Reading
Berks. and Hants. (Reading W. to Basing)	4	28	12	Trains to and from stations north of Reading
Didcot, Newbury and Southampton	No trains to and from stations north of Didcot		7+1Q	
Midland and South Western Jct.	No trains to and from stations north of Cheltenham		5	
Westbury–Salisbury	14	28	16	Trains to and from stations north of Westbury
Somerset and Dorset	8	32	nil	Trains to and from stations north of Bath

Q: Train runs if required.

CHAPTER VIII

The Development of Main Line
Train Services, 1845-1923

In 1845 the lines south of the Thames could boast of trains as fast as any in the country. The South Eastern, under the chairmanship of J. Baxendale, was praised by the *Westminster Review* for its equitable treatment of passengers of all classes.

Both these statements would have seemed incredible to the travelling public during the last quarter of the century. For in the succeeding years after 1850 the southern lines failed to keep pace with developments in speed and comfort elsewhere. With the possible exception of its West of England services, the South Western became a prey to creeping paralysis. In *Engineering* of 19 July 1867 appears the statement that 'The South Western, with its easy gradients, its splendid permanent way and its admirable Locomotive Superintendent [Joseph Beattie], only attains a through speed of 30–35 m.p.h.' The Brighton, faced with no real competition, was in like case, while the South Eastern and the Chatham, extending their limited resources in a ruinous warfare of capital development, had neither the money nor the inclination to improve services or comfort.

The situation did not change until the turn of the century. On the South Western there came to the West of England line a sudden and final flare-up of competition with the GWR, while Sam Fay reformed the lethargic Bournemouth line. The Brighton improved its services to and from its namesake, partly as a result of public criticism, and the Managing Committee began the work of reform on the lines under its control which the Southern was later to complete.

THE SOUTH EASTERN

Services in Kent on both the South Eastern and the Chatham were mainly concerned with handling the Continental, the Kent Coast and, in later years, the London suburban traffics.

In 1845 there were 8 scheduled passenger trains daily between London Bridge and Dover Town via Redhill. The fastest covered the 88 miles in 151 minutes, a speed of 36·3 m.p.h. At neither Folkestone nor Dover did the trains run alongside the boats and so the Continental and local passengers were not segregated.

Over the next twenty years there was little improvement in speed or frequency, but in the 'sixties two events brought some change. Prior to 1861 the South Eastern had concentrated its attention on Folkestone, but with the coming of the Chatham to Dover, the latter was to become the more important to both railways. On 1 May 1868 the shorter route via Sevenoaks came into use. The Folkestone boat trains were diverted, but the Dover ones ran via Redhill until 1 March 1869, when the times of the 'Mails' were cut by 15 minutes.

Sir Cusack Roney in his *Rambles on Railways* published in 1868 says 'for a short run the most rapid on the narrow gauge in England is between London and Dover'. The down Mail was scheduled to take 125 minutes (via Redhill), an average speed of 42·2 m.p.h. (Roney is quoted here – but Bradshaw of April 1868 shows the morning Mail as booked from Cannon Street to Dover Town in 115 minutes.) On 26 April 1868, however, the Australian mails were conveyed by a special train in 105 minutes, including a stop at Staplehurst for water. This works out at a fraction under 50 m.p.h., which was very respectable for the period.

In December of the same year, 1868, with the Sevenoaks route now in use, there were 8 down trains daily to Dover, including the 2 'Mails' and 3 others which by some stretch of the imagination could be deemed expresses. To Ramsgate there were 5 trains, including 3 expresses, but several of these were combined with Dover trains as far as Ashford.

In the eighties there were 4 up continental services, the 3.5 p.m. mail from Dover, the 4.10 from Folkestone (still called the 'Tidal', though now fixed), the 5.35 from Dover (Ostend boat) and the 3.5 a.m. Mail. Late starts were frequent, but the drivers were instructed to make up time, for track occupation was light and fast approaches to London could be made. Before 1895 there were neither station nor yards at Hither Green and the junction box would be passed regularly at over 70 m.p.h.

Throughout the period the rolling stock left much to be desired. In 1889 there were still 39 first-class saloons of 1849 in service and 73 coaches of 1854–59 vintage. Ahrons comments:

> In the seventies and early eighties the South Eastern carriage stock was Unique... Its colour was an unhealthy flesh tint above and a black line below by way of giving the impression that mortification had set in badly in the lower panels... Hardly any two coaches were alike in size and contours... The styles of the windows included Gothic, Norman and Early English in great variety... The partitions were so low that when the passenger sat down with his back to one of them his head nearly collided with the back hair and best hat of the female in the next compartment.

But though the South Eastern train, suburban or semi-fast, was a fearsome sight, a long string of four and six-wheel coaches with elderly four-wheel vans scattered at random through its length, there were compensations. In 1883 the first bogie lavatory coaches appeared on boat trains and after 1 October 1897 even third-class passengers were provided with bogies and lavatories on the Folkestone services.

In 1883, on a basis of the definition by the contemporary commentators Foxwell and Farrer of an 'Express' as being a train with an overall average of at least 39–40 m.p.h., there were 3 expresses down and 1 up between Cannon Street and Dover Town at over 40 m.p.h. and 2 between London Bridge and Ramsgate at 40·8 m.p.h. The two 'Tidals' from Folkestone and a train from St Leonards were booked at 39·5 m.p.h.

By 1888 the 11.7 a.m. down to Dover was averaging 47 m.p.h., one train each way to and from Folkestone 44 m.p.h., while the fastest time from St Leonards to London Bridge had been cut to 91 minutes. By way of comparison, the fastest up diesel-electric timing in 1958 was 88 minutes from St Leonards to Cannon Street, but we must take into account the vastly heavier train, greater number of stops and the very congested approach to London. The 90's were a period of increasing train weights, not speed.

THE LONDON, CHATHAM & DOVER

Steep gradients and sinuous curves prevented high speeds on the Chatham and the small locomotives were unable to work the trains punctually. The semi-permanent bankruptcy of the Company resulted in poor and antiquated rolling stock. 'From what nether depths the Chatham excavated most of its carriages, Goodness only knows' is all Ahrons could bring himself to say. But since there was no 60 m.p.h. limit, as there was on the South Eastern, an adventurous driver might make an occasional very fast run.

In 1868 there were 6 down trains daily to Dover, including 2 boat trains. All but the two last had portions for Ramsgate Harbour detached at Faversham. The working timetable of 1878 shows that the 7.40 a.m. from Victoria was due to leave Herne Hill, where all trains stopped to attach a City portion, at 7.50 and to reach Dover Harbour non-stop at 9.24 a.m. Thus $73\frac{1}{4}$ miles were covered in 94 minutes, 49·2 m.p.h. But generally speeds were very much lower and stops more frequent. Apart from the Dover trains, the *Granville*, named after an hotel in Ramsgate, was the best-known Chatham train. For many years it left Victoria at 3.15 for Ramsgate, and like all Chatham trains, except the boat trains, conveyed third-class passengers.

THE MANAGING COMMITTEE

Little was done to increase speeds. The new and much larger locomotives of H. S. Wainwright were used to deal with greatly increased train weights due to heavier traffic and to the new bogie coaches introduced by him. In 1895 he had been appointed carriage and wagon superintendent at Ashford and had instituted a 'new deal' for third-class passengers. By 1901 22 down passenger trains were due to pass Fawkham, on the Chatham line between Swanley and Rochester, on an ordinary weekday and one was due to terminate there. This was a considerable increase over Chatham days, but it should be compared with the 26 down passenger trains of the April 1925 timetable and the 39 of the December 1955. In 1901 there were only 2 down boat trains, one for Dover and the other for Queenborough. The Managing Committee was already concentrating on the Tonbridge route for boat trains.

THE BRIGHTON

The Brighton's chief interests were in the London–Brighton and London suburban traffics. On its secondary main lines and its rural branch lines conditions were wayward to an extent which cannot be appreciated in these days of interval electric services. The Newhaven boat trains never loomed as large as did the continental services on the Kent lines.

In November 1846 there were 6 trains each way between London Bridge and Brighton. Over the next decade there was a considerable growth of traffic, accompanied by a speeding up of the express services. The working timetable of March 1859 shows 5 expresses and 9 other passenger trains between London and Brighton. There were also 5 'short' trains from Haywards Heath to Brighton, as well as the London suburban trains as far as Croydon. The fastest service was the 5.0 p.m. from London Bridge, which took 80 minutes for the non-stop journey. There was one through train from Pimlico (Victoria not being open until October 1860).

From Brighton there were 8 trains on the West Coast line and 7 trains, not including the 5 'shorts' for Lewes, on the East Coast line. As a sample of branch line services, those to Horsham and East Grinstead from Three Bridges consisted of 12 and 8 passenger trains respectively.

In 1865 the 8.45 a.m. from Brighton to London Bridge was accelerated to 65 minutes, to remain the fastest time for thirty-three years. By now most trains had Victoria and London Bridge portions, combined or separated at East Croydon.

By 1875 the service to and from Brighton had assumed a pattern which remained unchanged until electrification. The best trains were the business services to and from London Bridge, the *City Limited*, 8.45 a.m. up and 5.0 p.m. down being the best known of all. There were also a few fast trains from Victoria, the best taking 70 minutes, but the semifasts took much longer.

On 1 November 1875 the first Pullman car was introduced – on the 10.45 a.m. from Victoria. On 1 December 1881 came the first all-Pullman train. It was soon withdrawn, but was permanently reinstated in 1892. During the 'eighties non-corridor bogie first-class coaches were introduced, but six-wheelers were the general rule until the turn of the century. An accident report reveals that on 1 May 1891 the up *City Limited* included 4 six-wheeled first-class coaches and 4 four-wheeled vans. On suburban lines 8-coach sets of close-coupled coaches, popularly known as 'bug-hutches', were in use.

In 1883 Foxwell and Farrer recorded 15 Brighton trains as being expresses according to their definition of a 39–40 m.p.h. average speed. All were between London and Brighton or Eastbourne. The fastest was still the *City Limited* with its 65 minute timing giving an average of 46·6 m.p.h. Ahrons unkindly compared this with an LNWR fish train booked from Tebay to Preston at 47·7 m.p.h.: 'Better a dead mackerel on the North Western than a first class passenger on the Brighton'.

In 1890 R. J. Billinton succeeded Stroudley as chief mechanical engineer and he and his successors built much larger and more powerful locomotives; as these became available, the service to Brighton became as good as it was to be prior to electrification. After 1893 trains from London Bridge and Victoria ran separately and the winter service that year consisted of 28 down trains, including 2 *Pullman Limiteds*.

In October 1906 there were 26 through down trains from London Bridge and Victoria to Brighton: 9 of these could be deemed expresses, taking less than 85 minutes. One took 65 minutes, one 72, one 75 and four 80. In the same year there were 19 down through trains to Eastbourne and beyond via Plumpton, together with 2 boat trains for Newhaven. The Mid-Sussex line had 13 down through trains.

On 1 November 1908 a new Pullman car set was placed in service on the *Limited*, which now became the *Southern Belle*. For a short time after 2 October 1898 the Sunday *Limited* was scheduled to do the trip in 60 minutes and in 1910 the *Southern Belle* was booked daily to do the journey in this time.

Coloured postcards of the train, hauled by a Marsh 4-4-2 tank or L. B. Billinton 4-6-4 tank, but apparently never by a tender engine, became increasingly popular and must have planted an undying enthusiasm in many a youthful breast. They probably romanticized the Brighton, however. Even in its last years a rather miscellaneous collection of bogie coaches with Pullmans scattered at odd intervals down the train represented the norm of expresses.

By 1923 the services to Brighton in particular and to the coast resorts in general, drastically cut during the first world war, had returned to their pre-war normal. At grouping there were 31 down trains and 28 up trains between London and Brighton.

THE LONDON & SOUTH WESTERN

There were in effect three main lines: the West of England via Salisbury, the Southampton and Bournemouth, and the Portsmouth Direct, though the last never received main line treatment, Portsmouth, as Ahrons put it, being regarded 'as an obscure and unimportant village'. Superimposed on the regular traffic on these lines were the ocean liner specials, often in large numbers, to Southampton.

In 1845, however, only the Southampton line was in operation and there were, as we have seen, but 27 trains of all descriptions in the 24 hours. The expresses were among the fastest in the country and were held up as models by the protagonists of the narrow gauge. But during the 'fifties and 'sixties, under Archibald Scott, speeds failed to improve and services stagnated generally. Routes to places other than Southampton were extremely circuitous, while the opening of the direct lines to Portsmouth in 1859 and to Salisbury in 1860 made little difference at first, for they were only single track.

The working timetable of April 1865 gives a good picture of the situation. It shows a total of 61 trains down the main line on an ordinary weekday, 44 passenger and 17 goods. Of these, 24 passenger trains were for destinations short of Woking and one for that station. One more was the Necropolis train, for Brookwood just beyond Woking. Nine passenger and 5 goods trains continued down the Guildford line, but of these only 5 passenger and a goods went on over the Direct beyond Godalming. Four passenger and 3 goods trains were for the Salisbury line, and over the Southampton line – always the most important – there were 7 passenger and 8 goods trains through from London. (Discrepancies in these figures are accounted for by the 7.5 a.m. and 3.50 p.m. from Waterloo being combined Exeter and Portsmouth trains to Woking.)

The fastest trains were those to Southampton. The 11.0 a.m.

and 3.10 p.m. took 137 minutes for the 79 miles (34·7 m.p.h.). The West of England trains ran moderately fast as far as Basingstoke, but had very easy timings beyond, while those to Portsmouth could under no circumstances be called expresses, even by South Western standards.

In 1874 the best down train was the 2.10 from Waterloo, unofficially the *Beeswing*, which combined Southampton and Exeter portions to Basingstoke. It was invariably double headed for the 47¾ miles and was booked at an average speed of 42¾ m.p.h. At Basingstoke the train was divided and one of the engines whirled the light four-wheeled coaches on to Salisbury at 42·9 m.p.h..The other part reached Southampton with an average speed of 34·1 m.p.h. Beyond, even this stately progress seemed rapid by comparison, for 'dry rot set in' over Castleman's Corkscrew and Weymouth was not reached until 6.25 p.m. This of course was the best, not the average.

But from 1880 onwards, under Sir Charles Scotter's management particularly, services underwent a revolution. By the late 'nineties they were not showy, but had become almost uniformly good. Express and semi-fast trains were frequent and conveyed all classes of passengers in comfortable bogie stock hauled by powerful and reliable locomotives. Lavatory-fitted bogie coaches had begun to appear as early as 1882.

Even in 1880 the improvements had begun. The *Beeswing*, now leaving at 2.20 p.m., reached Basingstoke at an average speed of 44·1 m.p.h. In 1883 it left at 2.30 p.m. and reached Salisbury with stops only at Basingstoke and Andover and with section averages of 45·5, 46·25, and 43 m.p.h. That year the fastest train of all was the 1.15 p.m. from Basingstoke (10.15 a.m. ex-Weymouth) which reached Vauxhall, then the ticket stop, in 56 minutes (51·5 m.p.h.). In 1884 C. Rous Marten, a pioneer of the indefatigable army of train timers, recorded runs behind the new 4-4-0s of William Adams to Basingstoke (47¾ miles) in 60¾ minutes and to Salisbury (83¾ miles) in 111 minutes. His account reveals how light the trains of those days were, 120 and 165 tons respectively.

In 1888 the Sway line to Bournemouth was opened. Though times were cut because of the reduced distance, speeds were slow to improve. In 1890 the best time to Bournemouth was 153 minutes, but by 1899, under Sam Fay, it was down to 125 minutes for the 108 miles. But Fay was not satisfied and sought to improve on this. He gave an account of his efforts in a letter to *The Times* of 19 August 1925:

I ran a Sunday experimental train from Waterloo to Bournemouth in 1 hour 50 minutes (110 minutes). On the Monday following the Chairman of the Company [Sir Charles Scotter] sent for me and said 'Don't do it again Fay, not in my time—not in my time.'

Not until 1911 was a regular timing of 120 minutes introduced and this was not improved on until the Southern's 116 minutes of 1936–9. In 1958 the 120 minute timing was re-introduced with the unprecedented feature of a stop at Southampton.

Meanwhile traffic was increasing on the West of England line. In 1901 a group of three trains left Waterloo for Exeter and beyond during the summer, at 10.50, 11.0 and 11.10 a.m., forerunners of the later system of running groups of reliefs to regular services at peak periods. On 1 August of that year vestibuled trains with diners were introduced. The South Western was never interested in developing overnight passenger travel. It took the second world war to allow the public on the 1.30 a.m. newspaper train east of Salisbury, and post-war travelling habits to require a heavy passenger train in its own right, expanding into 3 portions during the summer peak.

By 1923, the South Western had firmly laid the foundations of a service which was frequent, regular and punctual. Everywhere the average was excellent and there was nothing spectacular either in speed or waywardness. These were the foundations on which the Southern built up its own distinctive tradition.

POSTSCRIPT

Slip coach working, though never widespread, was introduced at an early date. There are indications in the South Eastern working timetable of January 1858 to suggest slip working; the first specific mention is of a slip from the 4.0 p.m. London Bridge to Brighton at Haywards Heath which appears in the LBSCR working timetable of April 1858. The first specific mention on the South

Eastern was in 1859 when the 12.20 p.m. London Bridge to
Ramsgate slipped a portion at Canterbury. An advertisement in
the *Kentish Gazette* states 'the train will convey first and second
class passengers to Canterbury where carriages are detached. The
train does not call there'. The South Western working timetable
of 1865 has a note alongside the 7.0 p.m. down Portsmouth stat-
ing 'a carriage for Weybridge will be detached from No. 53 Down
train by the Patent Break'. But the system never attained a wide
popularity in Southern England. In 1906 the Brighton had 5 slips
per day, the SE & CR had 3, while there were none on the South
Western. A solitary example, a portion for Forest Row off the
5·5 p.m. ex London Bridge was slipped at Horley until 30 April
1932.

From the beginning, second class was provided on all but a
few expresses, such as the *City Limited*. The South Western, after
a rather shady start in its treatment of third-class passengers, soon
became the best southern line in this respect. As a consequence of
a disaster in Sonning Cutting on 24 December 1841 which overtook a GWR goods train conveying third-class passengers in what
were virtually open goods wagons, it transpired that the South
Western was the only other line guilty of this practice. But the
Company became regenerate and soon after the Midland did so, it
provided third-class accommodation on all regular expresses, the
innovation being completed by 1883. Second was not finally
abolished until 22 July 1918, though electric services were first
and third only from their inauguration.

The Brighton, on the other hand, while it abolished second as
from 1 June 1911 on steam-worked suburban and a year later on
all other services except Continental ones, kept third-class passengers from its best trains until the first world war. Then even
the *City Limited* and the all-Pullman trains lost their first class
exclusiveness. In 1865, of the 12 down trains to Brighton, only
2 had third-class accommodation, while the *City Limited* was first
only. By the summer of 1867 third class was provided on 8 down
trains, but on none between the 11.0 a.m. and 5.5 p.m.; while
7 were first and second only and 2 first only.

The South Eastern started well in its treatment of third-class
passengers. In evidence before the Commission on Railways in
1844 the chairman said:

We give them seats; we give them sides above four feet high;
in fact we give them such accommodation that the number of
what we term the broad cloth is far greater than that of the
lower class . . .

Perhaps this was taken to heart by succeeding chairmen. Certainly during the Watkin régime third-class travel was not encouraged, for the declared reason that if that were done potential
second-class travellers would desert to it in large numbers. Third
class was therefore excluded from the best trains until the Managing Committee took over. Then, perhaps due to the more liberal
Chatham influence, third-class accommodation was, by 1906,
provided on all but the boat trains – as it had been from the start
on the Chatham, even on the *Granville* when it was inaugurated
in 1877. It was left to the Southern to abolish second class on the
South Eastern & Chatham section.

First class disappeared in 1941, permanently as it turned out,
on all trains starting and terminating their journeys within the
London Transport area. Three classes were retained on boat
trains until the introduction of the two-class system on the Continent in June 1956, when the British third class became second
everywhere.

In 1846 the single fare to Brighton was 14s. 6d. first and 9s. 6d.
second. This was very much less than coach fares, but ninety
years later, in 1936, the first and third single fares were 9s. 6d.
and 6s. 3d. respectively, while in 1958 (with third renamed
second) they were 12s. 6d. and 8s. 4d. This must be viewed against
the decline in the value of money since 1914, the increases in
monetary value of wages and incomes and the rise in their real
values. An average weekly wage for an unskilled worker in 1846
was 10s., in 1914 20s., in 1938 50s., and in 1958 200s.

Gladstone's Act of 1844 provided for one train a day on each
line to be run at third class fares not exceeding a penny a mile.
In due course this level became standard for all third class services
– by 1860 in the case of the Brighton. But railway managements
soon found that if a guaranteed full load could be found for a
train it could be run profitably even if considerably lower fares
were charged. Thus excursion trains were run from the very
beginning, either on special occasions such as race meetings or
military reviews, or regularly for day trippers to the seaside.

BRANCH LINES IN THE 'EIGHTIES

(37) *A '206' class ('Tadpole') diesel-electric unit on a train from Ashford crosses a train from Hastings ('205' class 'Hampshire' d/e unit) at Rye in 1981. Freight facilities have been withdrawn and the section to Appledore singled.*

(38) *Ryde Esplanade, August 1980. A train of '485' class (4-VEC) ex-London Transport units emerges from the tunnel that prevents the use of Southern electric stock.*

THE JUNCTION SCENE OLD AND NEW

(39) *Faversham, looking east. This scene, shortly before electrification in 1959, evokes a past age, not only by the steam locomotives but also the semaphore signals and the heavy mixed freight traffic.*
(40) *Fareham, looking west. The line to Southampton diverges immediately beyond the platforms. The tunnel on the original line to Eastleigh is through the wooded hill in the background, the later by-pass skirting it to the left. The aggregate terminal is on the right.*

CONNECTING WITH OTHER TRANSPORT MODES

(41) *Railair. A class '421/1' (4-CIG) unit arrives at Gatwick Airport on a misty March morning in 1980. The new air terminal is on the right, while alongside the rebuilding of the station nears completion. Contrast with the 1958 scene pictured in Plate 17.*

(42) *Continental boat train. A train from the Harbour branch leaves the reversing sidings at Folkestone East for Victoria in August 1981. It is headed by a motor luggage van (MLV), while behind is a '411' (4-CEP) unit.*

(43) *Park and Ride. A '423' class (4-VEP) unit leaves Guildford on a Portsmouth stopping service in 1980. The car park occupies the site of the locomotive depot.*

CONTEMPORARY FREIGHT

(44) *A class '73' (electro-diesel) loco heads a train of aggregate hoppers through Chichester on the short 7-mile run from the concrete plant at Drayton to the gravel pits at Lavant (July 1977)*

(45) *Speedlink. A '33' class (diesel-electric) locomotive, 33 052 'Ashford', leaves Dover Town with the 4.17 p.m. service to Warrington on 18 August 1981. The wagons had come over that morning from Dunkirk.*

(46) *A petroleum train from Fawley refinery to Salfords (for Gatwick Airport) takes the Fareham line at St Denys in September 1975. A '205' class unit leaves for Southampton.*

From the opening year, day return, season ticket, and excursion rates were in operation between London and Brighton. Nor were the excursions confined to third class. In 1845 a second-class excursion was advertised to Brighton on Sundays at 5s. return.

By the middle of the Victorian period, with the great growth of towns, the excursion habit had become firmly established. In *The Times* of 2 June 1865 excursions were advertised for Whit Sunday, 4 June, leaving Charing Cross at 7.30 a.m. for Canterbury, Ramsgate and Margate and at 8.5 a.m. for Folkestone, Dover and Hastings. On the Whit Monday there was an excursion at 7.30 a.m. for Ashford, Whitstable (via Canterbury), Herne Bay (via Sturry and coach), Sandwich and Deal. The fares to Whitstable and Herne Bay were 2s. 6d. by 'covered carriage' and 4s. 6d. second, and to all other stations 3s. 6d. and 5s. 6d. respectively. The reason for the exceptionally cheap fares to Herne Bay and Whitstable is revealed in the adjacent advertisement by the Chatham, who were charging the same fares to those resorts. In *The Times* of 3 June 1866 the Chatham was advertising day excursions to Calais via Dover at 7s. 6d. second and 10s. first.

These fares were cheap enough, and so were the season ticket rates. But both the Chatham and the South Eastern charged very high rates for ordinary first- and second-class travel – in an effort to recoup some of their excessive capital expenditure during the feud. It was this fact which prevented the fulfilment of the 1868 amalgamation proposals (see page 49), for the Brighton, a party to them, charged more normal fares. Foxwell and Farrer say of the South Eastern, 'its fares are enormous for first and second class'. But the Brighton did not escape criticism. 'The management', says Ahrons, 'naturally considered their railway to be a first class line and they backed up their opinion by making the best trains first class only and charging super first class fares.'

In spite of their comparatively short runs, the southern lines had a bad record for punctuality. It is true that with the reforms of Scotter and Fay the South Western managed to live down its former reputation, but the others were always bad time-keepers.

Writing in 1888, Foxwell says, 'The South Eastern is audaciously unpunctual, but so are all its southern neighbours'. Acworth in the same year complains, 'But habitual unpunctuality is another matter and there are too many trains in the South of

England which only exceptionally perform their work within the time alloted to them in the Time Table'. The Managing Committee was unable to make much progress and in a note on the Kent Coast services of 1912 the *Railway Magazine* says that some margins in the timetable are unrealistic and convey the impression that punctuality was neither expected nor obtained. In the case of the Kent lines this arose partly from congestion at Cannon Street and Herne Hill and partly from irregular arrivals of the steamers at the Channel Ports. But, concluded the *Railway Magazine*, it was also due to old and undersized locomotives and imperfect permanent way.

The Brighton was as bad. In September 1895 there was correspondence in *The Times* headed 'The Crawl to the South'. One letter describes a journey from Hastings:

> It was a light train running on a lovely afternoon. We swept on so rapidly the speed could not alarm the most timid. We did not escape a single stop, yet steamed into Victoria so proudly at 5.30 p.m. I felt sure we must have arrived unexpectedly early. The Time Table (a work of fiction) indeed made us arrive at 4.37, but this seems merely to be a printer's error.

Another correspondent, a regular traveller on the 10.31 p.m. Sutton to London Bridge claimed it was always at least 15 minutes late and on one occasion 93 minutes. Yet another correspondent complains that the progress of the 8.30 a.m. from Eastbourne north of Redhill 'seems to depend solely on the whim of the South Eastern signalman [at Redhill] whether he lets us through or holds us up to let a South Eastern slow train through'.

On 14 September 1895 *The Times* thundered forth with ponderous sarcasm in a leader alleging that the southern lines, unable to compete with the northern lines in speed, had apparently decided to set up unbreakable go-slow records.

The volume of traffic and consequently the service frequency increased over the years to such an extent that the southern companies were forced, often against their will, to become pioneers in signalling development.

From the very first, fixed signals were necessary on the London & Croydon Railway owing to the heavy traffic, while its signal engineer Hutton Gregory made history by interlocking signals and points at Bricklayers Arms Junction in 1844. But the trunk lines at first had none. They were forced to introduce them to supplement hand signalling in order to eliminate accidents similar to that on the approach to Nine Elms in 1840. A policeman had been sent by the Wandsworth station clerk to signal to an up fast that a mixed train had only just left. After waiting a minute or two the policeman returned, leaving the fast to go by without a signal and run into the rear of the mixed. On the South Eastern and the Brighton the fixed signals were semaphores after Croydon practice, but the LSWR used disc signals until the 1860s.

The trains were released into the section ahead under a caution or clear signal simply after an officially laid down interval had elapsed after the preceding train had passed. In practice this was sometimes when the latter was 'well out of sight' (Fay). The station staffs had no knowledge of the whereabouts of any train they could not actually see. The South Eastern however pioneered the use of the telegraph for reporting trains.

There remained the difficulty of stopping trains without continuous brakes, and this, together with the time interval system, was the greatest source of danger in the middle years of the Victorian era. The impossibility of pulling up at a signal at danger, because of some obstruction beyond, led to the erection of 'distance signals'. On the LSWR they began to appear between 1848 and 1850 and the South Eastern *Engineer's Report* of 18 August 1857 states that large numbers had been installed.

Drivers had thus some preliminary warning, but serious accidents were frequent. There are numerous macabre cartoons in *Punch* of the period. On 25 August 1861 a triple collision occurred in Clayton Tunnel due initially to three trains being despatched from Brighton at 8.28, 8.31 and 8.35 a.m. respectively. This was negligence by the assistant stationmaster, but the real fault was the time interval system. The inspecting officer urged the immediate adoption of the block system. This the LBSCR resisted on the grounds that 'by transferring much responsibility from the engine drivers, augment rather than reduce the risk of accident'. But public opinion forced it to give way.

The block system had been pioneered by Charles Walker on the South Eastern. Between 1852 and 1863 the whole railway had become so controlled and the Company was held up to the Brighton as a model at the time of the Clayton disaster. The Chatham was operated on the block system almost from its inception and by 1873 the whole line had been equipped. Soon after this the LBSCR and LSWR were converted to block working, the former by the end of 1877, when also all points and signals were interlocked.

Thanks to its signal engineer, W. R. Sykes, the Chatham kept in the van of progress. In 1874 he proposed to install his lock and block system, whereby the possibility of signalmen's errors were reduced by preventing a signal being pulled off again until the first train was clear and the next one properly accepted. Forbes opposed the scheme as the Chatham was virtually bankrupt, but the Board of Trade supported it. Lock and block was installed at Brixton experimentally and by 1882 the whole line to Dover had been equipped. In spite of delaying tactics from Watkin, the South Eastern soon followed suit, the introduction being hastened by a destructive rear end collision between two freight trains at Sevenoaks on 7 June 1884, caused by an error in working the Walker instruments. The other two lines were slower to adopt lock and block, but eventually it became standard throughout the region on suburban and main lines.

With increasing speeds the search for greater braking power began fairly early but without much success at first. On 9 June 1865 Creamer's patent chain brake did not stop the up 'Tidal' in time when some rails had been removed to repair a bridge near Staplehurst, even though a flagman had been put out and the day was clear. The accident was not unduly bloody, but became notorious by the presence of Dickens on the train. The shock contributed to his early death and indirectly hastened the introduction of air brakes. The LBSCR was a pioneer of the Westinghouse brake and sent an engine and 15 coaches so fitted to the Newark brake trials of June 1875. In 1882 the South Western standardized the vacuum brake. By 1889 when companies were required to return the number of vehicles equipped with the continuous brake, the South Eastern had 237 locomotives and 23 per cent of its coaches fitted and the LCDR 81 locomotives and 44 per cent of its coaches. The South Eastern had standardized the vacuum and the LCDR, not unexpectedly, the Westinghouse.

CHAPTER IX

The Southern and Electrification Policy

THE CREATION OF THE SOUTHERN

The Southern was the smallest of the four 'groups', each of 'constituent' and 'subsidiary' companies, established under the Railway Act of 1921, but in many ways it was the most efficient and the most successful. With an issued capital of £148·5 million and a route mileage of 2,178, the Southern Railway had a virtual monopoly of rail transport in Southern England.

Its constituents were the London & South Western, the London, Brighton & South Coast, the South Eastern, the London, Chatham & Dover, and the South Eastern & Chatham Railway Companies Managing Committee. To these were added fourteen subsidiary companies, including the lines leased and worked by the constituents, and the Isle of Wight Companies. The Southern was forced by the Railways Amalgamation Tribunal to accept the liabilities of three bankrupt companies, the Lee-on-the-Solent, the Brighton & Dyke, and the Freshwater, Yarmouth & Newport, but as already noted three others, the Hundred of Manhood & Selsey Tramways, the Kent & East Sussex Light, and the East Kent (Light), continued to be managed together with a number of other small railways elsewhere in Britain from the office of Lieut-Colonel H. F. Stephens at Tonbridge. The Southern inherited its predecessors' interests in joint lines, including the Somerset & Dorset, but the Midland & South Western Junction passed to the GWR.

The problems facing the Southern were numerous. The constituents had to be welded into a single unit, though the three sections into which the Company was divided – the Eastern, Central and Western – for long retained many features of pre-grouping origin. Arrears of maintenance resulting from the war had to be overcome: in this the Eastern section had the hardest task of all, for there still remained some aftermath of the Feud, and the Managing Committee's work was far from complete: it was not until 1924 that corridor stock could be introduced on the Kent Coast 'expresses'.

Then there was road competition. Though many routes had been started before the war, it was during the decade 1920–30 that the present close network of coach and rural bus services emerged. In addition, ex-Servicemen sank their gratuities in army-surplus lorries and joined in the almost unregulated free-for-all then obtaining in road haulage.

But the outlook was not unrelieved. Londoners were prepared to live further from their work to enjoy the benefits of less crowded housing and people everywhere were willing to spend a greater proportion of their income in travelling, both for work and pleasure. Living standards were rising and paid holidays becoming a condition of service in many industries. Finally, owing to the increased use of electricity, industry was no longer tied to the coalfields, but was migrating southward, especially to the Home Counties.

These opportunities the Southern grasped successfully. Commercial and operating statistics showed a constantly upward trend. This was accomplished by a large-scale programme of capital investment which had the double aim of increasing the operating frequency and reliability of services and decreasing the costs.

The greatest venture of all was electrification. It was not initiated by the Southern, but by two of its constituent companies prior to the first world war, who began suburban electrification. The London suburbs may be divided into a closely built-up *Inner Zone*, which had grown up by 1914 in connection with steam railway developments; a *Middle Zone* of lower density, growing up between the wars and dependent more on electric railways and on buses; and an *Outer Zone* which has developed discontinuously, chiefly since 1950 and with cars and railways as the main transport modes. The first two zones are covered in detail in Volume III, Chapters 3 and 4 dealing with the area served by the Southern Region. But passing reference must be made here in order to trace the emergence of the 'Southern Electric' system. In the early 1900s the South London line of the LBSCR, then its busiest suburban route, lost support at an alarming rate. Falling receipts could not be matched with lower costs, a reduction in the frequency of trains merely making the situation worse. The only alternative to closure was electrification. Operating costs would thereby be reduced, and the greater acceleration of electric trains would allow faster schedules and also a greater number of trains over the same track. These considerations, in fact, underlie all suburban electrification.

Some $8\frac{1}{2}$ route miles between Victoria and London Bridge were equipped with overhead lines at 6,600 volts A.C., and the public service began on 1 December 1909. The effect was immediate. Traffic which had fallen from 8 million to $3\frac{1}{2}$ million passengers annually quickly returned to 8 million and in 1920 reached 12 million.

Competition from electrified tramways and the District Railway had also been eating into the South Western's suburban traffic. In 1913, in announcing plans for electrification, the Company stated it had lost traffic worth £100,000 a year on the lines to be converted. These were to include the services to Wimbledon via Putney, the Kingston loop, the Thames Valley line to Shepperton, the Hounslow loop, and to Hampton Court and Guildford.

These projects, save the last, were inaugurated during the first world war. They are important to this history as they set the pattern for the post-1923 projects of the Southern. Partly as a result of a visit by Herbert Jones, the Company's electrical engineer, to the U.S.A. and partly because inter-running with District trains would be involved, the third rail system, using current at 600 volts D.C., was adopted.

By 1923 the Managing Committee had not embarked on any electrification project but had prepared schemes for the conversion of its inner suburban services. The Southern took over $24\frac{1}{2}$ route miles of A.C. traction from the Brighton, and 57 of D.C. from the South Western, together with the $1\frac{1}{2}$ miles of the Waterloo & City – 83 miles in all.

SUBURBAN ELECTRIFICATION

Electrification was urgent when the Southern took command partly because it would help solve growing congestion: from 1913 to 1923 the number of suburban passengers carried by the constituent companies had increased by 26 per cent, in addition to which the shortening of working hours meant shorter peak hours.

The plans already prepared by the constituent companies were therefore implemented as soon as possible. On the Western section electrification was carried out on the remainder of the 'new' Guildford line from Claygate to Guildford, together with the Raynes Park–Dorking North route and the connection between the two from Leatherhead to Effingham Junction. Public services on all these, 32 route miles, were inaugurated on Sunday 12 July 1925. It was a bold venture, for the areas served were still largely rural. But the expected traffic came. In 1927 the adjacent stations of Motspur Park and Worcester Park on the Dorking line issued 2,061 and 3,201 seasons respectively. In 1937 the figures were 22,808 and 31,984, a tenfold increase. At Dorking North itself sales of season tickets rose from 669 in 1924 to 2,737 in 1932.

On the Central section the electrification was completed between Balham, Selhurst and Coulsdon North and Sutton, just over 15 route miles. The new services were inaugurated on 1 April 1925.

The LSWR operated trains of one or two three-car units, but after 1920 marshalled trailers between the two units to make peak-hour trains of eight cars. The LBSCR used two- and three-car units and later sets of five vehicles, a motor-van in the centre of four coaches. Thus emerged the tradition, consistently followed by the Southern, of using 'multiple-unit' electric stock.

Meanwhile a most important decision had been reached, to electrify the Eastern section on the D.C. third rail system. Whether this was the result of South Western influence predominating in the new Company, or whether the system was actually cheaper to install and more efficient to operate, is not very clear. But it now became obvious that, since one or other system must go in the interests of standardization, it would be the A.C. This policy was officially announced on 9 August 1926.

From this stemmed a number of implications. First the Southern was now committed to the third rail system for future extensions, and the more lines converted the greater the commitment. Secondly, because of the gaps in the live rails at the numerous junctions and the danger of third rail in goods depots and marshalling yards, electric locomotives were not considered practicable. All freight, van and through passenger trains would therefore continue to be steam-hauled, and all electric services however distant the terminal points would be operated by multiple unit trains, the current being collected from a number of points all along the train. However far electrification extended, trains from destinations beyond would be steam-hauled all the way up to London. Even after electrification of the quayside lines at Newhaven, most of the boat trains continued to be headed by steam locomotives. Steam trains for the West of England traversed nearly 30 miles of electrified track extending to beyond Brookwood, and the Cardiff and Plymouth through trains reach Brighton over nearly 40 miles of electrified track from Farlington Junction.

The bulk of the Southern's revenue came from passengers, most of whom were travelling to and from London or going short distances between provincial centres. In 1931 £13·2 million was derived from passengers, £2·4 million from merchandise by passenger trains and £7·7 million from freight. In the same year the LNER, with three times the route mileage, took only £12·2 million from passengers but £29·9 million from freight. The Southern, in that year, ran nearly 24,500 passenger train miles per route mile, one of the highest figures in the world. Freight train mileage per route mile was only 3,000, however. Comparable figures on the LNER were roundly 10,000 for both passenger and freight trains.

Work on electrification of the Eastern section was started soon after grouping. Services were inaugurated in three stages. The first, covering 31 route miles, included the ex-LCDR main lines from Victoria and Holborn to Herne Hill and on to Bickley Junction to terminate at Orpington, the Catford Loop, and the Crystal Palace branch. Services began on 12 July 1925.

Stage two was inaugurated on Sunday, 28 February 1926, and consisted of the ex-South Eastern main line to Orpington, the Bromley North branch and the Mid-Kent lines to Beckenham Junction, Hayes and Addiscombe (25½ miles). Stage three (33½ miles) was the North Kent, Bexleyheath and Loop lines to Dartford. The full public service started on Sunday, 11 July 1926.

Strangely the main line from London Bridge to East Croydon was not yet electrified. This was partly because much of the traffic was carried in South Eastern trains to Caterham and Tadworth or Redhill. But it was the next section to be converted. Electric trains, now operated by the Central section, to Purley and thence to Caterham, and Tadworth and Tattenham Corner began running on 25 March 1928.

Meanwhile, work was going ahead on laying a third rail on the South London and Crystal Palace lines, together with extensions on lines hitherto steam worked; from Crystal Palace to Sydenham and to Beckenham Junction; and from Streatham to Sutton and thence to Epsom and to Epsom Downs. These very extensive new services were inaugurated on 17 June 1928.

Early on Sunday 22 September 1929, the last A.C. electric train left Victoria. The overhead coaching stock was converted to D.C. traction and the motor vans eventually became goods brake vans.

By the end of 1929 all the Central section services from London Bridge and Victoria to places within an area bounded by Beckenham Junction, Coulsdon North and Dorking North were operated by third rail electric trains. The new services were based on a 30 minute headway generally and 20 minutes to Caterham and Tattenham Corner.

There were now 277½ route miles of electrified track, representing 17 per cent of the track miles on the Southern. These were operated by 1,629 electric coaching vehicles, which ran nearly 35 per cent of the total passenger train miles. In the period since 1924 the electric train miles had grown from 5·0 million to 17·8 million, while the total steam passenger mileage had fallen only from 36·7 million to 33·8 million, an indication of the all-round improvement in service.

Electrification always involved much more than the substitution of a number of steam services by electric trains. To gain full benefit from conversion every opportunity was taken to reorganize track layout, modernize signalling and station accommodation, particularly in the central London area, where Cannon Street was provided with an entirely new layout and colour light signalling began to be installed.

On the operating side the timetables were completely recast to provide a more frequent service at regular intervals, considerably augmented during the morning and evening peak periods.

Fixed-interval services were introduced by the LSWR with the inauguration of its electrification and the Southern also made the practice a concomitant of all electrification extensions. This was due to Sir Herbert Walker, who urged that 'people don't like time-tables' and who insisted the best way to encourage rail travel was to make it possible for intending passengers to be at their local station at so many minutes past any hour and find a train stopping there.

It was to Sir Herbert Walker more than to any other one man the Southern owed the success of its electrification policy. Appointed general manager of the LSWR, the chairman described him as one of the most capable of the younger railwaymen. He went on to become general manager of the Southern until he retired in 1937, when he became a director until 1948. As *The Times* said, his great gift was that he 'knew what the public wanted . . . and he had the vision and will to scrap old ideas and old ways to make these things possible.'

THE EFFECTS OF ELECTRIFICATION

Electrification was the means of satisfying a rapidly developing social trend towards better and less congested housing. In many cases therefore conversion from steam working brought about social and economic changes in the country to the south of London as great as the building of the original lines there. Tens of thousands of houses were erected around existing market towns or rural villages or on agricultural land between. Many of them were built by the London County Council as slum clearance schemes and it is from this period that the large estates such as St Helier, Bellingham, Downham and Mottingham date. Many more were built by large firms of speculative builders, who invariably advertised the fact that their particular estate was contiguous to an electrified line.

In 1925 the continuously built up area of South East London extended no further out than Penge, Catford, Hither Green, Lee and Blackheath. Outside the built-up zone towns and villages were growing steadily, but outwards from their old centres with much open country between.

Today virtually the whole area up to and including the Cray Valley eastward and Hayes Common and Farnborough to the south is continuously built over save for public open spaces and sports grounds.

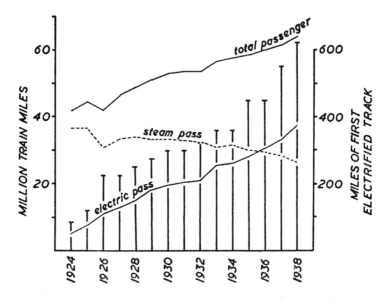

The effects of electrification on passenger train operation.

There was thus an enormous increase from stations within the area, which is covered in detail in the Greater London volume, but traffic trends on the Southern as a whole were revealing. According to the 1927 annual report the number of passenger journeys was up by 7½ million compared with 1926. But passenger journeys at ordinary fares were down by 12 million, compensated for by rises of 10 million in journeys at reduced fares, 4½ million at workmen's fares and 5 million on season tickets. Over the period 1930–39 passenger journeys on electrified lines of 1930 and lines subsequently converted rose by nearly 12½ million, but declined by nearly a million on the remaining steam services. It was only electrification and the reduced operating costs which allowed better services at cheaper fares. By those means rail transport was once more in a competitive position and new traffic was created.

MAIN LINE ELECTRIFICATION

Competition in the late 'twenties from bus, coach and private car
was increasing particularly fast between London and Brighton,
the distance being too short for the superior speed of the trains to
show to spectacular advantage. Frequent services, reliability, comfort and competitive fares provided the only solution.

In the 1929 Budget the Railway Passenger Duty (on first and
second class fares) was abolished on condition that the companies spent the capitalized value on improvement schemes. The
Southern's share was calculated at some £2 million and on 21
February 1930 it was announced that this would be spent on
electrification to Brighton.

The scheme included converting the 35 miles from Coulsdon
North to Brighton and the coast line to West Worthing. The short
section from Redhill to Reigate was also included. If the Quarry
and Redhill lines are counted as a single route, 47 miles were
converted in all.

In order to cover costs the chairman said an increase of 6 per
cent would be needed over the existing traffic. 'We are', he said,
'absolutely confident this result will be achieved, and we shall be
very much surprised if it is not achieved in the first year of working.' His estimate was conservative. The increase in the first year
proved to be 29 per cent.

Electric services were inaugurated as far as Three Bridges on
Sunday 17 July 1932. The Brighton services were officially inaugurated by the Lord Mayor of London on 31 December. At
12.5 a.m. on Old Year's Night the last scheduled steam train left
Victoria for Brighton, the full electric services going into operation on New Year's Day 1933.

The new services included features which are still standard
practices on the electrified main lines of the Southern. Overall
speeds were not greatly increased, if at all, over the fastest pre-
existing schedules. The fastest advertised time to Brighton was
60 minutes, a schedule first introduced in 1910 and remaining
until 1966, when it was reduced to 55. This has led to adverse
criticism, especially as 4-4-0 *Holyrood* with a 130-ton Pullman
special had done the trip in 48 minutes 41 seconds on 26 July
1903. The best recorded electric time is 47 minutes 44 seconds.

What is generally overlooked is that immediately prior to electrification there were only 7 down 60-minute trains. In the new timetables there was a train leaving Victoria every hour 'on the hour, in the hour'. In addition the great reserve of power was used to ensure regularity and punctuality. Summer and winter alike punctuality was exemplary and affected only in an occasional emergency.

In addition, the new services were frequent and at regular intervals; an express, semi-fast and stopping service from Victoria in each hour and a semi-fast and stopping service from London Bridge. 4·92 million train miles a year replaced 1·97 million steam train miles. Fares were made attractive and altogether much new custom was gained. Though the weather was bad, revenue in January 1933, the first month, was up by 5 per cent over the previous year. Over the Easter holidays tickets collected at Brighton were 78 per cent up and on the Bank Holiday, when 50,000 were collected, 127 per cent up.

Traffic continued to grow, especially with extensive post-war housing development along the line. In 1957 some 7,288 weekly seasons and 9,209 tickets for longer periods were issued at the single intermediate station of Horley. The siting of one of the New Towns at Crawley meant increased traffic, not only at Crawley, but also at Three Bridges on the main line.

The services were operated by multiple unit trains, the same system as the suburban lines. Initially there were 10 six-car express sets, each including a Pullman refreshment car. These sets are known as 6-PULs. Three five-car sets with increased first-class accommodation were provided for the *City Limited*, though since the war ordinary sets have been used, and 3 five-car all-Pullman sets for the *Southern Belle*, later the *Brighton Belle* (withdrawn 1 May 1972), which made three round trips a day. Stopping trains were operated by 33 four-coach sets. Many of the stopping trains carried an extra set for Reigate, detached at Redhill. This practice, inaugurated with the splitting of Caterham and Tattenham units at Purley, later became very widespread.

The immediate success of the Brighton electrification led to a decision to electrify the East Coast line to Hastings. There were still numerous steam trains on the main line, and the fewer of these there were, the greater the prospects of improved services.

But meanwhile some short extensions were carried out in the suburban zones. For example, on 6 July 1930 electric services were inaugurated to Windsor, and out to Gravesend. The first involved the conversion of 12¾ miles from Whitton Junction to Windsor and the replacement of steam trains from Waterloo. In the second case certain of the electric services already terminating at Dartford were projected over 7 miles of newly electrified route to Gravesend Central.

The lines to Sevenoaks were next dealt with: the new services to St Mary Cray began on 1 May 1934, and by both routes on to Sevenoaks on 6 January 1935. In this case the extensions were from Bickley Junction and from Orpington. Trains from Charing Cross, terminating at Orpington, were extended 8¼ miles to Sevenoaks. The Holborn–Catford Loop–Shortlands trains were projected on via Swanley Junction, involving 14¼ route miles of conversion. In the Sevenoaks area the increase in services was spectacular; wayside stations, hitherto served irregularly by a few stopping trains, now had a service with a headway of 20 minutes on the Swanley route and 30 on the Orpington. Sevenoaks (and Gravesend too) was still plentifully served by main line steam trains. Traffic from St Mary Cray greatly increased in consequence of the L.C.C.'s post-war housing estate built nearby at St Paul's Cray. There was also much housing development around Swanley and Chelsfield stations. But the more rigid enforcement of 'Green Belt' legislation in the post-war period prevented traffic increases elsewhere and it came as no surprise when the off-peak interval on the Swanley line was extended to 30 minutes in September 1958.

The Hastings electrification was completed in 1935, the new services being officially inaugurated on 4 July, the full public service beginning three days later. The lines converted included the East Coast line from Brighton to Ore, the station beyond Hastings. The reason for selecting Ore as terminus was the same as that for choosing West Worthing for the West Coast electrification, to reduce occupation of the limited platform accommodation at Hastings and at Worthing Central. The Keymer–Lewes line was also converted, together with the Eastbourne and Seaford branches. Finally the short connecting line from Copyhold Junction to Horsted Keynes was dèalt with. The official reason for this last was the relief of congestion at Haywards Heath if the local service from Seaford was terminated at Horsted Keynes. But one wonders if a shunting neck between up and down lines at Haywards Heath would not have been a cheaper solution. The Southern did however intend to electrify the Oxted and East Grinstead line, and thus this would have been a link in an alternative electrified route to Brighton. By the Hastings extensions 50 route miles were added to the Southern electric system.

Seventeen six-car pantry-equipped sets (6-PANs) were built in connection with this extension, but came to travel more widely. The normal practice was for a 6-PAN and a 6-PUL to run from Victoria to Eastbourne, whence only the latter unit continued on to Ore. For local services two-coach units were built; 10 had new steel bodies (2-BILs) and 33 were converted from steam stock (2-NOLs). Only the expresses ran through to London, the stopping trains working between Ore and Brighton, Seaford and Brighton, and Seaford and Horsted Keynes. There were now 26 per cent more through trains between London and Eastbourne and 55 per cent more to Hastings. 2·9 million electric train miles per year replaced 1·73 million steam train miles.

During the 1935 Parliamentary Session the Railways (Facilities) Act was passed. This was intended to stimulate capital investment in railway improvements at a time when the companies, though solvent, were suffering from the trade depression and road competition so much that there was little surplus to plough back. It was hoped too that capital expenditure would stimulate heavy industry and relieve unemployment. Under the Act the Treasury would guarantee principal and interest of loans floated by the railways. The Southern was quick to seize on the opportunity for further extensions, and stated it would convert all the important lines within a triangle London–Hastings–Portsmouth, and also to Reading and the Medway Towns.

In November 1935 plans for the 'Portsmouth Number One' project were announced. Ninety-five route miles were involved in the scheme. These included the main line from Hampton Court Junction to Pirbright Junction, the Portsmouth Direct from Woking Junction to Portsmouth Harbour, Pirbright Junction to Alton, and finally Staines to Weybridge via Virginia Water and

Chertsey. As in all previous main line conversions, power was taken at various points from the National Grid at 133,000 volts A.C., carried along the lineside at 33,000 volts and fed into the live rails through remotely controlled rectifying sub-stations. On the suburban system continuously manned rotary converter substations were used until the 1950s.

Public services for staff training began between Virginia Water and Weybridge on 30 November 1936 and from 3 January 1937 full services from Waterloo to Weybridge via Staines. At the same time some trains ran in steam timings out to Farnham via Guildford. Full services over the whole converted area began on 4 July.

For the Portsmouth expresses a departure was made from the six-car units. Four-car sets were built with gangways between the motor cars. Restaurant facilities in one unit would thereby serve the whole train. With gangway bellows swaying, a train approaching at speed was then a startling sight. With their usual flair for nicknames the railwaymen dubbed the new sets, with their single window on the near side of the bellows and 'blind' route indicator on the other, 'Nelsons'. Forty-eight sets were built, 19 with restaurant cars; 38 2-BIL and 2-NOL units were provided for local services.

Doubts were expressed of the wisdom of electrifying the Portsmouth Direct, with its scanty local traffic, the fluctuation between summer peak and winter minimum of the Isle of Wight traffic, and low level of commuting traffic. But the potential proved to be there and, as already said, in 1947 7¼ million passengers were carried compared with the 3 million in the year prior to electrification. This was partly the result of services on an unbelievably lavish scale for the line which had been the Cinderella of the South Western. The basic service was of one fast and two slow trains an hour each way, the latter detaching and attaching portions for Alton at Woking. 4·2 million electric train miles *per annum* replaced 2·2 million steam train miles. On summer Saturdays 4 fast trains an hour left Waterloo for Portsmouth and summer and winter alike the trains were well filled. Up to 100,000 people have used the services in a single Saturday. Commuting traffic from Farnham, Haslemere and Godalming grew considerably as did the station to station traffic.

Meanwhile, in the years since 1926 suburban traffic had grown.

Service frequencies were increased and 222 three-car sets converted from steam stock between 1928 and 1937.

The 'Portsmouth Number Two' project, which principally involved the Mid-Sussex line, was inaugurated on Saturday 2 July 1938. It had meant the conversion of 75 route miles; from Dorking North and from Three Bridges to Horsham and thence to the West Coast line at Arundel Junction; the West Coast line itself from West Worthing to Havant; and the Bognor Regis and Littlehampton branches. Once more the train mileage was doubled from 2 million steam train miles to 4 million, while steam train mileage on connecting branches was also increased. Again, the effects of frequent services at regular intervals and of competitive fares soon made itself felt, for in the first six months receipts rose by 13 per cent. The writer recalls how an examination of the books at Arundel in 1939 showed great increases not only in bookings to London but in short distance traffic to Littlehampton and Bognor. The $3\frac{3}{4}$ million passengers carried in the year ending July 1938 had swollen to $7\frac{1}{4}$ million in 1947.

Expresses left Victoria hourly, travelling via Sutton and Dorking. At Barnham they divided, one part going on to Portsmouth and the other to Bognor. The fast trains to Worthing via the Cliftonville curve were extended to Littlehampton. Local services ran between Brighton and Portsmouth and between Three Bridges and Bognor, ingenious dovetailing at Barnham and Ford ensuring good connections in all directions. Suburban services were extended from Dorking North to Horsham. Thirty-nine 4-COR sets, 13 with buffets, and 68 2-BIL sets were built.

In February 1938 steam locomotive enthusiasts in the rapidly widening aesthetic desert of multiple units had something of a reprieve when it was announced that the Sevenoaks-Bopeep line would not, after all, be electrified. There were two considerations given officially: that the narrow tunnels would entail special stock, thus reducing the inter-availability which was one of the advantages of electrification; and that new locomotives and coaching stock had in any case just been provided. The latter were narrow and therefore would not be of use elsewhere. In fact the 'Hastings' steam stock has been widely used elsewhere.

Electrification in the Thames Valley was going ahead, and on 31 December 1938 the last steam train left Waterloo for Reading.

This entailed the conversion of the 20¼ miles on from Virginia Water. On 1 January 1939 electric services were inaugurated on the branch from Ascot to Ash Vale, and from Aldershot Junction to Guildford, 19¼ miles. There were now two outer suburban services along the Windsor line from Waterloo, each at half-hourly intervals. The one split at Ascot to serve Reading and Guildford via Aldershot, the other split at Staines to serve Windsor and Weybridge. Thirty-six electric trains from Waterloo to Reading daily replaced 20 steam. The average time was reduced by 11 minutes. This seems a small saving, but the electric trains had additional stops, giving the intermediate stations a more regular service. Traffic from this much sought after residential area subsequently increased, while in the 1950s one of the New Towns took shape at Bracknell.

On 2 July 1939 the 53 route miles of the extensions in the Medway area came into service. The lines affected were from Swanley to Gillingham; Otford to Maidstone East; Gravesend to Strood and thence over the Toomer Loop to Gillingham; Strood to Maidstone West. To work the new services another type of unit, the 2-HAL, was introduced, 78 sets being provided. An hourly service from Charing Cross split at Strood for Gillingham and Maidstone, while Gravesend suburban trains were extended to Gillingham with connections at Strood for Maidstone. Hourly trains from Victoria were divided at Swanley for Gillingham and Maidstone. The local services in the area were thus greatly improved; that to Maidstone East was increased from 24 to 43 trains a day and the average time reduced from 106 to 93 minutes.

'SOUTHERN ELECTRIC'

This concluded the 1935 programme. Plans were already afoot for further extensions, notably the Oxted line, but the war and its aftermath prevented any further work being started until 1956.

By 1939 the 'Southern Electric' system, as it had come to be widely known, had grown into one of the largest electrified systems in the world. It was certainly the largest third rail system. In 1929 17·8 million electric train miles were run over 277½ route miles and 763 track miles. By 1938 these figures had increased to 622 route miles and 1,774 track miles over which 37·3 million train miles were operated. In 1936, for the first time, electric mileage exceeded steam passenger mileage and in 1938 it was all but 60 per cent of the total. The figures of train miles per route mile in 1929 and 1938 were practically identical, about 60,000 in each case. But it must be remembered that the more recently electrified lines had lower traffic densities than the approaches to the London termini, already converted in 1929. Route for route there had everywhere been a real increase in traffic.

This was the outcome of a continuous rise in passenger traffic. On the whole Southern Railway in 1923 there were 198 million passenger journeys at ordinary and workmen's fares, 208 million in 1932 and 237 million in 1938. In 1923 there were 170,000 season ticket holders, 183,000 in 1932 and 223,000 in 1938. In 1929 an average of 294,000 passengers arrived daily at the London Termini, in 1938, 370,000.

That electrification was the main factor in this increase was revealed by Sir Herbert Walker in 1929. Receipts on the Dorking and 'New' Guildford lines had increased 38 per cent since electrification, but on the steam-worked lines to Guildford via Woking and to Weybridge via Staines they were $\frac{1}{4}$ per cent down, in spite of similar traffic and level of fares. He also revealed in 1933 that 20 million electric-train miles had replaced 8 million steam, but working costs were increased by only £206,140. On the other hand receipts were up £1·3 million. The net increase represented $17\frac{3}{4}$ per cent on capital invested in conversion.

But the Southern shared with all suburban systems the discrepancy between the daily maxima and minima of traffic flow. 21·3 per cent of the trains entering the London Terminus in 1938 did so between 7.0 a.m. and 10.0 a.m. and they carried 65·7 per cent of the passengers. If in fact passenger flow had been constant, there would have been 150 passengers per train, a comfortable load for a three-car suburban set.

In addition the morning and evening peak traffics had steadily been concentrated into a shorter period. In 1929 102,000 passengers reached the London termini during the busiest hour, in 1939 123,812, and in 1956 171,000. As C. P. Hopkins, general manager of the Southern Region, said 'These figures summarize the whole problem of the Southern Region's suburban traffic.'

Plant provided for the peak period thus stood idle or under-used for most of the day. In addition the overcrowding, particularly on services to and from North-west Kent, had attained serious proportions. Services were increased by electrification and re-signalling to the maximum, but this was still not enough. It was therefore decided to increase the capacity of the trains. In 1941 appeared the oddly-nicknamed 'Queen of Sheba' (I Kings, chapter 10, verse 2: 'and she came to Jerusalem with a very great train'), a four-car set with increased seating capacity, including six-a-side, an innovation on the Southern. After the war the standard suburban formation came to be 2 four-car units and gradually the older sets were replaced by semi-open and open four-car sets. An unsuccessful experiment was the building of two double-decked four-car units which went into service on 2 November 1949. Instead of building more of these it was decided to increase accommodation by lengthening the trains by introducing two-car units to make 10-coach trains. The conversion scheme involved the lines from Charing Cross and was carried out between 1954 and 1957.

As has been said, the full benefits of electrification could not have been realized without concurrent improvements in signalling. On main lines numerous colour light intermediate signals were installed and junctions such as Woking were equipped with power signalling. By 1939 there was a total of 286 route miles controlled by colour lights. By 1954 the whole of the line from Victoria and London Bridge to Brighton via Quarry was so equipped. In addition the upper quadrant was adopted as standard on all semaphore installations.

The high signalling standards were reflected in the excellent safety record of the Southern Railway. In its quarter century of existence there were only three major train accidents. Of these only one, in which a suburban electric train ran into the rear of another between Purley Oaks and South Croydon on 24 October 1947, was the result of a signalling failure.

Much of the coaching stock taken over in 1923 was extremely antiquated. So concurrent with electrification an extensive programme of steam stock building was begun. All coaches had corridors and gangways and by the mid-thirties the average standard on the Southern was probably higher than on other railways. Its best might not be so opulent as the 'Louis Seize' restaurant cars of the LNER, but there were no such antiquities as the ex-North London four-wheel sets which were still trundling disgruntled commuters up to the Northern Heights in 1935.

A report on a minor accident at Cannon Street on 13 May 1925 reveals that the three trains involved, the 4.37 p.m. ex Erith, the 4.48 p.m. ex Bromley North and the 5.24 p.m. for Ashford were formed of 12 six-wheelers and a bogie coach, 10 six-wheelers, and 9 non-corridor bogies respectively. Ten years later this would have seemed scarcely believable and in 1936 the few remaining six-wheelers were seen for the last time on Saturday reliefs to the Kent Coast, and occasionally thereafter for a year or two on hop pickers' specials.

Passenger stock was built for the most part in sets, usually of three or four coaches. The pre-war coaches were good and the post-war sets among the best in the country. Pools of sets which could be used on any service were kept at the carriage depots and this, together with complex stock workings, led to the use of modern corridor stock even on local workings.

The Southern was fortunate in its two chief mechanical engineers. R. E. L. Maunsell joined the South Eastern & Chatham in 1913. During his years of office he welded the miscellaneous stock of the constituent companies into a coherent whole, and designed a number of most successful new locomotive classes. The best known were his passenger types, the 'King Arthurs', 'Lord Nelsons' and 'Schools', but his mixed traffic engines, 4-6-0 and 2-6-0, have borne the brunt of goods and holiday extras alike.

Maunsell was succeeded in 1937 by O. V. S. Bulleid, a man of revolutionary ideas. But unfortunately war and nationalization prevented the full flowering of his genius. As it is he has left his mark in his 'Pacifics' and in the powerful and ugly Q1 0-6-0s. He has also left his mark in his fine post-war passenger coaches.

The Southern took over 2,285 locomotives and in 1948 handed on 1,858. It had built 520 and 1,338 had survived from the constituent companies. Strangely enough, in spite of electrification, locomotives of Brighton origin had the highest survival rate.

Steam services from London were put on a standardized departure basis for the most part. Thus West of England trains left Waterloo on the hour and Bournemouth line trains at 30 minutes past the hour. Services to the Kent Coast and Hastings were improved, especially in business hours. The fastest trains now reached Salisbury, 83¾ miles, in 86 minutes, Bournemouth, 108 miles, in 116 minutes and Folkestone, 71 miles, in 80 minutes. But paths still had to be found for the numerous 'specials' that were a feature of Southern operating. In 1937 there were 11,874 non-scheduled trains of passenger stock on London Central Division alone. These included 1,023 race specials, 1,480 extra boat trains, 259 football specials, and 477 extra parcels and mail trains.

The Continental services received much attention. During the 'thirties the exchange rates with France were particularly favourable and there was a great increase in holiday traffic. On an August Saturday in 1937 one lineside observer recorded 80 boat trains to and from Folkestone and Dover.

Indeed there were so many boat trains that some were diverted to Cannon Street. The *Special Traffic Notice* of 9 July 1938 provides for 34 down boat trains, 16 up and 4 up empties. Of these 10 left and 5 arrived at Cannon Street. There was also an excursion from Tunbridge Wells to Folkestone Harbour for Boulogne. This was the heyday of the works outing and accommodation for 115 was to be reserved on it for 'Kelsey Brewery' party, while 4 first-class compartments were to be reserved for 'Directors'. We are left hoping Tonbridge duly arranged all this on the 7.5 a.m. (Empties) for Tunbridge Wells and that a good time was had by all in criticizing, doubtlessly unfavourably, the French beer.

On 15 May 1929 the all-Pullman *Golden Arrow* was inaugurated. Known to the enginemen on account of its weight as 'The White Elephant', it soon became so to the Traffic Department and in 1932 included ordinary coaches. It reappeared in all-Pullman guise on 15 April 1946 and during the succeeding austerity-ridden years its immaculate condition and luxurious furnishings served as a symbol of hope. In spite of air competition it maintained its Pullman exclusiveness until 1957, by which time its work was done, for the Southern was not only once more in possession of its high standards, but was ready for a great step forward.

An altogether bolder objective was the introduction of a train ferry service. Proposals for one from Dover were first made in 1868 and again in 1905, though then the South Eastern & Chatham proved unco-operative. In 1911 however the Brighton sought powers for one from Newhaven, but the first world war intervened. About 1930 the Southern began to consider the scheme seriously. At first it selected Richborough, from which a military train ferry had operated during the war. But Dover is less liable to silting, though tidal amplitude averages 25 feet. Eventually therefore Dover and Dunkirk were chosen as terminals and docks built to allow on or off loading at all states of the tide.

Three ferries were built, each accommodating 12 sleeping cars or 40 wagons and also 30 motor cars. They went into service on 14 October 1936. Goods wagons are conveyed by day and sleepers by night. By 1956 tonnage was double that of 1938 and by 1962 double again.

The outbreak of war in 1939 put an immediate end to any further developments the Southern was then preparing, though fortunately there was no major uncompleted work on hand. The heavy programme of capital investment just described had placed the railway on a sound footing for dealing with increased traffic and the general ravages of war.

The year 1945 however found all four main line companies in a similar predicament to that of their predecessors in 1918. Arrears of maintenance were very serious. But inflation had reduced the value of profits made during the war years which in any case had to be shared with the Government, and it was unlikely they could find unaided the vast capital sums needed for their rehabilitation. Nor was their task made more possible by a Government pledged to nationalization, which maintained a rigid control through the wartime Railway Executive – which continued after 1945. On 1 January 1948 the Southern was nationalized, and the Southern Railway Company was dissolved on 10 June 1949 after just over a quarter of a century of most useful service.

SOUTHERN REGION – THE EARLY YEARS

The Transport Act of 6 August 1947 authorized the vesting in the British Transport Commission from 1 January 1948 of all transport to be nationalized. Management of the main-line railways was delegated by the Commission to the Railway Executive. Its Southern Region took charge of all lines of the Southern Railway, together with any other lines south of the ex-GWR main line via Reading and Newbury that were not dead-end branches. The Southern Region thus took over the Reading–Basingstoke branch of the GWR, the Didcot, Newbury & Southampton's line south of Enborne Junction (Newbury), the former Midland & South Western Junction south of Grafton South Junction (near Savernake), and also the Kent & East Sussex and the East Kent (Light) Railway.

In Southern England there have been few boundary changes of importance, though control of the Southern end of the ex-Midland & South Western Junction was relinquished to the Western Region from 1958 to 1961. But the transfer of the West of England line west of Salisbury in 1963 had important consequences on services from Waterloo to the West. In 1968 eight trains were running daily to Exeter, but not beyond.

The first years of nationalization were ones of painful integration by the Railway Executive of the four large Groups. Material shortages prevented any serious beginning on the programme of capital investment, which was a declared advantage of nationalization. Nor did the co-ordination with other forms of transport, which was another, proceed very far.

But much was achieved by economies from standardization of equipment. From 1950 standard locomotives and coaches began to appear on the Southern Region's steam services, though by its nature the electric system remained highly individual. On the whole it was a period of slow return to something like the pre-war level of services, a much nearer approach on the Southern than in other parts of the country.

The Transport Act of 6 May 1953 was a landmark. It aimed at decentralization and also relieved the Transport Commission of its duty to promote transport co-ordination, thus reversing the policies underlying the 1947 Act. The Railway Executive was dissolved and from 1 January 1955 the Southern Region was controlled by a Board, responsible to the Commission, but with a considerable measure of autonomy.

Further decentralization was brought about by the creation of three Divisions with power to make important decisions in the commercial field. They were designated 'South Eastern' (1958), 'South Western' (1961) and 'Central' (1961) and it was regretted no title incorporating 'Brighton' or 'South Coast' could be devised for the latter. Thus the wheel of nomenclature had come almost full-circle, and most significant of all was the great, though unconscious, tribute to the Southern Railway, that 'South Eastern' could be proudly adopted in 1958, whereas in 1923 it was more a term of abuse.

The Southern soon began to re-assert the strong individuality which springs from the history and geography outlined in these pages. The first outward sign was the rapid return of the familiar green livery to the steam rolling stock, a livery the electric stock never lost. But of more moment was that by 1959 not only had 1939 standards been regained everywhere, on many routes they had been greatly surpassed.

In 1955 the Government turned its attention to the grave arrears of investment in the railways. They had for ten years been low on the list of priorities for allocating scarce capital resources, but by now the country had overcome the worst set-backs brought about by the war. It was therefore agreed the Transport Commission's £1,200 million modernization plan should be implemented.

But to justify this investment it was necessary to increase revenue by expanding traffic. While passengers and parcels increased slowly, coal and minerals remained more or less constant and merchandise showed a steady downward trend. The railways were failing to gain any real share in the expanding movement of goods and passengers which was overcrowding the main roads with 'C' licence lorries and with private cars. Since alone of the Regions the Southern depended more on passengers than freight and since it was the only means of transport for so many of its commuters, its position was the most secure.

It was thus less affected when it became apparent that parts of the 1955 plan had been hastily drawn up and the cost underestimated. A re-appraisal was therefore carried out in 1959, which stressed the need to concentrate modernization on traffic flows best suited to rail transport and to abandon over the next five years many services which could never become viable.

First fruits of modernization blossomed on the Tunbridge Wells and Hastings line, where rapidly increasing commuter traffic was swamping the ageing steam trains. 23 six-car diesel-electric multiple units were used to maintain a regular interval service of increased frequency. Running times were reduced, but even more important was the greater reliability attained. A few units were used along with steam trains from May 1957, the full service beginning on 9 June 1958. A 40 per cent increase in traffic was soon recorded. At the same time an interval service was provided by 4 two-car units on the Bexhill West branch and between Hastings and Ashford.

In September 1957 interval-services of greatly increased frequency were introduced in the Southampton area. These clearly demonstrated the advantages of diesel traction where traffic density does not warrant electrification. Operating costs were considerably reduced. A daily mileage of 6,058 replaced 2,587 steam train-miles. Yet this was maintained by 18 two-coach units instead of 20 steam locomotives and 42 coaches. This was made possible by the high availability of the sets, 17 being needed on the road each day. By the end of the first year a 56 per cent increase in passenger numbers and a 48 per cent increase in revenue had been attained. It was soon found necessary to add an extra coach to each set and, as the services were extended, another 11 sets were built. The 19 three-car units for the Oxted lines brought the Southern's diesel-electric multiple-unit fleet to 75 sets.

The first extension of electrification embraced the 78 route miles from Gillingham to Ramsgate, Faversham to Dover and the branch to Sheerness. The new services were inaugurated on 15 June 1959, almost exactly twenty years after the previous extension of electric services, to Gillingham and Maidstone on 2 July 1939. An hourly express now ran from Victoria to Ramsgate, from which a Dover Priory portion was detached at Gillingham. The hourly semi-fast trains from Victoria and Charing Cross to Gillingham were extended to Sheerness and Ramsgate respectively and an hourly Sheerness–Dover service started. At peak periods and at holiday times services were augmented. In the first six months ticket sales expanded by a third and excursion traffic doubled. That this was not solely due to an exceptionally fine summer was proved by the November 1959 traffic being 30 per cent up on that of the previous November. At Rainham there was an increase of 300 per cent and at Canterbury East one of 100 per cent.

Phase II involved converting another 132 route miles, bringing the Southern's electrified mileage to 924½; from Sevenoaks to Dover and Ramsgate; from Maidstone East to Ashford and Maidstone West to Paddock Wood; Ashford–Canterbury West-Minster; and the Folkestone Harbour branch. Progress was so rapid some electric trains began running in existing schedules between Dover and Ramsgate on 2 January 1961 and between Charing Cross and Dover on 12 June 1961. The full service, representing a proportionally greater increase in frequency than with Phase I, began on 16 June 1962. An express now left Charing Cross each hour for Ashford, where it was divided, the two parts reaching Ramsgate via Dover and via Canterbury West. A semi-fast left hourly for Margate via Dover, detaching an all-stations portion for Ashford at Tonbridge.

The third rail was then extended from Sturt Lane Junction to Bournemouth (80 miles). The 4½-mile Lymington branch was also converted. During 1966 some services were operated by electric trains, but the full service started on 10 July 1967. The fast trains reached Southampton in 70, and Bournemouth in 100 minutes. Steam was eliminated on the Southern.

Again it was realized the full benefits could not be attained without improvements in civil engineering and signalling works. Several short sections were quadrupled, electrified passing loops laid and junctions re-aligned. Ashford and Folkestone Central were completely rebuilt and 41 other stations modified. The lines between Victoria and Ramsgate and Charing Cross and Archcliffe Junction (Dover) were now controlled throughout by colour-light signals and on the latter only eight signal boxes were regularly open on the 70 miles between Hither Green and Archcliffe Junction. Farnborough–St Denys (44 miles) was controlled by two.

In Kent 59 four-car corridor sets (BEP/CEP now 410/411) and 46 two-car sets (EPB now 416) were provided for normal services and boat trains. But operation of other trains showed new features. In 1941 the Southern Railway put in service a practicable third-rail locomotive on the Central section and built two more after the war. The Kent project included 24 electric locomotives and these were used on the 'Golden Arrow' and the 650-ton 'Night Ferry'. They were also used on parcels and freight trains, especially the *Grand Vitesse* services of train-ferry wagons, of which there were four each way daily in 1967.

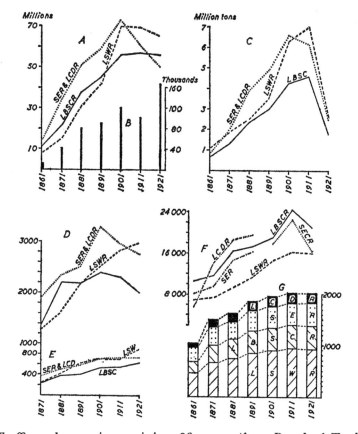

Traffic and operating statistics 1861–1921 (from Board of Trade returns 1861–1911) Ministry of Transport 1921.

A. Passenger tickets sold (all classes except seasons)
B. Number of season ticket holders
C. Freight traffic (goods and minerals)
D. Number of coaches (including electric motor coaches and trailers)
E. Number of locomotives
F. Passenger train miles per mile of route per annum
G. Route miles open to traffic (including leased and worked lines)

Note:

1. Decline in SER and LCDR passenger journeys 1901–21 due to tramway competition in the inner London suburbs not met, as by the Brighton and South Western, by electrification.

2. Coal strike of 1921 accounts for low freight figures for that year.

3. Number of coaches somewhat misleading. Fewer bogie coaches are required to seat the same number of passengers, but separate figures for bogie, six and four wheel stock are not available.

4. Figures for the LSWR are for the whole railway. In figure F therefore the inclusion of the lines with low traffic densities west of Salisbury give lower traffic density figures than would be the case if separate figures for the LSWR in Southern England could be given.

5. The particularly dense traffic of the LCDR due to the very intensively occupied lines between Longhedge, Herne Hill, and Ludgate Hill.

These locomotives were equipped with pantographs, but although some yards have overhead lines, it would be too costly to equip all sidings. So diesel locomotives were used on many freight trains over electrified routes as well as for operating unconverted branches. From 26 February 1962 steam was eliminated from the South Eastern Division, and by January 1964 there were only 34 daily steam duties on the Central Division, mostly on services scheduled for early withdrawal.

In 1962 six 'electro-diesel' locomotives were put into service. This was a new departure. Current was normally obtained from the third-rail, but a 600-h.p. diesel engine was fitted to allow operation over non-electrified lines. In 1964, 30 more were ordered and later a number of electric locomotives were converted. They can be used in multiple with ordinary electric stock, as can the motor-vans used on boat trains, which have batteries to allow them to be worked on the Dover quayside.

Experiments with these locomotives proved high speed 'pull and push' trains possible. On the Bournemouth line 4-REP (class 430) power units (11) propel one or two non-motored 4-TC units (491) (28) to Bournemouth Central whence they are taken on to Weymouth by diesel locomotives which propel them back, eliminating shunting movements. Trains of old 'Brighton' electric stock, displaced by the 54 new four-car units, powered by a diesel locomotive on the 'pull and push' system were used on the Oxted line. The system was later used between Edinburgh and Glasgow and is capable of further extension.

The 1950s were for the Southern mainly a period of rehabilitation and consolidation after the war; a period during which all arrears were made good. But the early 1960s brought with them several signposts to the future of the Region.

In the first place the 1961 census revealed how much faster Southern England was growing than was the rest of the country. The 1951–61 intercensal increase for England and Wales was 5·3 per cent, but Kent, Surrey and East Sussex all had increases of between eight and nine per cent, while Hampshire had one of 11·6 per cent and West Sussex 27·4 per cent.

Allied to this was the continued decline in the population of the County of London coupled with an increase in employment there. Long-distance commuting was obviously increasing. At the same time most south-country towns were attracting new industries at much faster rates than the national average. The opportunities and the problems facing the Southern Region in the early 1960s were similar to those the Southern Railway so successfully faced in the early 1920s.

But ultimate policy decisions lay beyond the Regional Board and the attitude of the Government was changing. On 1 August 1962 yet another Transport Act became law. In almost all but de-nationalization the intentions of 1947 were now finally reversed. Transport co-ordination, a dead-letter, was officially buried, and above all the railways were no longer to be a utility. Commercial viability, not service, was now their prime duty. To this end they were given almost complete freedom to vary rates and also passenger fares outside the London Transport Area. At the same time they were relieved of common-carrier liability. Transport Users' Consultative Committees could no longer pronounce on quality or cost of service, but only on the possibility of hardship from withdrawal of passenger services. There was no means of questioning the sometimes suspect figures produced by British Railways to support any measure they deemed necessary.

Under the Act the Transport Commission was dissolved and from 1 January 1963 British Railways were vested in the new Railways Board. Meanwhile, pursuing these new policies, the Minister of Transport appointed the Stedeford Group to enquire into the future part to be played by the railways. Its findings have not been published, but one of its members, Dr Richard (later Lord) Beeching, was appointed Chairman of the Transport Commission (and later of the Board) for five years from June 1961.

THE BEECHING PERIOD

Charged with seeking commercial viability, Dr Beeching presented his proposals in March 1963 in the report popularly known as the 'Beeching Plan'. In the light of the 1959 re-appraisal it was by no means revolutionary, and, within the terms of reference, many of its proposals were sound enough. Briefly, the only way to viability was to concentrate on keeping and attracting traffic suited by its nature to rail and to relinquish attempts to carry the rest. This would entail the abandoning of one third of the railway system, which carried an estimated one per cent of the total traffic.

But the detailed reasoning of the report was disappointing. Technological developments were ignored, particularly the potentialities of electrification, so important to the Southern. Also no account was taken of any regional differences, the whole railway system being assumed to be homogeneous. The unique place of the Southern was unrecognized. The approach to a period of rapid economic change was also inflexible. The plan failed also to recognize the consequences of the imminent 'container revolution' on the ports, or the rapid growth of continental traffic.

In addition, two traffics were singled out as being no longer profitable and therefore to be shed as soon as possible, holiday and commuter (though the railway was recognized as being vital to London's suburban traffic). Rigid application of this policy boded ill for the Southern, for even in the early 1960s these traffics remained the core of its carrying.

In some basic assumptions, therefore, the Beeching Plan was antipathetic to the equally significant 'Buchanan Report' of November 1963, which was just as eagerly accepted by the Government. Professor Buchanan underlined the revolutionary social consequences of the explosive increase in urban motor traffic, and stressed that public transport must always play a vital part and therefore should not be allowed to decay. In many senses Southern England was fast becoming a vast urban region.

Traffic density in Southern England was generally too high to entail the drastic curtailment of the system experienced in other regions. The closures have been detailed elsewhere in the book but it can be said that virtually all affected non-electrified lines, even though some carried more passengers than certain electrified lines. There were to be no bold experiments such as reducing stations to 'bus-stops' (though this was subsequently tried for a time south of Tunbridge Wells) or the singling of double track. Faith in the potentialities of frequent diesel-electric services had also been lost, for both the new Hampshire and East Sussex services suffered heavily.

CHAPTER X

1965–80: The Unfinished Story

CHANGES IN GOVERNMENT POLICY

The appointment in 1965 of Mrs Barbara Castle as Minister of Transport resulted in Government recognition of the continuing role of railways and of the importance of overall transport planning. In 1967 Mrs Castle announced that the rail network would be stabilized at 11,000 route miles (as against the 8,000 envisaged in the 1965 British Railways Board Report, 'The Development of the Major Railway Trunk Routes', often called 'Beeching II'). The Beeching period of extensive line closures was ending. In spite of periodic alarms, the system, especially in the Southern Region, has shown a remarkable stability, at least to the time of writing. In addition, the 1968 Transport Act introduced two new and important concepts. It empowered the Minister to make infrastructure grants for rail schemes in urban areas on the same basis as road grants and to subsidize 'socially necessary' passenger services.

In the event the Southern received no infrastructure grant like that by which the Great Northern suburban electrification was carried out. But the London and South East suburban services were supported *en bloc*, while other individual services, such as that between Brighton and Portsmouth, were identified and costed for support. Under the 1974 Railways Act, however, grant-aid to individual services under the 'Cooper Formula' (named after the accountants who prepared it) was given up. Instead a single Public Service Obligation (PSO) grant was paid on the whole network of passenger lines. Freight only lines, such as the Hundred of Hoo and the Fawley branches, were expected to cover the whole of their costs. On passenger lines, such as Reading–Redhill–Tonbridge, the freight traffic was expected to cover its direct operating costs and pay a 'rental' towards fixed track and signalling costs.

The 1973 Local Government Act laid transport planning duties on the 'shire' counties and empowered them to support the re-opening of passenger stations and improvements to services. Perhaps because station closures and the run-down of local services had been less, these measures have had little effect on the Southern Region. Unfortunately the 1970 London (Transport) Act, under which the London Transport Railways and Central (red) Buses came under GLC control, made no statutory provision for co-ordination with BR. Nor has there been much sign of co-ordination between the latter and the National Bus Company. Green Line services (since 1971 an NBC responsibility) still carry declining numbers of passengers to Central London instead of focusing on railheads such as East Croydon, while in the mid-1970s Southdown were operating express buses in direct competition with the very adequate Brighton–Portsmouth rail service.

Unfortunately, since the passage of the 1973 Act successive Governments have failed to formulate any coherent and long-term transport policy. This is reflected in the 1980 Transport Act, which encouraged diversion of medium- and long-distance passenger traffic from rail. If effective, rail revenue will decline faster than costs, as always. Losses will mount, but widespread closures, especially in Southern England, will be politically unacceptable, so subsidies will increase. In any case, in view of the uncertainties attached to long-term petroleum supplies, any run-down of electric railways would be an act of short-sighted folly, but one which Governments seeking short-term savings might well commit.

CHANGES IN PASSENGER TRAFFIC

The period has been one of considerable change in traffic flows and in service patterns. Between 1960 and 1975 commuter traffic increased on the longer-distance services, particularly between Sevenoaks and Ashford, Gillingham and Herne Bay and Woking and Basingstoke. On the latter section season-ticket sales virtually doubled between 1965 and 1970. At the same time peak-period traffic declined on the inner suburban services. But since 1975 there has been something of a reversal of these trends. At the same time office employment in Central London declined from 1970 onwards, while peripheral centres grew. In the case of Croydon the increase was from 14,000 jobs in 1967 to 28,000 in 1977. There have also been increases at smaller centres such as Sutton and Dorking. After 1975 industrial employment, for long buoyant in Southern England, began to decline.

The importance of London-bound journeys must not obscure that of short-distance flows. For example in 1977 416,000 passengers made the 3½-mile journey between Brighton and Falmer (the station for the University of Sussex), and 194,000 travelled the 2 miles between Sheerness and Queenborough.

During the 1970s the Southern Region gave much greater attention to marketing, including research, advertising and fare manipulation. Thus in May 1972 the Brighton–Portsmouth and Brighton–Hastings services were marketed under the names 'Coastway-West' and 'Coastway-East'. Particular attention was paid to encouraging off-peak traffic. For while commuters remained the largest market sector, in 1979 leisure traffic accounted for 25 per cent of all journeys. Sales of off-peak reduced-fare tickets grew from 43 to 84 million between 1972 and 1979.

In response to changes in traffic flow, particularly those identified by the comprehensive market-research surveys of 1966 and 1971, patterns of service were extensively modified. By 1978 the original service on the Chatham Line to the Kent Coast (page 201) had become one of a fast and semi-fast train hourly from Victoria. These divided at Faversham for Ramsgate and Dover, the fast service continuing to Western Docks (as the Marine Station has been named since 1979). In addition there were two stopping trains, to Gillingham and Faversham respectively. Trains from Charing Cross now terminated at Gillingham and a self-contained shuttle served the Sheerness Branch. On the Ashford Line the basic service consisted of a fast train (first stop Ashford) to Ramsgate, a semi-fast, dividing at Ashford for Margate via Dover and Ramsgate via Canterbury, and a stopping train to Ashford, all from Charing Cross.

The diesel-electric trains to Hastings no longer divided at Tunbridge Wells, the stopping portion running through from Charing Cross.

The Brighton line services, essentially unchanged since 1938, were drastically revised from 8 May 1978 to take into account the increasing importance of East Croydon and Gatwick. As a result all trains, even the Brighton non-stops, now called at the former. The pattern of services on both the main and Windsor lines from Waterloo were also changed.

In general there has been an increase in frequency on the basic services, which has gone far to counteract the periodic and highly publicized cuts introduced in response to financial crises. The lasting reductions have been in Sunday frequencies, in weekend opening of stations, and in buffet- and restaurant-car services.

Unfortunately the Southern Region did not share in the advances in speed, frequency and comfort which followed the West Coast electrification and the introduction of the HSTs on the Western and Eastern Regions. This was partly because in 1965 Southern standards were higher than on other Regions, and partly because, with the conversion of the Bournemouth line, electrification was almost complete.

During the 1950s and 1960s not only was new stock provided for the electrification schemes, but the class '421' and '422' (CIG & BIG) units replaced the original electric stock on the Central Division and Portsmouth services. But by 1980 the rolling-stock of the 1960s was soldiering on with little prospect of replacement, other than the '508' class (sliding-door) units for the elderly inner-suburban slam-door stock. Otherwise the newest sets were the '423' class (VEP) introduced in 1966.

At the same time labour relations declined, to the detriment of discipline, service reliability and cleanliness. This was partly due to the high turnover of staff, especially in certain grades – guards, platform staff and cleaners. The situation was exacerbated by disputes and strikes, particularly by drivers and guards, which seemed aimed at the customers rather than the management.

But in some ways the undoubted decline from the very high standards with which the Southern came to be associated was more vivid in the view of the media than in that of the objective observer. G. T. Moody describes how on several occasions, following press campaigns on late running, his own investigations found time keeping good, if not exemplary. Again, contrary to widespread belief, the Southern had not become a major loss-maker. In 1979 the receipts from the Kent Coast services (via Chatham and via Ashford) amounted to £33 million. Operating expenses were £21·3 million. Thus £11·8 million (36 per cent of revenue) was available as a contribution to the fixed costs of track and signalling. Even the 'inner-suburban' services to Dartford and Gillingham had an operating ratio of 70 per cent, with 30 per cent of revenue available for the fixed costs contribution. These figures are comparable with those of the so-called 'profitable' Inter-City services on other Regions.

The Report published in 1980 by the Monopolies Commission on the London commuter services, though not without some criticism, largely exonerated the Southern Region from being responsible for the basic difficulties. Instead it blamed successive Governments for imposing conflicting objectives. In effect, since 1968 successive Governments have recognized the rail services of Southern England as being socially necessary, but at the same time have expected those services to remain 'profitable', without defining profitability. The Southern Region has been kept particularly short of capital, while road improvements have been pushed ahead without real consideration of relative cost-effectiveness.

CHANGES IN FREIGHT TRAFFIC

Alongside the controversial passenger closures of the 1960s, rationalization of freight facilities has been quietly pursued. In 1962 the Region had 620 freight depots. Of these, 70 handled 75 per cent of the traffic. On the other hand 350 handled only 7 per cent, each dealing with a daily average of only 1½ wagons. But by 1964 there were only 13 depots in Kent dealing with 'sundries'. In 1958 there were about 300 depots dealing with coal, but by 1973 these had been reduced to 11 large mechanized depots, such as the two on the Chessington Branch, and

25 smaller ones. Many lines such as those to East Grinstead and Uckfield and the Portsmouth Direct, now had no freight depots and therefore no freight trains.

But on the other hand, during a period when freight traffic on BR as a whole was in decline, that on the Southern was buoyant. In 1961 freight revenue on the Region was 11 per cent up on the previous year and between 1964 and 1973 originating tonnage grew from 5 million to 8·3 million.

More and more freight came to be handled by the new technology which became available after the mid-sixties. For example, in 1970 a new cement plant and associated rail terminal were opened at Northfleet on the North Kent line. The terminal is equipped for 'merry-go-round' (mgr) working. At the time of writing over one million tonnes of coal annually are brought in from Welbeck and other East Midland collieries by about 16 block trains weekly with pay loads of 1,264 tonnes. About 240,000 tonnes of gypsum are brought from Mountfield (page 36) in nine trains a week of 660 tonnes pay load. In the outward direction some 1½ million tonnes of cement are railed in bulk wagons to distribution depots throughout the country. Other North Kent cement plants (in 1980 there were 3 private sidings between Strood and Maidstone) and the ones at Southerham (Lewes) and Beeding are also sources of traffic.

Aggregate traffic has also become important. To an increasing extent London and the South East are in deficit and in 1975 5 million tonnes were being railed in from the Mendips and other sources. By 1976 there were 12 aggregate terminals on the Southern Region. Making use of Section 8 (1974 Railways Act) grants for private sidings, further ones were opened at Eastleigh and Hothfield (near Ashford). Sea-dredged aggregates were railed from Cliffe (Hundred of Hoo) and Angerstein Wharf and locally produced gravel from Lydd and Lavant. Internal aggregate movements totalled 2½ million tonnes in 1975.

The two large oil refineries at Fawley and Grain and the small one at Kingsnorth between them railed over two million tonnes of petroleum products, and in 1980 there were ten oil terminals in the Region. As a result of a breakthrough in fuel technology, Kent coal became a useful source of coke and in the later 1970s was being railed in block trains to steel plants. Uniquely for Southern England, a steel plant was established at Sheerness in 1972, scrap being railed in and finished products dispatched. The extension of the private sidings in 1974 received one of the first Section 8 grants. Other trainload traffics of the later 1970s included china clay to Sittingbourne (for paper manufacture), fertilizers to Andover Junction, steel to Farningham Road, and motor vehicles from Ramsgate and Eastleigh. Mention must also be made of the Transfesa continental railhead established at Paddock Wood in 1974. This is an example of bad siting as there is no near access to the trunk road system.

But the Southern has derived little benefit from freightliner development. By 1979 there were two terminals, dealing mainly with shipping traffic, at Southampton, which had ten trains daily as early as 1973. There was also a small terminal at Poole Harbour. But there were none in the industrial area south of the Thames. There would appear to be potential sites at Chatham or somewhere on the line to Brighton. The 1980 Speedlink Development Plan proposed that there should be up to 19 trains a day each way to and from Dover, and that there should be established 20 terminals in Southern England for feeder services. One such terminal is the modernized freight depot at Poole.

CHANGES IN INTERNATIONAL TRAFFIC

The role of the Southern in international traffic has been one of the themes of this book. In this, as in so many other aspects of the Southern's activities, changes have been fundamental. Gatwick Airport, second only to Heathrow in traffic levels, by chance adjoins the four-tracked Brighton line. In 1935 Tinsley Green station was opened north of Three Bridges. The next year the airport was opened with the terminal near the station, which was renamed Gatwick Airport. After the war the airport was greatly enlarged and a new combined terminal/railway station opened in 1958, a mile north of the original station and on the site of the disused Gatwick Racecourse station. At the time of writing the new station is being rebuilt and enlarged. In

1978 the airport dealt with 5·4 million passengers, a figure expected to grow to 16 million by 1990. About 45 per cent arrive at or leave the airport by rail. By 1980 the London rail service was being marketed as 'Rapid City Link'. There was a basic service of eight departures an hour for London; an all-night hourly service to Victoria; an hourly departure to Reading via Redhill; and two daily through trains to Manchester via East Croydon, Reading and Birmingham.

Almost equally spectacular was the increase in the cross-Channel ferry traffic between 1960 and 1980. At Dover passenger traffic grew from 5 million in 1970 to 9·2 million in 1979. In the same period accompanied cars grew from 87,000 to 506,946 and commercial vehicles from 83,277 to 506,946. Folkestone and Newhaven had more modest increases, but a number of new services were started from Sheerness and Southampton and particularly from Portsmouth, as new operators moved in to challenge the monopoly of Sealink and its Continental associates and Townsend Thoresen. We must also remember the Hovercraft services from Dover and Pegwell Bay (Ramsgate).

The rail share of this increase has been much smaller. But more passengers were using the boat trains to Dover and Folkestone, while bus connections (the vehicles in Sealink and Seaspeed liveries after 1977) were provided between Dover Priory station and the Eastern Docks and Hoverport. But the erstwhile prestige trains were axed, the 'Golden Arrow' in 1969 and the 'Night Ferry' in 1980. Growth in train ferry traffic has been somewhat erratic, but it increased from 600,000 tonnes in 1976 to one million in 1980, aided by connecting 'Speedlink' services and aggressive marketing.

These changes have been accompanied by corresponding changes in the layouts of the ports. All the ferry ports have been provided with ramps for loading roll-on–roll-off (ro–ro) vessels, while the last passenger-only Sealink ferry, the *Caeserea* was withdrawn in 1980. At Dover there were five ro–ro berths in the Eastern Docks by 1978 and the new Hoverport (1978) had been provided on reclaimed land at the old Prince of Wales Pier. The rail lines to all berths except the Admiralty Pier and train ferry dock had been removed, though there were plans to provide the Hoverport with a rail link. At Folkestone a new terminal, incorporating the Harbour station, was opened in 1968.

The pattern of deep-sea traffic, notably at Southampton, also changed. In the first place the passenger traffic virtually disappeared, and by 1979 was confined to a few cruise liners and transatlantic summer sailings. Break-bulk cargo traffic has largely given way to containers, handled at the five new berths at the west end of the Test Quays.

This has had major consequences on the rail services and layout. The boat trains largely disappeared and in 1979 there was only an occasional one to the Ocean Terminal. In 1972 there were ten daily freight trains conveying 300,000 tons of imports, but this had shrunk to 170,000. Any dock traffic is now dealt with at Bevois Park Depot, which along with the neighbouring Northam Yard/Mulfords Sidings deals with wagon-load traffic and such specialized traffic as bulk cement. The two freightliner terminals are between Millbrook and Redbridge. Central Station was rebuilt in 1971. Finally, at Eastleigh Marshalling and East Yards are used to sort wagon-load traffic, while there are four important private sidings.

All the small ports from Sheerness to Poole have experienced increased trade, particularly at Shoreham and Portsmouth. But with the exception of Poole, which in 1980 had adequate rail connection, rail's share of the traffic has virtually vanished.

OTHER CHANGES AND RATIONALIZATION

One of the features of the period after 1965 was the extensive re-signalling programme. For example in 1966 the Surbiton–Southampton section, and in 1974 the Portsmouth Direct line, were converted to multiple aspect (mas) colour light signalling. In 1971 it was announced that the 3,187 track miles in the Region would eventually be controlled from 13 power signal boxes. This entails not only conversion from semaphore to mas signalling, but the re-signalling of sections already converted to colour-lights since electrification. Thus the line from Victoria to Brighton will be controlled from only two boxes – Clapham Junction (ready 1984) and Three Bridges (ready 1987), the latter designed to control 280 track miles. Other power boxes already open are at Eastleigh, Feltham, London Bridge, Dartford, Chislehurst and Tonbridge.

Track simplification has also been pursued. For example, at Bournemouth Central (page 162), after electrification there were only two through roads, at the platforms, and a short bay platform line for the stopping trains. At the west end there are two sidings, one long one for turning round 12-car trains and a short one for the diesel loco waiting to take on the Weymouth portion. The goods depot was closed in 1979 and all traffic concentrated on the modernized terminal at Poole.

Perhaps the principal on–off project has been the Channel Tunnel. Agreement in principle was reached in 1964, the biggest step forward since the scheme was mooted in 1802. In 1974 it was cancelled, but in 1980 BR and the French SNCF were proposing a modified scheme to their respective governments. Obviously completion of the Channel link would have very great implications for the Southern.

MILITARY LINES

As frequently mentioned already, there have been a number of military lines in Southern England. The chief of these was undoubtedly the Longmoor Military Railway. In 1905 it was decided to extend the Bordon Branch (page 130) to Longmoor, 3 miles to the south, using railway troops. By 1914 the Woolmer Instructional Railway, as it was to be called until 1935, was sufficiently complete to allow a simple train service to be operated and for the emphasis to change from training in construction to operation. After the first world war the line was allowed to run down, but a change in War Office policy towards the role of railways in war led to rehabilitation, improvement and extension to Liss on the Portsmouth Direct line, reaching there in 1933, though physical connection was not provided until 1942. The Hollywater Loop was constantly laid, torn up, rebuilt and finally completed over the years between 1932 and 1942.

In the 1930s about 50 passengers a day were conveyed free of charge by a train service the frequency of which reflected the training programme and not the traffic. Trains were controlled by a variety of demonstration signalling systems, including that specially developed for military lines. The second world war saw an enormous increase in traffic. Numerous sidings were laid in and by 1945 the track mileage had reached 71. By 1943 there were 27 passenger trains daily from Liss to Longmoor and 19 on to Bordon, carrying 3,650 passengers daily, together with freight trains bringing in nearly 500 wagons a day.

After 1945 the line was gradually run down. The Hollywater Loop was closed, followed by the Bordon–Martinique section on 4 April 1966. Passenger services ceased altogether after 31 October 1969, freight continuing to be moved until the Liss connection with BR was severed on 31 October 1971. Before closure the line figured in several films, including *The Great St Trinian's Train Robbery*, which involved operating practises that BR would have refused to allow. The railway troops were moved to a short branch from the line to Fawley at Hythe.

An earlier training line was laid out by the Royal Engineers shortly before the South African War. With a single track of 2 foot 6 inches, the CHATTENDEN & UPNOR LIGHT RAILWAY led up from the Medway at Upnor Hard to Chattenden Barracks and Lodge Hill ammunition depot. When the REs were transferred to Longmoor in 1904 the Admiralty took over the line and operated it to transport workmen and stores until 1961, when the last scheduled service ran on 19 May, with total closure following on 31 December. But passenger and freight stock and a diesel locomotive could be seen, at the time of writing, in service on the Welshpool & Llanfair.

The Admiralty also connected Lodge Hill with Sharnal Street on the Hundred of Hoo branch (page 63) by the 2-mile standard gauge CHATTENDEN NAVAL TRAMWAY, authorized by a Light Railway Order of 1901. In 1915 the line was extended to Kingsnorth to serve an ammunition plant and to reach tidewater. In 1929 the extension was transferred to the unsuccessful KINGSNORTH LIGHT RAILWAY, which closed in 1940. The CNT lasted until 1961.

To bring in materials for Dover Harbour, the contractors built a line to the Eastern Arm from Martin Mill along the cliff-tops and down the cliff-face by a zig-zag. When the harbour was completed in 1909, it was planned to convert the line to a passenger-carrying DOVER & MARTIN MILL LIGHT RAILWAY, but eventually it was taken up. The formation on the cliff-top was re-used and extended during the second world war so that rail-mounted guns could be fired from different positions.

INDUSTRIAL LINES

Since Southern England's period of industrial growth, with some exceptions, came after the motor age, since the area had no major coalfield or mineral resources, and since coal and heavy raw materials for the North Kent plants could be brought in by water, there were relatively few industrial lines. Most connections between industrial plants and main lines were more in the nature of extended private sidings than branches or systems. As it is not possible to give a complete picture here, a few important examples follow.

The most important group is the lines serving the cement plants of North Kent. Each plant was connected with the chalk pits supplying the raw material and with piers on the Thames and Medway, from which most of the production was shipped, while some were connected with the North Kent and Maidstone lines. Because many were not linked with the main lines, there was a wide variety of gauges, including such peculiarities as 3 foot 9½ inches and 2 foot 8½ inches. Rolling stock was equally varied, including locomotives which were modified Aveling & Porter 'traction engines' and self-propelled electric hoppers to convey cement from a plant at Greenhithe to the pier. Closure of plants, exhaustion of chalk pits, the use of slurry pipes and the transfer of cement despatches from water to rail have greatly reduced the number of lines. The reader wishing to know more is referred to *Cement Railways of Kent* by B. P. Stoyle and R. W. Kidner.

The paper industry is well represented in North Kent. The largest complex is that of Bowaters at Sittingbourne. Pulp was landed at Ridham Dock, which went into service in 1919. It was connected with the Sittingbourne Mill by 3½ miles of 2-foot 6-inch gauge. When Kemsley Mill was opened half way along the line, the northern section was doubled. Because

Ridham and Kemsley (which supplied steam to Sittingbourne) were served by sidings from the Sheerness branch, it was decided to dispense with the narrow gauge line in 1969.

Mention must be made of the passenger-carrying line opened in November 1916 from Davington, the nearest point to Faversham station which could be reached without extensive demolition of property, for 2 miles to munitions factories at Uplees on the Thames marshes. The gauge was 3 foot 3 inches. By 1920 the plants were closed and the line dismantled.

The largest industrial systems in use at present are those in the oil refineries at Grain and Fawley.

PRESERVED LINES

As is to be expected in such a well-populated area, Southern England has its fair share of preserved lines operated by steam, the multiplication of which was such a feature of the 1960s.

The stormy later history of the Bluebell line was related on page 98. This aroused sufficient interest to float the Bluebell Society, which leased and re-opened in 1960 the section from Sheffield Park to a point just outside Horsted Keynes. Eventually agreement was reached to share the station with BR, with the Society becoming sole user in 1963 (page 98). Plans include extension to meet BR at East Grinstead. In 1979 291,162 passenger journeys were made over the 4½-mile line.

The former Kent & East Sussex line remained open between Robertsbridge and Tenterden until 1961 (page 69). Preservationists immediately moved in, envisaging running regular passenger and freight services as well as steam specials. But they were frustrated by the Ministry of Transport, who refused to allow occasional interruptions to road traffic where the line crossed the A21 on the level at Robertsbridge. Eventually the TENTERDEN RAILWAY company was formed and the line re-opened between Tenterden Town and Rolvenden in 1974 and on to Wittersham Road in 1977, 4 miles in all. The eventual goal is Bodiam. 50,148 passengers were conveyed in 1978, on the line marketed as the Kent & East Sussex.

In 1973 the Alton–Winchester line was closed (page 124). Even before closure a company was set up to save at least part of the line. There were also plans, supported by Hampshire County Council, to take over the whole line and run a regular diesel service with week-end steam. The company, however, failed in 1975 to raise a share issue. It was left to the Winchester & Alton Railway Company to re-open a part. They obtained a Light Railway Order, the first to be made direct to a preservation company, and on 30 April 1977 the 3-mile section between Alresford and Ropley opened as the WATERCRESS line. 64,747 passengers were carried in 1978. At the time of writing authorization had been obtained and plans advanced for re-opening the $7\frac{1}{2}$ miles on to Alton.

In the Isle of Wight the line between Smallbrook Junction and Newport was closed in 1966 (page 152). A preservation society later re-opened the $1\frac{1}{2}$ miles between Haven Street and Wootton. Finally, Bowaters were anxious that their narrow gauge line should be preserved, along with the steam locomotives and passenger stock. The southern section between Sittingbourne and Kemsley, which could be conveniently isolated, was handed over as a going concern to the Locomotive Club of Great Britain on 4 October 1969, on advantageous terms.

Mention must be made of the VOLK'S ELECTRIC RAILWAY, the only municipally owned line in Southern England and of great historic interest. On 4 August 1883 Dr Magnus Volk opened what was then a great rarity, an electric line, along the Front at Brighton for $\frac{1}{4}$ mile eastward from the Aquarium. By 1901 the line had been extended to $1\frac{1}{4}$ miles. The Corporation took over in 1940. In 1977 the 2-foot 9-inch gauge line operated in the summer, the seven cars carrying over 350,000 passengers.

CONCLUSION

The complex story of railway and social and economic development in Southern England has been outlined. The period covered since 1830 has been one of continuous change, fundamentally altering both the appearance of the landscape and the way of life. The railway has been a principal instrument in this change. Basically the network evolved over forty years – 1840 to 1880. Though it had then all but reached its present extent, it had yet to undergo a long period of technical development which brought it to the forefront of the British system. In the opening pages of the book the differences between railways north and south of the Thames were stressed. But since 1965 declining freight traffic, the spread of fixed-formation trains, lighter and more frequent trains and signalling progress have all brought the other Regions more in line with the basic characteristics of the Southern.

But the story is not yet at an end. Railways now have a great potential for development, a fact recognized everywhere, except perhaps in the land of their birth. Automation, started in manufacturing and now spreading to commerce, must also affect transport. Rail, by its nature, is more suited to this development than is road. There is also the spectre of the coming energy crisis, and rail is more conservative of energy and more flexible in the type of energy used. The task of railways in Southern England is still uncompleted. Today they play as vital and almost as central a role in the economy and the society of the region as at any time in their history.

Bibliography and Acknowledgments

The selection of works consulted is given below to serve as a starting point for further reading either on the railways of Southern England generally or on some more localized aspect.

Original sources include the relevant Local Acts of Parliament, the papers of the committees preparing them and the Deposited Plans for the various lines for which Acts were sought; the Half Yearly and Annual Reports of the various companies and their Minute Books; the statistical Returns issued by the Board of Trade (Ministry of Transport since 1919) from 1866 onwards; the Accident Reports issued by those bodies (which reveal much of contemporary operating conditions); working timetables and, of course, *Bradshaw's Guide* and *Bradshaw's Manual* for railway shareholders.

Files of the periodical and daily press are invaluable and fall into three classes. First the railway press of the nineteenth century such as *Herapath's Journal*, the *Railway Times* and the *Railway Magazine* (not to be confused with the existing journal). For the present century there are the *Railway Gazette*, *Modern Transport* and 'house magazines' of individual railways. Secondly, there is the national Press of which *The Times* and the *Illustrated London News* are the most useful. Thirdly there are the various local newspapers.

Local guides and directories of counties and towns are of much value, particularly of course early railway guides. Among these are *The London and Southampton Railway Guide*, by J. Wyld, 1839; *Guide to the London and South Western Railway*, by A. Freeling, 1842; *The Railway Excursionist's Handbook to Brighton*, by J. Lundie, 1852; and *Illustrated Guides* to the LSWR (1856), LBSCR (1853) and SER (1858), by G. Measom.

Nor can any serious work be done without constant reference

to the *Ordnance Survey* topographic maps, one inch and 25,000 scales.

Of secondary sources the most important are the local studies, many of them of a high order of scholarship, which have appeared in the *Railway Magazine*. Without them this book could never have been written, but unfortunately they cannot be listed here. *The Journal of Transport History* has a number of excellent papers, among them 'The rivalry and working union of the South Eastern and London, Chatham and Dover' by P. S. Bagwell in Vol. 2.

Of general works consulted covering Southern England the County Reports of the Land Utilization Survey in *The Land of Britain*, edited by L. D. Stamp, are of particular value. Also *The Weald*, by S. W. Wooldridge and F. Goldring, Collins, 1953; *Brighton*, by E. W. Gilbert, Methuen, 1951; *A History of Kent*, by F. W. Jessup, Darwin, Finlayson, 1958; *The Gateway of England*, by R. Scott, Nelson, 1957 (Dover Harbour); and *The English Seaside* by H. G. Stokes, Batsford, 1947. Also there is *The Canals of Southern England*, by C. Hadfield, David & Charles, 1955.

General Railway history includes *Early British Railways* (1938) and *The Railway Mania and its Aftermath*, (1939), by H. G. Lewin; *The Railways of England*, by W. M. Acworth, 1889; *Express Trains*, by E. Foxwell and T. E. Farrer, 1889; *Our Iron Roads*, by F. S. Williams, 1852; *Red for Danger*, by L. T. C. Rolt, Longmans, 1955; *A Handbook of Closed Passenger Lines*, by M. D. Greville and J. G. Spence, 1955.

Works specific to Southern England include *The Southern Railway 1923–1947*, by R. A. Savill, Oakwood Press, 1951 (facts and figures); *Southern Electric*, by G. T. Moody, Ian Allan, 1979; *Locomotive and Train Working in the Nineteenth Century* – Vol. 5, by E. L. Ahrons, Railway Publishing Co., 1955 (reprints of the author's articles in the *Railway Magazine* between 1915 and 1928); *A Royal Road*, by Sam Fay, 1883; *The L. & S.W.R.*, by G. A. Sekon, 1896; *The South Western Railway*, by C. H. Ellis, Allen and Unwin, 1956 (mainly mechanical history); *Boat Trains and Channel Packets*, by R. Bucknall, Vincent Stewart, 1958; *The South Eastern Railway*, by R. W. Kidner, Oakwood Press, 1952; *A History of the South*

Eastern Railway, by G. A. Sekon, 1895; *A History of the Canterbury and Whitstable Railway*, by R. B. Fellows, 1930; *The Isle of Wight Railways*, by R. M. Robbins, Oakwood Press, 1953; *The Caterham Railway*, by J. G. Spence, Oakwood Press, 1952; *Early Railways in Surrey*, by C. E. Lee, 1944; *The London and South Western Railway: Vol I, The Formative Years*, by R. A. Williams, David & Charles, 1968; *The Somerset and Dorset Railway*, by R. Atthill, David & Charles, 1967; *A Southern Region Chronology and Record, 1803–1965*, by R. H. Clark, Oakwood Press, 1964.

The period since the third edition of this volume has seen the publication of a number of significant works. These include R. W. Kidner's revision of C. F. Dendy Marshall's classic *A History of the Southern Railway*, Ian Allan, 1968; *The Railways of Southern England* (3 vols), by Edwin Course, Batsford, 1976; and *Sir Herbert Walker's Southern Railway*, by C. F. Klapper, Ian Allen, 1973, a rare event – an authoritative biographical study of a railway administrator. Also to be mentioned: *The London Brighton and South Coast Railway* (3 vols), by J. T. Howard Turner, Batsford, 1979. No student of railway history can do without G. Ottley's *A Bibliography of British Railway History*, Allen & Unwin, 1965, while the *Branch Line Index*, compiled by G. C. Laithwaite and published by the Branch Line Society, is valuable. There are also three contributions to the literature on the 'independent' lines: *Cement Railways in Kent*, by B. D. Stoyal and R. W. Kidner, Oakwood Press, 1973; *The Longmoor Military Railway*, by D. W. Ronald and R. J. Carter, David & Charles, 1974; *The Colonel Stephens Railways*, by J. B. Morgan, David & Charles, 1978.

Many dates have been checked and in some cases discovered by Mr C. R. Clinker, for whose patient and painstaking work the author is deeply indebted. The author is also indebted to the help he has received from Mr David St John Thomas and from Prof. J. A. Patmore, editors of the series Grateful thanks are also due to Mr L. C. Johnson, formerly Archivist to the British Transport Commission, and to his staff for their assistance in gaining access to source material and for his permission to publish it; to the Curator of British Transport Historical Relics, for his permission to reproduce old photographs and to photograph relics; to Mr F. D. Y. Faulkener, Public Relations and Publicity Officer, Southern Region, for statistical information, permission to publish photographs and for other valued assistance; to the Council and the Librarian of the Institute of Transport for use of their Library. Especial thanks are due to Mr S. Miles Davey, formerly proprietor of Locomotive and General Railway Photographs, for his generosity in making his unique collection available for publication.

Railwaymen of all ranks have patiently answered the author's questions, and numerous other people have contributed information. The following must be mentioned individually as they have placed their own files at the author's disposal or read and commented on the manuscript; Mr H. V. Borley, Dr E. A. Course, Messrs. M. D. Greville, H. M. Madgwick, B. N. Nunns, Michael Robbins, J. G. Spence, R. H. G. Thomas, R. A. H. Weight and G. F. A. Wilmot.

Index

Heavy type is used to indicate pages giving opening dates of sections (not individual stations).
Branch openings are indexed at the stations at the farthest end (from London). *Popular names of lines as well as those of promoting companies are listed.*
Abbreviations: d/e = diesel-electric; elec. = electrification; tfc = traffic